Shari Buxbaum
Editor

Library Services for Business Students in Distance Education: Issues and Trends

Library Services for Business Students in Distance Education: Issues and Trends has been co-published simultaneously as *Journal of Business & Finance Librarianship*, Volume 7, Numbers 2/3 2002.

Pre-publication REVIEWS, COMMENTARIES, EVALUATIONS . . .

"**O**FFERS NUMEROUS SMALL TIPS AND BIG IDEAS for managing library services and collections for distant business students. . . . Covers the range of problems from circulation to bibliographic instruction. Copyright issues are well addressed. . . . Any librarian can gain a better perspective on the needs of the many users who use our Web pages but do not visit the library."

Brenda Reeb, MLS
Director
Management Library
University of Rochester

The Haworth Information Press
An Imprint of The Haworth Press, Inc.

Library Services
for Business Students
in Distance Education:
Issues and Trends

Library Services for Business Students in Distance Education: Issues and Trends has been co-published simultaneously as *Journal of Business & Finance Librarianship,* Volume 7, Numbers 2/3 2002.

The *Journal of Business & Finance Librarianship* Monographic "Separates"

Below is a list of " separates," which in serials librarianship means a special issue simultaneously published as a special journal issue or double-issue *and* as a "separate" hardbound monograph. (This is a format which we also call a "DocuSerial.")

"Separates" are published because specialized libraries or professionals may wish to purchase a specific thematic issue by itself in a format which can be separately cataloged and shelved, as opposed to purchasing the journal on an on-going basis. Faculty members may also more easily consider a "separate" for classroom adoption.

"Separates" are carefully classified separately with the major book jobbers so that the journal tie-in can be noted on new book order slips to avoid duplicate purchasing.

You may wish to visit Haworth's Website at . . .

http://www.HaworthPress.com

. . . to search our online catalog for complete tables of contents of these separates and related publications.

You may also call 1-800-HAWORTH (outside US/Canada: 607-722-5857), or Fax 1-800-895-0582 (outside US/Canada: 607-771-0012), or e-mail at:

getinfo@haworthpressinc.com

Library Services for Business Students in Distance Education: Issues and Trends, edited by Shari Buxbaum, MLS (Vol. 7, No. 2/3, 2002). *Explores approaches to providing library services for distance education business students; examines the standards and guidelines for measuring these services.*

Library Services
for Business Students
in Distance Education:
Issues and Trends

Shari Buxbaum
Editor

*Library Services for Business Students in Distance Education:
Issues and Trends* has been co-published simultaneously
as *Journal of Business & Finance Librarianship,* Volume 7,
Numbers 2/3 2002.

The Haworth Information Press
An Imprint of
The Haworth Press, Inc.
New York • London • Oxford

Published by

The Haworth Information Press®, 10 Alice Street, Binghamton, NY 13904-1580 USA

The Haworth Information Press® is an imprint of The Haworth Press, Inc., 10 Alice Street, Binghamton, NY 13904-1580 USA.

Library Services for Business Students in Distance Education: Issues and Trends has been co-published simultaneously as *Journal of Business & Finance Librarianship*™, Volume 7, Numbers 2/3 2002.

The development, preparation, and publication of this work has been undertaken with great care. However, the publisher, employees, editors, and agents of The Haworth Press and all imprints of The Haworth Press, Inc., including The Haworth Medical Press® and The Pharmaceutical Products Press®, are not responsible for any errors contained herein or for consequences that may ensue from use of materials or information contained in this work. Opinions expressed by the author(s) are not necessarily those of The Haworth Press, Inc. With regard to case studies, identities and circumstances of individuals discussed herein have been changed to protect confidentiality. Any resemblance to actual persons, living or dead, is entirely coincidental.

Cover design by Anastasia Litwak.

Library of Congress Cataloging-in-Publication Data

Library services for business students in distance education : issues and trends / Shari Buxbaum, editor.
    p. cm.
    Co-published simultaneously as Journal of business & finance librarianship, v. 7, nos. 2/3, 2002.
    Includes bibliographical references and index.
    ISBN 0-7890-1720-2 (alk. paper)–ISBN 0-7890-1721-0 (pbk. : alk. paper)
    1. Libraries and distance education–United States. 2. Academic libraries–Off-campus services–United States. 3. Business libraries–United States. 4. Financial libraries–United States. 5. Internet in higher education–United States. I. Buxbaum, Shari II. Journal of business & finance librarianship.
Z718.85.L54 2002
025.5–dc21   2002020518

Indexing, Abstracting & Website/Internet Coverage

This section provides you with a list of major indexing & abstracting services. That is to say, each service began covering this periodical during the year noted in the right column. Most Websites which are listed below have indicated that they will either post, disseminate, compile, archive, cite or alert their own Website users with research-based content from this work. (This list is as current as the copyright date of this publication.)

Abstracting, Website/Indexing Coverage . . . . Year When Coverage Began

- *BUBL Information Service: An Internet-based Information Service for the UK higher education community <URL: http://bubl.ac.uk/>* **1996**

- *CNPIEC Reference Guide: Chinese National Directory of Foreign Periodicals* **1996**

- *Current Awareness Abstracts of Library & Information Management Literature, ASLIB (UK)* **1992**

- *FINDEX <www.publist.com>* **1999**

- *IBZ International Bibliography of Periodical Literature <www.saur.de>* **1996**

- *Index Guide to College Journals (core list compiled by integrating 48 indexes frequently used to support undergraduate programs in small to medium sized libraries)* **1999**

- *Index to Periodical Articles Related to Law* **1992**

- *Information Science Abstracts <www.infotoday.com>* **1992**

- *Informed Librarian, The <http://www.infosourcespub.com>* **1993**

- *INSPEC <www.iee.org.uk/publish/>* **1992**

(continued)

Special Bibliographic Notes related to special journal issues (separates) and indexing/abstracting:

- indexing/abstracting services in this list will also cover material in any "separate" that is co-published simultaneously with Haworth's special thematic journal issue or DocuSerial. Indexing/abstracting usually covers material at the article/chapter level.
- monographic co-editions are intended for either non-subscribers or libraries which intend to purchase a second copy for their circulating collections.
- monographic co-editions are reported to all jobbers/wholesalers/approval plans. The source journal is listed as the "series" to assist the prevention of duplicate purchasing in the same manner utilized for books-in-series.
- to facilitate user/access services all indexing/abstracting services are encouraged to utilize the co-indexing entry note indicated at the bottom of the first page of each article/chapter/contribution.
- this is intended to assist a library user of any reference tool (whether print, electronic, online, or CD-ROM) to locate the monographic version if the library has purchased this version but not a subscription to the source journal.
- individual articles/chapters in any Haworth publication are also available through the Haworth Document Delivery Service (HDDS).

Library Services for Business Students in Distance Education: Issues and Trends

CONTENTS

ABOUT THE EDITOR

Shari Buxbaum, MLS, is Head of the Gast Business Library at Michigan State University. She participates in projects to integrate library resources into distance learning courses offered by the Virtual University at MSU. Her interest in library service to distance learners grew out of the demand to meet the needs of the business students who were enrolling in the growing online program at MSU. She is a member of the Special Libraries Association, Michigan Library Association, and Academic Business Libraries Directors Group.

Introduction

Shari Buxbaum

The first documented case study of library service to distance learners may have been when Moses came down from Mount Sinai bearing the stone tablets of law. He delivered the assigned text from God, the teacher, to his pupils, the children of Israel, who were assembled at the foot of the mountain.

Since that event, the tools have changed but the concept is still valid: students who are not on the premises have the same needs as those who have immediate physical access to the study materials.

As people who are responsible for business students' access to information, our work is clear: we must continue to improve access for the growing cadres of business students who are participating in distance learning, be it a single course or a complete degree program. As we take on this responsibility, we find ourselves playing new roles. Not only are we providing traditional library services via new delivery mechanisms, in many cases we are responsible for the delivery mechanism as well. Technical troubleshooting has been added to our list of skills needed to provide service.

Many approaches are reflected in this collection of articles. However, several common themes become apparent as they are studied. Collaborating with faculty, a key factor in successful library service, is discussed in many ways. Collaboration with faculty was at the top of the list of research priorities that resulted from a survey conducted April-June 2000 by the Research Committee of the *ACRL* Distance Learning section. Also, overcoming technical barriers is a concern that

[Haworth co-indexing entry note]: "Introduction." Buxbaum, Shari. Co-published simultaneously in *Journal of Business & Finance Librarianship* (The Haworth Information Press, an imprint of The Haworth Press, Inc.) Vol. 7, No. 2/3, 2002, pp. 1-5; and: *Library Services for Business Students in Distance Education: Issues and Trends* (ed: Shari Buxbaum) The Haworth Information Press, an imprint of The Haworth Press, Inc., 2002, pp. 1-5. Single or multiple copies of this article are available for a fee from The Haworth Document Delivery Service [1-800-HAWORTH, 9:00 a.m. - 5:00 p.m. (EST). E-mail address: getinfo@haworth pressinc.com].

1

surfaces repeatedly. The definition of a distance education student is becoming less clear-cut as on-campus students take advantage of online courses. This leads into the question of differentiating between the student populations with (separate but equal?) library services. For example, at Pace University, distance education students are given document delivery services for which on-campus students would be charged. Other places do not try to keep track of a student's physical proximity to campus. Leslie Behm, in her survey of service models, touches on this issue.

Leslie Behm outlines several service models in the article "Distance Learning and the Impact on Libraries." She gives an overview of the issues facing libraries as they begin to integrate the changes necessitated by accepting the responsibility for library service to distance education.

A number of the contributions come from the librarians at Michigan State University. Beginning as "outreach" to off-campus programs in 1993, the MSU Libraries realized that its role in the success of distance education would be vital. Thus, the job of the Outreach Librarian grew into a new library unit, Library Distance Learning Services (LDLS), which was created in order to support the program.

Michael Seadle in the article "The Copyright-Distance Learning Disconnect" presents the copyright issue as it relates to the need to make materials available electronically. He examines the question of copyright from each stakeholder's perspective. The solution he proposes is a vigorous campus-wide education program for all concerned parties: students, faculty, librarians, and administrators. Also, he sees the ultimate value of teaching students the research skills they need to find information so that faculty rely less on prepackaged information in online courses.

Business information resources are increasingly available in electronic format. Every effort made to improve the user's ability to locate valuable Internet sites will help in retrieving useful information. Heidi Frank in the paper "Cataloging the Wide World of Web" discusses the need for cataloging Web pages as a means of making the Internet with its vast array of resources more available and reliable as a research tool for distance learners. She presents several metadata schemes that would impose a measure of order on the chaos of the Web, were they to be more widely adopted.

The experience of the business librarians at Michigan State University showed that access to library material was not a concern when distance education courses were designed. They conducted a survey of faculty who were preparing online courses for a newly proposed masters program in international business, Master of International Business Studies (MIBS). The conversations with the faculty as the survey was conducted alerted the librarians to discrepancies in perceiving how to provide library support for online courses. Fraser, Buxbaum and Blair describe the process of finding the library's role as the distance education phenomenon is becoming an integral part of the curriculum at MSU.

Lisa Robinson in her essay "The Role of Libraries in Global Distance Business Education" suggests that it is the responsibility of librarians to ensure that the role of the library is understood by distance educators. The way we define ourselves and our profession is evolving as we integrate the role of technology support for distance learners. Robinson also discusses in her article the tension between the tendencies toward providing prepackaged information to distance learners and the desire to educate students to be information literate.

Central Michigan University has been recognized as a leader in distance education for many years and the CMU library program is very strong in the support given to remote students. The article "Library Services for Off-Campus Business Professionals" from Anne Marie Casey of CMU outlines the services CMU librarians have developed to support the business courses. The goals for the future that CMU has identified should resonate with all librarians who are designing services that incorporate new technology to meet the students' needs for library assistance.

At Pace University the new off-campus MBA program needed library support. The librarian was able to quickly respond to a call for help from the faculty. The initial collaboration was subsequently fine-tuned as the needs of faculty and students were communicated to the library. The lines of communication that were established led to the library's firm inclusion into the University's planning process for distance education. Medaline Philbert narrates the process in the article "Bridging the Distance: Pace University Library and Remote Users."

The article by Jill S. Markgraf and Robert C. Erffmeyer "Providing Library Service to Off-Campus Business Students: Access, Resources and Instruction" is a case study that illustrates many of the points of the ACRL Guidelines. In transferring a traditional marketing course to a Web-based environment, many adjustments were made to course content, bibliographic instruction, and ultimately, faculty expectations. Librarian-faculty collaboration was a key element in the project. The approach they chose recognized the need to make the online students "information literate." A post-course survey of students yielded interesting insights about the value they placed on their newly-acquired research skills.

Again the theme of collaboration with faculty appears in the article from McFarland and Chandler at Royal Roads University in British Columbia "'Plug and Play' in Context: Reflections on a Distance Information Literacy Unit." At this adult education institution, librarians worked with faculty to integrate information literacy instruction into the syllabus. In addition, the librarian also taught and monitored that particular portion of the course work.

Amanda Wakaruk, in the article "Creating a Distance Education Tool-Set for Course Based Business Information," has very practical advice for librarians in using video conferencing technology to instruct business students in library research. Incorporating research guides and tutorials in her presentation, she explains how she utilizes the video classroom environment to deliver her message of learning how to conduct business research to distant students.

At Drexel University, Ken Johnson serves distance learners as part of his job as business librarian. He describes in the article "Library Services for Distance Learners at Drexel University's LeBow College of Business" that he has provided specialized instruction and participated in a review and revamping of the journal collection so that the needs of distance learners are met with electronic access.

The ACRL Standards are referred to repeatedly in the articles in this collection. In "Guidelines and Standards Applicable for Library Services to Distance Education Business Programs" Lessin, McGinnis and Bean present four sets of standards and examine their usefulness to librarians who are designing library services for distance learners. They suggest that in addition to using the standards as accreditation tools, they are very useful in opening a dialog with university administrators and faculty when planning and launching new programs in distance education.

Professor Michael Moch teaches Management at the Broad College of Business at Michigan State University. He has taught distance education courses, and also integrated electronic resources into his on-campus classroom. His article, "Using Computer-Based and Electronic Library Materials in the Classroom: It's Not the Technology, It's the System!" presents his efforts to integrate a multitude of electronic tools and resources into a coherent system. His frustrations and his successes give librarians a taste of one faculty person's experiences.

The National Education Association and Blackboard Inc. commissioned a study in 2000 which was conducted by the Institute for Higher

Education Policy. The study, entitled "Quality on the Line, Benchmarks for Success in Internet-Based Distance Education," examined six distance education programs considered to be leaders in the field. The pre-publication executive summary can be found at the Web site <http://www.ihep.com/qualityonline.pdf>.

Of the twenty-four benchmarks outlined in the study, three speak to the role of libraries:

1. "Students are instructed in the proper methods of effective research, including assessment of the validity of sources."
2. "Students have access to sufficient library resources that may include a 'virtual library' accessible through the World Wide Web."
3. "Students are provided with hands-on training and information to aid them in securing material through electronic databases, interlibrary loans, government archives, new services, and other sources."

These benchmarks are helpful when examining the standards and guidelines against which library service to distance education is evaluated. They provide us with clear direction in striving to improve these services.

Is the importance of library service in distance education for business students as well understood as the role of the library in classroom-based instruction? Librarians will need to draw upon all of their communication and marketing skills in order to ensure that the message of equal access to library service is heard by faculty and administrators.

Distance Learning
and the Impact on Libraries

Leslie M. Behm

SUMMARY. Distance learning is changing the landscape of education. Along with education, libraries will need to change to be able to provide services to distance-learning students. This paper discusses several models currently in existence for delivery of services to distance-learning students and raises questions regarding the provision of services for these students. *[Article copies available for a fee from The Haworth Document Delivery Service: 1-800-HAWORTH. E-mail address: <getinfo@haworthpressinc. com> Website: <http://www.HaworthPress.com> © 2002 by The Haworth Press, Inc. All rights reserved.]*

KEYWORDS. Libraries, distance learning, victim libraries, education

INTRODUCTION

"Distance learning is an old concept given new meaning by the development of the Internet and the World Wide Web."[1]

Leslie M. Behm, BS, MSLS, MPH, is Health Sciences Librarian, Michigan State University Libraries. She has taught courses via interactive TV and the Web, as well as in the classroom. She is currently a doctoral student at Capella University, in Education with an emphasis on instructional design.

[Haworth co-indexing entry note]: "Distance Learning and the Impact on Libraries." Behm, Leslie M. Co-published simultaneously in *Journal of Business & Finance Librarianship* (The Haworth Information Press, an imprint of The Haworth Press, Inc.) Vol. 7, No. 2/3, 2002, pp. 7-18; and: *Library Services for Business Students in Distance Education: Issues and Trends* (ed: Shari Buxbaum) The Haworth Information Press, an imprint of The Haworth Press, Inc., 2002, pp. 7-18. Single or multiple copies of this article are available for a fee from The Haworth Document Delivery Service [1-800-HAWORTH, 9:00 a.m. - 5:00 p.m. (EST). E-mail address: getinfo@haworthpressinc.com].

7

Learning will need to continually take place even after formal education has been completed in order to be successful in the current global society. Brophy[2] states three reasons why he believes lifelong learning will be necessary: (1) a massive rate of change in society, (2) individuals will need to be better informed in a global society, and (3) competitiveness between individuals, trading blocs, companies, and nations.

AN OVERVIEW OF DISTANCE EDUCATION

Distance learning is not a new concept. Correspondence studying was common during the years between 1873-1897 in America.[3] There is evidence that correspondence study goes back as far as 1728. Technologies began to transform distance education starting first with the audiotape, followed by video capabilities, and now the computer and the Internet are having a major impact on distance learning.

Fudell[4] suggests the following six historical phases of distance education: (1) print primarily as correspondence schools, (2) print and audio including the incorporation of radio and audiocassette, (3) print, audio, and video adding the use of television, satellite and videoconferencing, (4) print, audio, video, and computer basically continuing the incorporation of the current technology, (5) blending the technologies by using the computer to deliver compressed audio and video, and (6) virtual learning environments by using the Internet to create both synchronous and asynchronous learning environments for students. Phase five and six do not include paper; this premise could be debatable. Paper is still the most durable form of storage we have and many of the current adult learners are still more comfortable curling up with a book than curling up with a monitor to read. Until there is a full shift to using computers exclusively for information and we have a generation of learners completely comfortable with using monitors only, I would suggest paper would continue to exist.

Phase one (correspondence) primarily covered the 18th, 19th, and early years of the 20th century. Libraries did not play a significant role during the early correspondence phase of distance learning. Phase two (print and audio) covered mainly the early decades of the 20th century. Phase three through five (print, audio, video, early computer assisted instruction (CAI)) covered the middle decades of the 20th century. A significant shift occurred during these phases when libraries began providing textbooks and course packs (copies of articles, pamphlets, government publications) designed by the professor of record and assembled by the library staff.

Currently distance education is in Phase six. Recent advances in computer and communication technology have forced a shift in how distance education is offered. In today's learner-centered paradigm of instruction in both distance and traditional environments, librarians will occupy a primary role in facilitating learning. With the current emphasis on self-learning and directed study learning, librarians have an opportunity to reinvent themselves and become the gatekeepers of the institution's information resources. Education will need to change to a more business/market philosophy to survive, and the library can be in the front of this movement if they, also, become aggressive marketers.

LIBRARY GUIDELINES

In 1931, the American Library Association (ALA) first recognized that distance-learning students were at a disadvantage educationally because they were without access to library resources. The first guidelines for distance education were developed by the Association for College & Research Libraries (ACRL) in 1967, and a second revision was approved in 1990.[5] In 1998, ACRL and ALA approved the third revised ACRL guidelines for distance learning library services[6]

> Library resources and services in institutions of higher education must meet the needs of all their faculty, students, and academic support staff, wherever these individuals are located, whether on a main campus, or off campus, in distance education or extended campus programs, or in the absence of a campus at all; in courses taken for credit or non-credit; in continuing education programs; in courses attended in person or by means of electronic transmissions; or any other means of distance education.[6]

While ACRL and ALA have developed guidelines for libraries for providing services to off campus students, without the parent institution's philosophical as well as economic commitment to the distance learning and off campus students, library services will most likely not be adequate. Once there is a commitment by the parent institution, the library will then need to decide the best way to provide services.

MODELS

Four basic models exist for library services for distance learning:[7]

1. The first model is onsite collections and library resources at the remote centers.
2. The second model focuses on interlibrary loan, resource sharing, and students using unaffiliated libraries.
3. The third model provides delivery of materials from the parent institution to the student.
4. The fourth model pertains to the use of technologies to access electronic information sources remotely.

A fifth model not mentioned by Slade is contracting services from another library. In general the models are not mutually exclusive and features of all four models will exist in tandem.

The first model is the onsite or branch campus structure. A mini-library is created at the location where students are taking classes. This model only works if there are sufficient students in one location to have facilities available for use as a branch campus, which would include library facilities. Advantages to this model are that materials are readily available for the students who do not need to travel or to use interlibrary loan to get basic resources for their classes. Also, local libraries are not overburdened trying to meet the needs of the students. Disadvantages are the cost of supplying duplicate book collections at more than one location, issues of copyright clearance for journal articles for reserve readings, and the need for additional staffing at remote locations. The more locations, the greater the costs of providing library services.

Examples of an onsite library model include Illinois Institute of Technology (http://www.iit.edu/libraries), Washington State University (http://www.wsulibs.wsu.edu), and Pennsylvania State University (http://www.libraries.psu.edu/). All three of these institutions have both a main library on campus and branches at locations remote from the main campus and library. This model works well if the parent institution supports an onsite campus remote from the main campus to serve a large number of students in a given area.

The second model involves interlibrary loan and the use of unaffiliated libraries. Advantages are no additional staff is needed, no additional resources need to be purchased, and there are no copyright issues to worry about. Disadvantages of this model are students do not have ready access to the materials for class, unaffiliated libraries may very likely not have the resources for classes that are outside their mission and collection policies, and students are unfairly disadvantaged over students on campus. This model places an undue burden on the local libraries as well as not being in line with the ACRL guidelines for distance learning library services.

A third model for services for distance learning is the separate department dedicated to distance-learning students. Advantages are students have one place to call for services, the materials are readily available to the students, and students do not unduly victimize local libraries. Disadvantages are materials are not available onsite so students need to plan ahead for their library needs, higher costs for additional staffing, and possible copyright issues will exist.

Examples of this model are Central Michigan University (http://www.cel.cmich.edu/), Michigan State University (http://www.lib.msu.edu/outreach), Regis University (http://www.regis.edu/library.asp), University of Kentucky (http://www.uky.edu/Libraries/), and Utah State University (http://www.usu.edu/~distedli/index.html). Regis University is an interesting model in that it has both a distance-learning department in the library as well as branch libraries at other campuses.

The fourth is the use of technology that allows students to access electronic materials remotely. Given the number of electronic resources libraries now subscribe to or own and the fact that even on-campus students and faculty appreciate the convenience of accessing library resources remotely, this model should not be considered a separate model but a feature of any model of distance-learning library services adopted by an institution. Advantages include ready access to the materials owned by the parent institution and reduced reliance on unaffiliated libraries. Disadvantages are students need to have the resources to access materials remotely and the general issues of providing access to licensed and copyrighted materials remotely. Examples would be all the institutions mentioned in the section such as Michigan State University, Central Michigan University, and any institution that provides remote access to their materials.

The fifth model is contracting services from another library. A new type of educational institutional is a university without a campus. There are office buildings, a staff, and faculty that generally work on a contract basis. As a result, the institution does not have library services or a facility; thus contracting services makes a great deal of sense. Advantages are the institution does not need to develop a library, which is costly today, and all students are provided equal access to material, as all students are distant from campus. Disadvantages are students need to have the resources to access materials and students are dependent on a third institution for their resources. Copyright issues will also come into force, depending on how the institution sets up the library services and also the arrangements faculty make for reserve readings for students.

Two examples of contracting services are Capella University (http://www.capellauniversity.edu) and Western Governers' University (http://www.wgu.edu). Capella University contracts with the University of Alabama-Huntsville (UAH) to provide library services for the students and Capella pays the salary of a full-time librarian. Western Governers' University is unique in that it essentially brokers educational offerings from affiliated education providers to its students. Western Governers' University has a virtual library–WGU Central Library operated by the University of New Mexico (UNM) Central Library, contracted by WGU to provide library services. In addition to services provided by UNM, education providers agree to provide access to their library collection and services.

No matter which model is adopted, a Web page is used as an interface to information about and the services from the library. Looking at the Web pages of the institutions given as examples, one finds a wide variation on the sophistication of each gateway. Most pages are simply a collection of links to the library's catalog and to the databases owned by the library, and forms for requesting materials. A small number of libraries have created tutorials for learning how to use the library and its resources. Distance students are entitled to the following services: instruction on use of the library and resources; contact information for requesting services; information about requesting materials not held at a local site; quick turnaround time in receiving materials from the collection; quick response for reference assistance and guidance; and quick response to non-library related questions. Library Web pages will need to be designed to take into account these services as more students take distance-learning classes.

STUDENTS

Universities and their libraries will need to redefine their mission in light of the shift in the field of education towards life-long learning and adult learners. The Internet and the World Wide Web will transform on-campus learning as well as distance learning. Collaborative learning, team learning, and group learning will become the focus of the educational experience. Online will be a great place to blend all the various ways to learn.[8] Students are becoming more consumer-oriented and active in their learning, demanding expert teaching, quality resources, flexibility, fair assessment, and marketable skills. Distance learners are more likely to be adult learners[9] who differ from younger learners in that their goals are often more clear cut; they are more likely to prioritize the forces that compete for their attention, and they are more likely to take an active role in their learning because their motivation is higher. In other words, the adult learner has greater expectations in having resources available for their use.

ISSUES OF DISTANCE LEARNING LIBRARY SERVICES

Equity of Services

ACRL guidelines[9] indicate that distance-learning students should have comparable service for on campus students. What does comparable mean? Is it the same level of service with no additional cost to the student? Does the library cover the cost of the extra work and supplies to provide the materials?

If the institution does not have a library but contracts out in some manner for library services, there would be fewer issues about comparable services and the cost. All students either pay the same cost or pay for materials as needed. The main issue of what is comparable arises when an institution has both on-campus and off-campus students. At Michigan State University, it might be said that distance-learning students get better library service. There is an 800 number for them to call, copies of articles are made and mailed at no cost to the student, books are mailed out to the student, and searches are done for them. In contrast, campus students paying the same tuition rate must come to the library building and make their own copies, check out their own books, and do their own research. Is the service comparable? It could be argued that it is not, but which student is disadvantaged? On-campus students must do their own library research, make their own copies, and check out books themselves and return them. Off-campus students do not need to learn how to use a library if they do not have the skills already, nor will they develop information seeking skills that will be needed to continue their lifelong learning. It is hard to say which group of students is more disadvantaged!

Libraries will need to keep pace with the demands of the students. One question that looms large for libraries already dealing with shrinking budgets for books, journals, and electronic resources will be how to provide equitable service to distance-learning students. Another is whether or not it is the library's responsibility to come up with the resources to provide the service or whether the parent institution should be responsible if it has chosen to provide distance learning.

Victim Libraries

Parent institutions are more aware of the issues of library services for distance-learning students now than when distance education first started to expand. In the early 1990s, most of the time the students were expected to find their own resources to complete term papers and other projects. This presented problems for local libraries with limited resources to meet their own patrons' needs and were now facing additional demands on their resources from the distance learners.

If there is a cluster of students in a given area, then the parent institution should consider an informal or formal agreement with the local library to provide services for the students. The larger problem comes when there is not a cluster of students in a given geographic area. It would not be feasible for the parent institution to set up lots of agreements with large numbers of libraries to provide services to their students. Given that most students will have privileges at local libraries as residents of the area, the student could then take the responsibility to see what services the local library would be able and willing to provide. Students should be aware that their public library does not collect academic material and may be unable to obtain some books for them. Likewise academic libraries in the student's area may not be open to the public and if they are, there may be a different level of service for non-school patrons.

Dugan[10] has written a very cogent summation of the issues of provider and victim libraries. Two of the more important issues as he sees them are the logistics and management of providing library services offsite and meeting the needs of distance-learning students for information and information instruction. Traditional universities tend to utilize their own resources to provide services to their distance-learning students rather than local libraries. Some newer entrepreneurial institutions do not have libraries; therefore there is no tradition of providing library service. These institutions often believe that the students should be able to use their local libraries since the students live and work in their community. Unfortunately, this attitude does not take into account the differing needs a student has from the local patron using a public library. In addition, even if there is an academic library in a student's home area, it may not be open to non-school patrons. All libraries have licensing and/or copyright agreements for the electronic resources they either subscribe to or own. Generally, those agreements preclude the use of the materials by non-institutional members. Simply being a member of the community is not sufficient to be able to use the collection. Both victim and provider libraries should have written policies to describe their mission, to outline what services they provide to their core constituents, and for victim libraries, to explain to what extent services will be provided to students of other programs.

What Level of Research Should Librarians Provide?

Goodson[11] wrote a provocative paper on librarians' expectations of student information skill levels. She states that "instead of truly serving our library customers . . . , we instead mislead and frustrate them by tacitly promising they can acquire the same sophisticated skills that we possess after a brief bit of instruction . . . " Are we in danger of losing out on our jobs and professions because we have spent decades trying to convince people that they can do their own library research easily? We spend time going to school and training and then turn around and state that individuals should be able to do their own intensive research.

With the advent of the Internet and the World Wide Web, our skills will be all the more crucial for students. A certain level of information skills will be needed by all individuals of a society in order for the society to remain viable. However, with the proliferation of Web-based resources and the current lack of organization and filtering of those resources, it will be vital for librarians to provide the necessary services.

QUESTIONS RAISED

Libraries are at a crossroads, driven in part by budgetary constraints but also by the shift at their parent institutions to distance education classes. We need to reconsider what, how, and where we offer the services we provide and perhaps also the why. ALA Guidelines state that the distance-learning student has the same right to access of library resources as does the traditional on-campus student.

Questions raised by the issue of equity are: Is it fair that off-campus students do not necessarily pay more tuition yet also have copying and library research done at no cost to them? Does a library disadvantage a distance-learning student by not providing tutorials to learn how to do their own library research? Are students missing out on life-long skills that will be needed to be successful? Should library services become more fee-based for students as the shift moves to more off-campus students than on-campus students?

Victim libraries provide yet an additional list of questions: Should informal or formal agreements be made with local libraries when there is a cluster of students? Should the distance-learning institution expect local libraries to serve as the library of record with no support? Will we see more and more services contracted out to traditional libraries, possibly ending up with a cadre of a select number of libraries that provide services to their own community and to a number of distance-learning programs? And if that is the case, what level of service should distance-learning students be able to expect from the contracted libraries?

The idea of who does the research–the librarian or the student looking for the information–provides yet a third round of questions to be answered or at least discussed. With the proliferation of information, should students be expected to keep up with how to find material on their topics or not? Do librarians really do a disservice to students and to ourselves when we expect a student to have the same level of sophistication in finding information that we have trained to be able to do? What levels of information seeking skills are truly needed by students? Are critical analysis, problem solving, and ability to think and synthesize information of greater importance than being able to find the information?

CONCLUSION

The Internet, Web, and distance learning have had and will continue to have a dramatic impact on library services. We are very much in a transition between print and electronic, between traditional on-campus and off-campus learning, and between getting a degree and a lifelong learning process. Much writing has been done on the issues related to library services to distance-learning students. What is clear is there are more questions than answers. The movement to journals and books in an electronic format will also impact all of a library's users. Librarians will need to rethink how services are provided for all students, not just distance-learning students. If it were possible to fill your information needs without leaving your dormitory room, apartment, or office, why would you want to go to the library? Equity of service questions will begin to answer themselves as more and more material is available online and on-campus students begin to demand the same type of access that benefits distance-learning students. The issue of victim libraries will become less of a problem as more and more material is available online from the provider library.

Students will need to learn specific skills for navigating the vast amount of information available on the Web. Librarians will play an increasingly crucial role, if we are pro-active and do not allow others to co-opt our roles in the acquisition, organization, and access of information. Better and more sophisticated search engines will need to be developed. Librarians' organizational skills position us in an ideal place to become the gatekeepers of information: to develop useful cataloging of Internet resources and Web interfaces for easy navigation of electronic information. Librarians will need to create online tutorials for students to learn how to search for information, how to use the traditional tools that will continue to exist, and how to navigate around each library's resources.

Medical librarianship is a model that should be considered in the future. Physicians often do not do their own searching for information. They stop in the library, call, or send an e-mail requesting information on specific topics. The librarian searches for the information, evaluates the resources, selects the ones most able to answer the question, and then provides copies for the physician to read. What will be different for undergraduate and graduate students are the middle steps. The librarian will provide the information on the resources available and the student will need to review and decide which references are of importance to them. The better the student defines the topic and request at the start, the more relevant the retrieval they receive back.

In closing, I would like to comment that while technology is changing how librarians look at their profession, it will be student and faculty needs that will drive the ultimate changes. Without the shift in how students are learning, there would only be a shift in the media used for information. Librarians must become pro-active in working with students, and in developing resources that teach and foster independent thought and critical analysis of the information available. We will become gatekeepers providing an easier way for students to find their way through the morass of information available to them. It is an exciting time to be in the library field. We can reshape our institutions and ourselves to what we think will best benefit our profession and our patrons.

REFERENCES

1. William G. Jones, *Distance Learning* [Web Page] (Association of Research Libraries, October 12, 1999 [cited January 18 2000]); available from <http://arl.cni.org/transform/dl/index.html>.

2. Peter Brophy, *Distributing the Library to the Learner* [Web Page] (Marc Fresko Consultancy, February 18, 1999 [cited January 18, 2000]); available from <http://www.ukoln.ac.uk/services/papers/bl/blri078/content/repor~22.htm>.

3. Edward Erazo, "Distance learning and libraries in the cyberspace" (paper presented at The Internet–Flames, firewalls and the future, Roswell, New Mexico, 1995 [cited January 18, 2000]); available from <http://www.checs.net/95conf/PROCEEDINGS/erazo.html>.

4. David Fudell, *Distance education a primer: overview* [Web page] (University of Texas, 9/1998 1998 [cited 3/21/2000]); available from <http://www.utexas.edu/cc/cit/de/deprimer/overview.html>.

5. Gloria Lebowitz, "Library Services to distant students: an equity issue," *Journal of Academic Librarianship* 23 (1997): 303-308.

6. Harvey Gover, ed., *ACRL Guidelines for Distance Learning Library Services* [Web Page] (American College and Research Libraries, 1998 [cited January 18, 2000]); available from <http://caspian.switchinc.org/~distlearn/guidelines/>.

7. Alexander L. Slade, "Library Services for Distance Learning: What Librarians Need to Know!" *PNLA Quarterly* 63, no. 1 (1998): 19-21.

8. Ronald Watts, *Re-engineering the learning process* [Web Page] (Marc Fresko Consultancy, January 19, 1999 [cited January 18, 2000]); available from <http://www.ukoln.ac.uk/services/papers/bl/blri078/content/repor~23.htm>.

9. John A. Niemi; Ehrhard, Barbara J.; Neeley, Lynn, "Off-Campus Library Support for Distance Adult Learners," *Library Trends* 47, no. 1 (1998): 65-74.

10. Robert E. Dugan, "Distance Education: Provider and Victim Libraries," *Journal of Academic Librarianship* 23 (1997): 315-318.

11. Carol Goodson, "I have seen the future, and it is us!," *Journal of Library Services for Distance Education* 1, no. 1 (1997); available from <http://www.westga.edu/library/jlsde/>.

The Copyright-Distance Learning Disconnect

Michael Seadle

SUMMARY. Many people seem to think that copyright and distance learning must interconnect in some logical and perhaps even convenient way. Unfortunately they do not. One reason stems from the differences in speed between legislative action and technological invention. Another comes from people's attempt to understand copyright in terms that connect logically and comfortably with the rest of their lives, ambitions, and responsibilities. This article explains some copyright basics that apply to distance education, and examines how faculty, students, publishers, and administrators each view copyright issues for Web-based works. One solution to their differences lies in educating each of the interest groups about the statutes, the case law, the guidelines, and even the (best) practices of other institutions. *[Article copies available for a fee from The Haworth Document Delivery Service: 1-800-HAWORTH. E-mail address: <getinfo@haworth pressinc.com> Website: <http://www.HaworthPress.com> © 2002 by The Haworth Press, Inc. All rights reserved.]*

KEYWORDS. Copyright, fair use, moral rights, distance education

Michael Seadle is Digital Services and Copyright Librarian, Michigan State University Libraries, East Lansing, MI.

[Haworth co-indexing entry note]: "The Copyright-Distance Learning Disconnect." Seadle, Michael. Co-published simultaneously in *Journal of Business & Finance Librarianship* (The Haworth Information Press, an imprint of The Haworth Press, Inc.) Vol. 7, No. 2/3, 2002, pp. 19-29; and: *Library Services for Business Students in Distance Education: Issues and Trends* (ed: Shari Buxbaum) The Haworth Information Press, an imprint of The Haworth Press, Inc., 2002, pp. 19-29. Single or multiple copies of this article are available for a fee from The Haworth Document Delivery Service [1-800-HAWORTH, 9:00 a.m. - 5:00 p.m. (EST). E-mail address: getinfo@haworthpressinc.com].

INTRODUCTION

*To a Platonic mind, everything in the world is connected with ev-
erything else, and perhaps it is. Everything is connected, but some
things are more connected than others.*

–Simon, 1973[1]

Many people seem to think that copyright and distance learning must
interconnect in some logical and perhaps even convenient way. Prominent along the true believers are a class of energetic, technologically active business faculty for whom the realities of the law come as a shock
and disappointment.

One cause of this disappointment stems from the differences in speed
between legislative action and technological invention. Major legislative changes, such as the last thorough rewrite of the U.S. copyright
code in 1976, measure their pace in decades. Since 1976 networking
technology alone has undergone multiple revolutionary transforma-
tions from Arpanet to NSFnet to the current highly commercialized
World Wide Web where browsers, bandwidth, and the user base expand
annually. It is little wonder that the prescience of the statute writers
failed in the face of such fundamental alternation.

But the strained connection between existing law and evolving technology represents only one of the factors causing havoc. Another
equally important cause comes from divergent understandings of the
"social contract" regarding intellectual property. Generally people
know little about the law itself, and tend to understand copyright chiefly
in terms that connect logically and comfortably with the rest of their
lives, ambitions, and responsibilities. The issues break down by groups.
Faculty believe in an analogy to face-to-face teaching, students believe
in the freedom of the "net," publishers believe every use should be licensed and paid for, and administrators believe variously that they are
helpless against or responsible for preventing infringement.

METHODOLOGY

The methodology for this article is fundamentally anthropological. I
have, in a sense, lived among the natives for the past couple of years in
my role as copyright librarian at Michigan State University (MSU). My
office seeks copyright permissions for all of the official distance educa-

tion classes, including those for our college of business. We also provide copyright information (not advice, since we are not lawyers) to faculty, staff, and students throughout the university and occasionally beyond.

This context is important. As with surveys, the truth of anthropological generalizations depends on the representativeness of the data behind them, in this case the people and problems I encountered and observed at MSU. It is a large (43,000 student), Midwestern, land grant, Carnegie-Research-I type university with a particularly clear sense of its land grant mission to serve people throughout the state, and distance education ranks as part of that mission. Although the law will be the same from institution to institution, the interplay of interest groups and their understanding of the law may vary.

The law and associated guidelines will be discussed first, because they provide the context for everyone involved in providing informational support for distance education.

COPYRIGHT BASICS

No brief characterization of the copyright law can possibly express the complexity represented by authoritative tomes like Nimmer,[2] monographs like that of Kenneth Crews,[3] or Web-sites like the Indiana University-Purdue University Indianapolis Copyright Management Center.[4] But the most basic of copyright basics can be understood via a set of five broad labels: protected, public domain, fair use, licensed, and moral rights.

What Is "Protected"?

Understanding which works are *protected* is clearly the most important concept. The rule of thumb should be that everything created since 1978 is protected from the moment it is saved or "fixed" in some reasonably permanent form, including storage on a magnetic disk or tape, on paper, on film, or carved in granite. This means that almost everything on the Web has protection. Copyright does not just cover texts. It includes pictures, graphics, sculptures, architecture, pantomimes, dramatic works, music (both scores and recorded performances), almost everything where we give verbal or visual expression to something which meets the criteria for having a minimum of originality.

There are exceptions. Copyright does not protect ideas per se, only the expression of them. This means that anyone may take someone else's idea, as long as the expression of it seems sufficiently different to be original. Copyright also does not protect facts, such as the boiling point of water. Compilations of facts can be protected if their organization meets the test of originality, and a new law in Congress may extend that protection to cover the labor involved in compiling the facts, much as the "Database Directive" has in the European Union. Since 1989 the © (or the word copyright or copyr.) has not been required for protection, and in fact the requirement was eased considerably in 1978. Since 1978 registration has also been optional, except to obtain statutory damages for an infringement (anyone may receive actual damages, whether a work has been registered or not).

The term or duration of protection has changed twice in the last quarter century. Until 1978, the law allowed two terms of 28 years each for a total of 56 years of protection since publication. In 1964 the renewals became automatic. Previously they were not. In 1978 the term of protection for newly created works began to be measured from the death of the author, plus 50 years, or for an anonymous or corporate work, 75 years from publication or 100 years from creation. In 1998 the term was extended to life of the author plus 70 years, and 20 years were added to other durations. In effect, this means that, with a few exceptions, everything published in the U.S. since 1923 is protected and will be protected until 2018. U.S. law also grants protection to works protected in other countries that signed the Berne Convention.

What Is "Public Domain"?

Public domain works encompass everything that is not protected. In general, this means works from before 1923 (if published in the U.S.), works published before 1978 without proper notice of copyright, and works created by U.S. Federal government employees in the course of their duties. The latter does not include works created by state employees, or works created by foreign governments. Works created for the Federal government under contract do not fall immediately into public domain. Works which the Federal government happens to publish or distribute, including e-mail lists run from Federal agencies, do not fall into the public domain unless the author happened to be a Federal employee writing on Federal business. Public domain works may be copied freely, used on the Web, or published without permission or royalty payment. The King James version of the Bible, the works of Shakespeare, and Federal court decisions are all examples of public domain works.

What Is "Fair Use"?

Fair use has a specific legal meaning. The U.S. copyright law bases it on the following four criteria:

1. *the purpose and character of the use, including whether such use is of a commercial nature or is for nonprofit educational purposes;*
2. *the nature of the copyrighted work;*
3. *the amount and substantiality of the portion used in relation to the copyrighted work as a whole; and*
4. *the effect of the use upon the potential market for or value of the copyrighted work.* –17 USC 107[5]

If the purpose of a use is educational, if the original work is scholarly or factual rather than fictional, if only a small amount is copied (and that amount does not include the heart and soul of a work), and if the copying has no negative effect on sales, then a use *may* be said to be fair. But if a whole of a work gets copied (and the whole of a diagram counts as a whole work), or the copying means that someone can escape buying the work, then the use is not fair in the legal sense of the word. A number of guidelines have tried to reduce the troublesomely vague "amount" clause to a formula. These guidelines can be helpful, but court decisions have shown that they are not always reliable.

What Is "Licensed"?

A *licensed* work means that two parties have agreed to a contract which binds them to terms which may override fair use or other exemptions in the law itself. The contracts which libraries enter into with database vendors are just one example of these. Often the library will agree to some kind of limitation on who may use the database, and specify a mechanism for how that limitation will be enforced (for example, by checking the Internet address of an incoming request). The library may also agree not to provide access to the information outside the interface that the vendor provides. And that interface may have a "click through" license whose terms bind users before they get to the data they want. Penalties can be specified in the contract too, even the venue, if court action is needed to settle a dispute. Simpler forms of licenses exist as well. Each permission from an individual author is itself a mini-contract, and may specify duration, payment, or other terms. Licensing is growing rapidly in importance for Web-based information.

What Are "Moral Rights"?

Like fair use, *moral rights* has a specific legal meaning, and in U.S. law (17 USC 106A) they pertain only to visual art.[6] Moral rights include the right to claim authorship; to prevent false attribution; to deny attribution to a distorted or mutilated work; to prevent distortion, mutilation, or destruction of a work. Moral rights differ from economic rights in that they cannot be transferred, and they are for the author's lifetime only. In continental European law, moral rights apply to a much broader range of works, including textual works, and they include more rights, including (in German law) the right to withdraw a work the author no longer agrees with.[7] Moral rights do not belong to the users of a work, only to the creators.

DISTANCE EDUCATION PROVISIONS

Congress thought about distance education when writing the copyright law in 1976, but at that time cutting edge distance education meant televising images to remote classrooms of faculty engaged in face-to-face teaching, along with the informational materials on their black-boards or on their desks or in their hands. Today the law still constrains those wanting to take advantage of the distance education exemption to follow that norm:

> *Notwithstanding the provisions of section 106, the following are not infringements of copyright: . . . (2) performance of a nondramatic literary or musical work or display of a work, by or in the course of a transmission, if–(A) the performance or display is a regular part of the systematic instructional activities of a governmental body or a nonprofit educational institution; and (B) the performance or display is directly related and of material assistance to the teaching content of the transmission; and (C) the transmission is made primarily for–(i) reception in classrooms or similar places normally devoted to instruction, or (ii) reception by persons to whom the transmission is directed because their disabilities or other special circumstances prevent their attendance in classrooms or similar places normally devoted to instruction, or (iii) reception by officers or employees of governmental bodies as a part of their official duties or employment; –17 USC 110[8]*

Performance is the key word. The intent was to allow the reading of a short story or singing a song.[9] It might well apply if an instructor performed a dramatic reading of a chapter of an accounting text, but would not stretch to cover that same chapter presented only in text in HTML. Also paragraph C(i) represents a serious limit because most students do not use the Web from classrooms.

The desire to update this part of the law has foundered on fears about the ease of Web-based copying that were not a significant issue for televised distance education. The facilities to do the transmissions are expensive and not readily available to individuals. While illegal copies of broadcasts could be made, they would suffer the same kind of degradation as ordinary videotape copies, and would have a limited market at best. HTML copies of an important chapter in a text could, however, be copied easily, cheaply, and perfectly, and could easily undercut the market for the original work. Congress has not yet come to terms with this problem.

VIEWS OF THE SOCIAL CONTRACT

Outside a small body of lawyers and librarians, few people have any concrete knowledge of the copyright law itself. They have no reason to know it in detail, and in so far as they have to deal with it at all, they tend to connect it with their interpretation of a fair balance between ownership rights and use rights.

No one should be surprised that balance means radically different things to different groups. But how it differs, and who espouses which views, does much to determine how copyright affects distance education and those librarians who supply information in support of the classes.

Faculty

Fairness in the minds of faculty has a lot to do with the rules for face-to-face teaching, which do in fact allow for duplication of protected material for each student under certain circumstances:

- The work must be brief, e.g., an article of less than 2,500 words.
- The idea to use the work must be spontaneous and so close to the time of the class that getting permission would be impractical if not impossible.

- The copy is used for only one course, no more than three excerpts from the same author, and no more than nine instances of copying during the term.
- Each copy includes a notice of copyright.

The full "Agreement on Guidelines for Classroom Copying" are available online.[10]

It seems reasonable to most faculty that copyright not acquire a new and stricter meaning in an asynchronous, Web-based distance education environment. To them, the Web, or e-mail, or any other Internet tool is nothing more than a faster, easier, cheaper way of doing what they would do if the student happened physically to sit under the same roof and take a paper handout from a pile on a chair near the door or on a desk at the front.

Recently a business faculty member had to be discouraged from putting digital copies of recent newspaper articles online, and from distributing them via e-mail. Neither fit the fair use statute nor any of the specific library or teaching exemptions, and it violated the university's contract with an online vendor. One counter-argument the faculty member made was:[11]

> [We have] a subscription to the [newspaper], both hardcopy and online/interactive. Fair use with hardcopy would allow me to put articles on reserve, and allow each student to make one copy of all of them. I am not even asking for this . . .

He went on to say that the university "has an obligation to the students and to its own right to access materials it paid for." He also made the point that he was not acting on a whim: " I've spent 2 years working on the online system and the last 6 months building the articles to be used next Fall, so I also have considerable effort invested in this."

This situation was particularly interesting precisely because this was a dedicated and energetic teacher, an early adopter of new technology who had thought intelligently about the issues and took a strong, readily defensible moral stance. The only factors against him were the law itself (or rather a set of case law interpretations of the statutes), a license agreement that he never saw or signed which prohibited copying, and an institutional risk aversion that he felt (perhaps reasonably) to be exaggerated. He acted and argued based on a consistent system of equity derived from his own prior experience with copyright and teaching.

As a practical matter, he resolved the problem by persuading the newspaper to grant him a license, but he never ceased to feel that he had been right from the start. Web-based distance education would certainly be immensely easier and more effective if he were.

Students

Students tend to view the Web as free. This may change as more commercial enterprises charge for viewing. But for now only pornographic sites and a few business-oriented newspapers charge per view. Universities normally provide free access to databases to tuition-paying students. Even students who would never shoplift in a store feel no qualms of conscience about downloading an image or plagiarizing a paper.

Recently a teacher in an ethics class discovered that a significant number of students had copied whole papers from the Web.[12] The students simply did not see Web-copying as anything like cribbing another student's paper, which they said they would never have done. To them, written works on the Web were free for the taking: a form of intellectual communism where all such goods existed in a world wide ownership-free zone.

When students apply the same attitudes toward course-pack type material put behind password-protection as part of a distance education class, it leaves little doubt that access privileges will be abused. This need not, however, be considered an in-born and genetically inescapable trait. Students who have been exposed to a moderately stiff dose of copyright information seem ready to revert to an almost excessive caution. But they get that dose rarely, and then usually not from regular faculty, but via a guest-lecturer copyright expert.

Publishers

Although publishers are not always the copyright holders, they have more resources to defend their copyrights against infringements than individuals, and are more likely to have significant financial interests at stake. They view both students and faculty with the wary eye of a plump rabbit watching out for foxes. This fear has led them to support lobbying efforts to prevent the circumvention of copyright protection systems, even when done in the name of fair use. The Digital Millennium Copyright Act of 1998, which contains such language, also has a delay clause to allow for a 2 year study by the registrar of copyrights.[13]

The legal and technical copyright protections may well mean as little in our society as speed limits. Withdrawing a database because of abuse means that a publisher would be cutting off its own revenue source, while prosecuting individual, probably impoverished, students for infringements would cost more in lawyers' fees and bad publicity than it would be worth in income. And any salutary effect on potential infringers would accrue equally to the publisher's competitors.

This sense of vulnerability makes some publishers reluctant to cooperate with institutions and with those faculty who in fact have enough respect for the copyright laws to request permission. Each denial or exorbitant charge (to compensate for rampant theft) only makes compliance harder, though, interestingly enough, apparently not rarer.

Administrators

Administrators have the unhappy role of fending off the worst excesses of infringement by faculty and students on the one hand, and legal retaliation and public embarrassment by publishers on the other. They must persuade their two most independent-minded constituencies that a genuine legal danger to the institution exists, while success in preventing the worst undercuts the reality of that threat.

Copyright lawyers frequently talk about risk assessment as a critical component of any copyright use decision. Administrators are the ones who must make that assessment, because the institution's deep pockets offer a far more enticing target than any individual infringer. There appears to be no strong correlation between institutional size or wealth and risk aversion. Instead these decisions seem to rest more on personal morality than institutional demography. Those who clamp down too much on infringement may make distance education harder for libraries to support without a significant infrastructure and costs devoted to getting permissions. Those more incautious may foster growth now and pay the price later. Winning is not a matter of extremes, but of balance.

CONCLUSION

Distance education matters to most business school deans today, and any library that fails to support it runs the risk of falling into a moneyless antiquarian backwater. If it were not for copyright, every paper information resource and every face-to-face teaching aid could go seamlessly if not inexpensively onto the Web. This puts copyright-wise librarians at odds with most of their patrons, most of their suppliers, and some of their sources of funds. The situation is awkward, but not impossible.

The solution lies in educating each of the interest groups about the statutes, the case law, the guidelines, and even the (best) practices of other institutions. This does not mean that people will abandon cherished beliefs about how copyright ought to be. Faculty especially seem ready to cling to the ultimate rightness of their original understandings, even when bowing to a discomforting reality. From the library viewpoint, persuasion matters less than cooperation.

A good copyright education program is not hard to devise. The bigger challenge is getting an audience to listen. It is, however, a critical step in delivering information for business distance education classes. Once faculty in particular recognize that they must emphasize materials in licensed databases, and that doing that may make it necessary to train students in search techniques, half the battle is won.

NOTES

1. Herbert Simon, "The organization of complex systems," in *Hierarchy Theory: The Challenge of Complex Systems,* ed. H. H. Pattee, (New York: Braziller, 1973), p. 23.

2. Nimmer, Melville, Marcus, Paul, Myers, David, and Nimmer, David, *Cases and Materials on Copyright, and other aspects of Entertainment Litigation,* 4th Edition (St. Paul, MN: West, 1991).

3. Crews, Kenneth D., *(C)opyright, Fair Use, and the challenge for Universities: Promoting the Progress of Higher Education,* (Chicago, University of Chicago Press, 1993).

4. Indiana University-Purdue University Indianapolis, *Copyright Management Center.* Available (February 2000): <http://www.iupui.edu/~copyinfo/home.html>.

5. Available (February 2000): <http://www4.law.cornell.edu/uscode/17/107.html>.

6. Available (February 2000): <http://www4.law.cornell.edu/uscode/17/106A.html>.

7. Schulze, G., *Meine Rechte als Urheber: Urheber- und Verlagsrecht,* 3rd edition, (Munich, Deutscher Tachenbuch Verlag, 1998), p. 76.

8. Available (February 2000): <http://www4.law.cornell.edu/uscode/17/110.html>.

9. Hoon, Peggy (1997), *Guidelines for Educational Use of Copyrighted Materials,* (Pullman, WA: Washington State University Press, 1997), p. 17.

10. Available (February 2000): <http://www.musiclibraryassoc.org/Copyright/guidebks.htm>.

11. Private communication, 1 July 1999.

12. Private communication, Fall semester, 1999.

13. Digital Millennium Copyright Act of 1998, 105th Congress. Available (February 2000): <ftp://ftp.loc.gov/pub/thomas/cp105/hr796.txt>.

Cataloging the Wide World of Web: Organizing the Internet for Distance Learners

Heidi Frank

SUMMARY. The Internet has become one of the leading forms of communication and information dissemination in the world today. Furthermore, the Internet provides great opportunities for librarians to supply their remote patrons with an invaluable research tool that will provide access to a vast amount of information and services. However, the Internet is currently a disorganized mesh of a variety of information resources, which makes it difficult for researchers to locate resources that are relevant, authoritative and reliable. This paper demonstrates the need for better organization of the information resources on the Internet, and then discusses various methods and initiatives towards resolving these issues of organization. Some methods mentioned for organizing the Internet include improving the capabilities of search engines, and the use of metadata both within and separate from Web documents. The new roles of librarians in the electronic environment are also discussed. *[Article copies available for a fee from The Haworth Document Delivery Service: 1-800-HAWORTH. E-mail address: <getinfo@haworthpressinc.com> Website: <http://www.HaworthPress.com> © 2002 by The Haworth Press, Inc. All rights reserved.]*

Heidi Frank, BS, MA, is Electronic Resources Cataloging Librarian, with a secondary appointment as a Reference Librarian, Michigan State University Libraries. She is a participant of OCLC's CORC initiative for cataloging Internet sites, and is also involved with developing a system that utilizes XML for automating the cataloging of Electronic Theses and Dissertations (ETDs).

[Haworth co-indexing entry note]: "Cataloging the Wide World of Web: Organizing the Internet for Distance Learners." Frank, Heidi. Co-published simultaneously in *Journal of Business & Finance Librarianship* (The Haworth Information Press, an imprint of The Haworth Press, Inc.) Vol. 7, No. 2/3, 2002, pp. 31-45; and: *Library Services for Business Students in Distance Education: Issues and Trends* (ed: Shari Buxbaum) The Haworth Information Press, an imprint of The Haworth Press, Inc., 2002, pp. 31-45. Single or multiple copies of this article are available for a fee from The Haworth Document Delivery Service [1-800-HAWORTH, 9:00 a.m. - 5:00 p.m. (EST). E-mail address: getinfo@haworthpressinc.com].

KEYWORDS. Cataloging, Internet, World Wide Web, WWW, distance learners, distance education, search engines, metadata, Dublin Core, DC, Cooperative Online Resource Catalog, CORC

INTRODUCTION

The Internet is becoming one of the key forms of communication to patrons of the library. The ability to transfer information via this format gives the potential to significantly broaden the library's clientele. This paper intends to demonstrate the need for better organization of the Internet, and then to explain various methods that can be employed to achieve a higher level of organization.

In academic libraries, there has long been discussion concerning the equality of library services provided to the distance education student versus the traditional college student. It is true that accommodating the requests of students who are able to make a personal visit to the library is usually easier than for those requests coming from remote students; however, due to the increased capabilities of technology, more and more patrons are accessing the library remotely. The Internet, in particular, has made, and continues to make, an incredible impact on equalizing the quality of services provided to both types of students. A number of questions and issues have been discussed by Julie Linden regarding library services that could be offered to distance education students over the library's Web site, including circulation transactions, interlibrary loan requests and delivery, and reference services.[1]

A brief look at the past will demonstrate the tremendous improvements that have been made in the process of information transfer. Life in the nineteenth century could be considered primitive compared to life as we see it today. For example, the telephone was barely an invention, automobiles were just starting to be considered a serious form of transportation, and mail delivery across the States took days at best.[2]

Consider for a moment, how information traveled just one century ago. Sending information across the United States involved a long and elaborate process, as shown when Marshall Cushing tracks a letter from Exeter, New Hampshire, to Elk Lawn, Siskiyou County, California.[3] The letter moves from train to train, and is handled by many postal workers before it finally reaches its intended destination. In speaking of the Railway Mail Service in the late 1800s, Postmaster General Wanamaker said:

It thunders on day and night, over every railroad, full of bustling clerks, taking up sacks of mail, sorting them between stations, and laying them down at proper destinations. Over six thousand men, full of intelligence and pluck, are on their feet swinging to the motion of the train, exposed to danger, deprived of their homes, making ready tons of letters and newspapers for quick deliveries. The railway mail is the spinal column of the service.[4]

This gives an accurate description of the process of information transfer in the past, and in fact, the traditional mail system today, though maybe a bit faster, works in much the same way. However, an analogy for the Internet could be made, as follows:

It thunders on day and night, over every cable system and satellite, full of bits and bytes, taking up files of information, sorting them between networks, and laying them down at proper monitor screens. Over a million servers, full of artificial intelligence and resilience, are on their desks pulsing down the information super-highway, exposed to computer hackers, deprived of their downtime, making ready billions of e-mail messages and document files for quick deliveries. The Internet is the spinal column of the service.

There are many similarities that can be made between the nineteenth century postal system via railways, and the modern process of information transfer via the Internet. For example, letters and e-mail that are misaddressed are returned to the sender as undeliverable mail. Also, the "Dead Letter" can be associated with the "Dead Link." Fortunately, there are two major differences–the Internet is capable of reaching the masses all at once and is able to perform closer to the speed of light. Although the Internet exhibits great potential for disseminating information, it has been described as "a library with all of the books piled in the middle of the room, in no particular order, and with no card catalog."[5] There has been much concern regarding the disorganized state of the millions of documents that reside on the Internet, and libraries, in particular, should have a vested interest in organizing and cataloging these resources, which are bound to become a major component of library collections.

NEEDS FOR ORGANIZING THE INTERNET

Distance education students, especially those in the business discipline, have many information needs when working on their research. They need access to current, scholarly information that is valid and reliable, and the Internet is oftentimes the first tool they will employ. Sarah Thomas mentions that some users even "question the need for physical libraries since they find all the references they require for their writing available online."[6] In a recent study on perceptions of the Internet, it was also found that students often use the Internet to complete assignments, and that they considered the library and the Internet to be "two separate and unrelated entities."[7] This study revealed that many students do not consider asking a librarian for assistance with Internet searching. Some reasons mentioned were because these students are often remote users, and it does not occur to them to ask a librarian, or they do not expect librarians to have this expertise.[8]

The Internet is a powerful tool that is able to link a mass of information, as well as the library's collections and services to these remote users. Nevertheless, accomplishing this goal effectively will not only require librarians to educate and direct their users to the appropriate information that they need, but also to promote their skills and knowledge on using the Internet. Most importantly, successful research on the Web will also require better organization and structure of the Internet than its current state.

One argument for better organization is the need for currency of information. The Internet provides an excellent means to distribute information much more quickly and broadly than for traditional print publishing; and immediate access to information, especially in the business world, can be extremely advantageous to the end user. Yet, if this information is buried among the list of irrelevant results retrieved by a search engine, the user will never realize it even exists. A more organized Internet will be better equipped to connect the user to the information at the time it is needed.

Another concern is the authoritativeness of the information found on the Internet. The Internet is a great form of free speech, and does not attempt to discriminate or censor the information that is placed there. Unfortunately, this may create a problem for the user who needs to determine if the information they find is authoritative and reliable. For example, a person who knows nothing of business and finance is capable of creating a very convincing Web page that may appear to contain official stock information from an expert. And since there is not any type of review process for information placed on the Internet, this Web page would be intermeshed with similar pages that actually were created by experts. Also, there are not any standards or rules that require the creator of the content to state their credentials, or to even state who they are for that matter. As illustrated by Peter Steiner, "On the Internet, nobody knows you're a dog."[9] Given this simple scenario, it is easy to see the obstacles in determining the reliability and trustworthiness of Internet content. In a study on the accuracy of Web information, it was found that about 73% of Web pages retrieved resulted in some degree of failure.[10]

The ability to regulate the content on the Internet in its entirety is not necessarily desirable because that type of control would likely hinder the freedom of expression and dissemination of information in the public domain. However, there is a need for ensuring the reliability of information intended for research or scholarly activities, and even for personal information needs. Thomas Pack questions the quality of Internet content and agrees that "anyone can put up a Web site, and it often is difficult to tell how frequently the information is updated, how well the facts have been checked, and whether or not the digital publisher is trying to promote a biased view of the data."[11] Pack also mentions a number of resources, written or compiled by librarians, which provide guidelines for the evaluation of Internet content. Due to their role as information professionals, librarians have become the leaders in evaluating Web sites.

Another reason for examining the structure and organization of the Internet is because there is a lot of information stored on the Internet that is not searchable by search engines. This information has been termed the "Invisible Web," and "generally refers to content contained in databases connected to the Web."[12] Much of this type of information is viewed "on the fly" and is not actually stored on the Internet for retrieval. If a user approaches the Internet by employing the numerous commercial search engines that are available, they may be missing out on much of the scholarly information that they are trying to target for their research. Furthermore, access to the content of most online journals and databases are subscription-based and are unavailable to the user who does not enter using certain authorization codes. Users are often unaware that many of these online resources may be accessed through their institution's library; but if the library provides descriptive Web pages for these resources, then search engines will have a means to retrieve them for the user.

METHODS OF ORGANIZING THE INTERNET

The Internet is a conglomerate of both scholarly and frivolous information, so that trying to locate that specific piece of relevant information is nearly impossible for the average user. Due to the amount of information available, it is difficult for search engines to efficiently and effectively weed through the entire Internet and track down only that information which is relevant. Also, the keywords that are entered for the query may be taken out of context, resulting in false hits. The realization of the need for better structure and organization of the Internet has generated many attempts to improve the access and searching capabilities on the Internet, both in the academic and in the commercial realm. Some of these approaches have involved the use of search engines, the creation of directories and pathfinders, and the use of metadata.

Search Engines (Computer-Indexed Searching) vs. Directories (Human-Indexed Searching)

The commercial world has been relentlessly trying to improve the efficiency and effectiveness of Internet search engines.[13] Nevertheless, usability studies have shown that "search does not work on the Internet."[14] In fact, most commercial search engines have proven to be inadequate in successfully locating relevant research-oriented or scholarly information. One of the big issues has been the use of computers versus humans for indexing Web resources. The key difference between the two is that computerized indexing of Web resources allows for a much larger quantity of Internet resources to be indexed, while human indexing greatly enhances the quality of the indexing.

There are various methods of computerized indexing, but one of the most commonly known is the use of "spidering" software that wisps through millions of Web pages creating an index for all the words it encounters. Todd Coopee explains how "a software robot, called a spider or crawler, automatically fetches sites all over the Web, reading pages and following associated links. . . . Results from spidering are recorded in the search engine's index or catalog."[15] Then, when a user enters a search query of keywords, the search engine looks for those keywords in the index and retrieves all the matching documents associated with those keywords. This automated method of indexing means that the search engine is only searching for strings of characters, without taking into account the context or meaning of the words. Also, many search engines do not have a thesaurus to rely on for cross-referencing. The

AltaVista index[16] is an example of a search engine that is primarily based on automated indexing and has been listed as having about 350 million Web pages indexed. Even that amount of Web pages is said to be less than 35% of the Web,[17] so one can imagine that human-indexing cannot come close to competing with the great quantity of information indexed by automation.

Therefore, it is evident that the major advantage to automated indexing of the Internet is the quantity of information that can be indexed. When it was apparent that automated indexing was not sufficient for determining the context of words and often resulted in false hits, many developers of Internet search engines decided to use humans for indexing or creating directories of Web sites. This means that each Web page must be compiled and cataloged manually. This method of organization has many benefits because each Web site can be evaluated as a whole when determining the subject or context of the Web site; then, the Web site can be placed in the proper directory for retrieval. The Yahoo! index is an example of this type of a manually created directory of Web pages, which is aggregated by human editors, and is both browsable and searchable.[18]

The major benefit of human indexing is that it can greatly improve the relevancy of the results of a query because the context of the information can be determined. As once said, "People are slower than computers, but they provide context."[19] The drawback of human indexing is the low number of Web sites that can be indexed, relative to that of automated indexing. Without automation or adequate resources, it is nearly impossible to index a sizeable portion of the Internet. Thus it is clear that search engines need to have a good balance between computerized and human indexing in order to retrieve both quantity and quality. In fact, it appears that this solution is already being put into practice both by AltaVista and by Yahoo!, as well as by many of their competitors.

Pathfinders

Another form of human-guided searching is the creation of Web pathfinders, which is basically a Web bibliography for a given subject area. Librarians have excelled in the creation of pathfinders in order to guide their patrons to the most relevant and authoritative information on a given subject. This role for librarians is "to identify, rate and present to their customers some of the better Web sites which are available around the curricular and research needs of the University."[20] This is not saying that librarians are meant "to replicate work done by the major search engines or other services, but tailored filtering of Web resources can be a very useful tool for both the on-campus and distance education student."[21] Since librarians have been well trained in evaluating the quality of information resources, it is apparent and necessary that this role should be extended to include Web resources.

Metadata

The use of Internet search engines and directories is currently the key method of retrieving information on the World Wide Web, and it was found that 88% of the online population uses search engines.[22] However, there is much that can be done to improve the effectiveness of this method of searching. One way is through the use of metadata. The term "metadata" may seem ambiguous to many, but really, it is just a term used for the bibliographic information that describes a resource, such as the title, author or publication date of a book. Gregory Wool describes how "metadata are essentially the cataloging and other identifying data that librarians (and other information workers) have always recorded and used–but with new forms and capabilities in the online environment."[23] Metadata in the form of a print card catalog has its usefulness in many aspects; however, the use of metadata in an electronic environment (such as the Internet) is able to provide much more potential and flexibility both in searching and in organizing information. For example, Kim Guenther explains how "metatags are the most important pieces of information you can provide to have your site and pages indexed properly and to reap the publicity you deserve."[24] The incorporation of metadata within Web pages not only helps to increase publicity, but also greatly enhances how the Web page will be indexed and searched by search engines.

Metadata *schemes* refer to various standard sets of defined pieces of information or "tags." For example, the MARC format is a metadata scheme consisting of numerous MARC tags, each of which is defined to hold a specific piece of information about a book, document or other information resource. To illustrate, the 245 tag is used for the main title of the item, while the 260 is reserved for publication information. By separating and placing each piece of information into a different tag, one is able to be more specific in a search query by specifying which tag or tags to search. This is a basic search function of the library OPAC, when patrons choose to perform a specific search for author or title rather than a general keyword search. Furthermore, employing a metadata scheme for structuring bibliographic information allows for the use of controlled vocabulary, which is necessary for the collocation of similar materials and for cross-referencing synonymous or related search terms.

The set of MARC tags as a whole is considered a standard metadata scheme. The MARC format is probably the most familiar to librarians since it has been used in library catalogs for years for describing and providing access to each resource in library collections. Some other examples of metadata schemes are the Encoded Archival Description (EAD), the Text Encoding Initiative (TEI), and the Dublin Core (DC) element set.[25] These other metadata schemes may be less familiar, but serve much the same purpose as the MARC format. This discussion will focus on the Dublin Core metadata element set, which was specifically designed for describing Internet resources and other electronic materials.

Dublin Core (DC)

The Dublin Core (DC) metadata element set has originated from the Online Computer Library Center, Inc. (OCLC), and was originally designed to be a very simple metadata scheme. It was hoped that this simplicity would induce Web authors, who may not be experienced in "cataloging," to use the DC scheme within their own Web pages. One application of the DC element set is to enter the metadata into the source code of Web documents using the eXtensible Markup Language (XML), which is a subset of the Standard Generalized Markup Language (SGML).[26] There are currently 15 DC elements that may be used for describing a Web resource. These include:[27]

Title	Contributor	Source
Creator	Date	Language
Subject	Type	Relation
Description	Format	Coverage
Publisher	Identifier	Rights

This set of DC tags accommodates any level of use, from simple to detailed, because each tag is optional and repeatable, meaning that each tag can be used as often as needed or not at all. Furthermore, these tags structure the descriptive information given in the header of an HTML Web document and allow search engines to be able to specify which part of the description to search, rather than just matching a keyword to a string of characters anywhere within the document. For example, the search for documents published by a particular publishing company could be much more effective if the search engine was able to limit the search to the DC "Publisher" tag, rather than randomly searching all the text of a document. This type of metadata scheme is meant to organize Web information in the same way that the MARC scheme is meant to organize the materials in a library's collection.

Using metadata schemes to structure the coded data of a Web site would greatly enhance the effectiveness of search engines because it would assist the search engines in determining the context of the keywords entered in the search query. Norm Medeiros describes the DC scheme as "a rich structure that will provide for very specific retrieval if adopted by search engine proprietors."[28] In fact, users would be able to target their search to a particular field of data. For example, since the most current information is often needed for research, this method of searching would allow users to search the DC "Date" tag for a range of publication dates or a "date last updated" in order to retrieve the level of currency they require.

Two methods of utilizing the DC metadata are: (1) incorporating the metadata directly into the source code of a Web page, such as the Cataloging-In-Publication (CIP) data found in a printed book; or (2) using the metadata for description and access through a database that is separate from the Web page, such as a MARC record in an online library catalog.

Metadata Incorporated into the Source Code of Web Documents

The application of the DC element set using XML gives the creator of a Web site the ability to include the bibliographic description directly within the source code of the Web page using HTML metatags. As an example, Figure 1 shows the current HTML source code embedded within the header information of the Web site for The American Institute of Certified Public Accountants (AICPA Online),[29] which currently only includes the "Title" and "Keywords" HTML metatags for the bibliographic description. However, a more detailed description could be included using the DC metadata shown in Figure 2.

Incorporation of these additional metadata tags is one method of improving the searching and indexing of Web resources because the structured metadata allows computers to determine the context of the strings of characters to be searched. In other words, a computer is able to identify whether the search terms might refer to an author, a title, or a publisher by reading the DC tags that are encoded around those terms. Unfortunately, the average individual or business Webmaster who cre-

FIGURE 1. Current HTML Source Code for AICPA Online (http://www.aicpa.org/index.htm)

```
<HTML>
  <HEAD>
  <TITLE>AICPA</TITLE>
    <meta name="owner" content="006 3788 05167 01/23/01">
    <script language=javascript>
function newWindow(form)
{window.location=form.sel.options[form.sel.selectedIndex].value}
</script>
</HEAD>
<META NAME="KeyWords" CONTENT="a-133, accountant, accountant services, accounting, accounting career,
accounting conferences, accounting course, accounting discussion, accounting education, accounting guidance,
accounting guide, accounting information, accounting journal, accounting laws, accounting legislation, accounting
links, accounting literature, accounting news, accounting periodical, accounting practice, accounting products,
accounting products catalog, accounting professional, accounting professional standards, accounting publication,
accounting resources, accounting services, accounting software, accounting standards, aicpa, aicpa catalog, aicpa
conferences, american institute of certified public accountants, american institute of cpas, assurance services, attest,
attest function, attestation, audit, certified public accountant, code of professional conduct, committee on assurance
services, continuing professional education, cost accounting, cpa association, ...">
</HEAD>
```

FIGURE 2. Dublin Core Metadata for AICPA Online (http://www.aicpa.org/index.htm)

```
<meta name="DC.Title" content="AICPA Online">
<meta name="DC.Title.alternative" content="American Institute of Certified Public Accountants online">
<meta name="DC.Title.alternative" content="AICPA">
<meta name="DC.Creator.nameCorporate" scheme="MEntry" content="American Institute of Certified Public
Accountants">
<meta name="DC.Publisher" content="American Institute of Certified Public Accountants">
<meta name="DC.Publisher.place" content="New York, NY">
<meta name="DC.Date.issued" scheme="MARC21-Date" content="1998-9999">
<meta name="DC.Description.summary" content="Information about the Institute: membership, job postings,
publications, products and services, educational programs, and links to sites of interest to CPA's">
<meta name="DC.Identifier" scheme="URI" content="http://www.aicpa.org/index.htm">
<meta name="DC.Language" scheme="ISO639-2" content="eng">
<meta name="DC.Subject.nameCorporate" scheme="LCSH" content="American Institute of Certified Public
Accountants">
<meta name="DC.Subject.topical" scheme="LCSH" content="Accountants · United States">
<meta name="DC.Subject.topical" scheme="LCSH" content="Accounting · United States">
<meta name="DC.Subject.topical" scheme="LCSH" content="Accountants · United States · Directories">
<meta name="DC.Relation.requires" content="Mode of access: Internet via the World Wide Web">
```

ates a Web page either does not know how to apply the DC metadata scheme or does not even realize it exists. For these reasons, the majority of Web page authors are not currently utilizing this system. As the DC metadata set becomes more widely accepted and incorporated into Web documents, search engine developers will be able to enhance the searching capabilities of their products.

Metadata Used Separate from the Web Document

Metadata schemes, such as the DC element set, can also be used to create bibliographic databases, just as the MARC scheme is used to create most library catalogs. One such initiative for organizing the Internet using metadata schemes is the Cooperative Online Resource Catalog (CORC) system, which was also developed by OCLC. This system relies on both the MARC and the DC metadata schemes, and is able to convert the data from one scheme to the other.

A useful aspect of this system is that it is programmed to read the HTML or XML source code of a Web page and extract the bibliographic information, placing it into a structured record in the CORC database. For example, the CORC system is able to extract the DC metadata code shown in Figure 2 and use that information to create the structured MARC record seen in Figure 3. This is one major reason for encouraging Web page creators to properly encode the bibliographic information within the source code of their Web pages using the DC scheme. If the DC metadata scheme is used correctly, the CORC system is able to automatically create a clean record in the CORC database that should not require much editing by librarians in order to meet the cataloging standards.

The CORC database has been merged with OCLC's WorldCat database, which is accessible to subscribing libraries and individuals through the Web-based interface of FirstSearch. Also, these records in the CORC system are available in either the DC format or the MARC format; therefore, once librarians have selected and cataloged Web re-

FIGURE 3. MARC Record for AICPA Online (http://www.aicpa.org/index.htm)

110	2-	American Institute of Certified Public Accountants
245	10	AICPA Online
246	3-	American Institute of Certified Public Accounts online
246	3-	AICPA
260	--	New York, NY : |b American Institute of Certified Public Accountants, |c c1998-
538	--	Mode of access: Internet via World Wide Web.
520	--	Information about the Institute: membership, job postings, publications, products and services, educational programs, and links to sites of interest to CPA's
610	2-	American Institute of Certified Public Accountants
650	-0	Accountants |z United States
650	-0	Accounting |z United States
650	-0	Accountants |z United States |v Directories
856	4-	|u http://www.aicpa.org/index.htm

sources in the CORC database, these records can be exported from CORC and input into the library's OPAC. This would allow patrons to seamlessly search and access these Web resources directly from the library's catalog along with the rest of the library collection.

The CORC system allows librarians to use their skills in evaluating, selecting, and providing access to valuable Web resources for their patrons. Since the CORC database contains descriptions of only those Web documents selected by librarians, librarians have the opportunity to pre-select resources that are valid and reliable, which ultimately saves patrons from having to weed through all the unscholarly and irrelevant information that is found on the Internet.

CONCLUSIONS

The Internet is greatly affecting all aspects of library services, and is becoming a major part of library collections whether we like it or not. For this reason, librarians must get involved and continue to play a major role in developing ways to organize, catalog, and provide access to Web resources. By doing this, the library will also be helping to equalize the quality of services and access to information for remote students in distance education programs.

Many reasons for organizing the Internet have been discussed here, including the need for current, reliable and authoritative information, as well as the need for scholarly and relevant information. Also, it is obvious that the Internet is vast and difficult to search in its present state, and that a lot of the information found is useless to serious researchers. Furthermore, many valuable Web documents do not contain much bibliographic information, and if any description is present, it is often not in any type of structured metadata scheme, which would improve the searching capabilities of search engines.

So what can librarians do to take the initiative in organizing the Internet? First, they can continue working cooperatively on cataloging projects such as the CORC system. Cataloging is the first crucial step towards organizing the Internet. In fact, quality cataloging not only assists search engines, but it also greatly influences the effectiveness of the library's reference service, collection management, resource sharing, and database automation.[30] In a discussion on the value of cataloging, it was agreed that since "information sources–both print and electronic–are so numerous that even sophisticated search engines can't find the right source, cataloging is clearly more valuable than ever."[31]

Subsequently, librarians can strive to educate patrons and themselves in creating Web documents that contain structured bibliographic descriptions using standard metadata schemes. Librarians can also continue to improve on methods of providing library services and training through the library's Web pages, because it is obvious that the Internet is here to stay so we might as well make it work for us as well as our patrons.

REFERENCES

1. Linden, Julie. "The Library's Web Site *is* the Library." *College & Research Libraries News* 61, no. 2 (February 2000): p. 99,101.

2. Scheele, Carl H. *A Short History of the Mail Service.* (Washington, DC: Smithsonian Institution Press, 1970), p. 96, 113.

3. Cushing, Marshall. *The Story of Our Post Office: The Greatest Government Department in all its Phases.* (Boston, MA: A. M. Thayer & Co., 1893), p. 51-56.

4. Ibid., p. 47-48.

5. Dees, Tim. "Using Search Engines." *Law & Order* 48, no. 5 (May 2000): p. 23-24.

6. Thomas, Sarah E. "Abundance, Attention, and Access: Of Portals and Catalogs." *ARL: A bimonthly report on research library issues and actions from ARL, CNI, and SPARC* no. 212 (October 2000): p. 2.

7. D'Esposito, Joann E. and Rachel M. Gardner. "University Students' Perceptions of the Internet: An Exploratory Study." *The Journal of Academic Librarianship* 25, no. 6 (November 1999): p. 458.

8. Ibid., p. 459.

9. Steiner, Peter. "On the Internet, nobody knows you're a dog." *The New Yorker* 69, no. 20 (July 5, 1993): p. 61.

10. Connell, Tschera Harkness, and Jennifer E. Tipple. "Testing the Accuracy of Information on the World Wide Web using the AltaVista Search Engine." *Reference & User Services Quarterly* 38, no. 4 (Summer 1999): p. 366.

11. Pack, Thomas. "Can you trust Internet information?" *Link–Up* 16, no. 6 (November/December 1999): p. 24.

12. Cohen, Laura B. "Searching the Web: The human element emerges." *Choice* 37, Supplement: Web IV (August 2000): p. 26.

13. The following two references discuss various commercial search engines and their strategies to improve Internet searching: Wiley, Deborah Lynne. "Beyond Information Retrieval." *Database* 21, no. 4 (August/September 1998): p. 18-22; and, Zetter, Kim, Harry McCracken, and Yael Li-Ron. "How to Stop Searching and Start Finding." *PC World* 18, no. 9 (September 2000): p. 129-143.

14. Sherman, Chris. "Search Engine Strategies 99." *Information Today* 17, no. 1 (January 2000): p. 1, 70.

15. Coopee, Todd. "How to climb the search engine rankings." *InfoWorld* 22, no. 24 (12 June 2000): p. 61, 64.

16. "About AltaVista." <http://doc.altavista.com/company_info/about_av/background.html>.

17. Coopee, p. 61.

18. "Yahoo! Help–Search." <http://help.yahoo.com/help/us/ysearch/ysearch-18. html>.

19. Hanrahan, Timothy. "The Best Way to... ...Search Online: Finding what you need on the Web is getting easier and easier (But it's still not easy)." *The Wall Street Journal* (Eastern Ed.), 6 December 1999, section: The Internet (A Special Report), p. R25.

20. "Key elements on using technology for library support in distance education." *Information Intelligence, Online Libraries, and Microcomputers* 15, no. 12 (December 1997): p. 1-6.

21. Ibid.

22. Hanrahan, p. R25.

23. Wool, Gregory. "A Meditation on Metadata." *The Serials Librarian* 33, no. 1/2 (1998): p. 169.

24. Guenther, Kim. "Publicity Through Better Web Site Design." *Computers in Libraries* 19, no. 8 (September 1999): p. 66.

25. For more information about EAD and TEI, see: "Encoded Archival Description (EAD): Official Web Site." <http://lcweb.loc.gov/ead/>, and "Text Encoding Initiative (TEI) Home Page." <http://www.uic.edu/orgs/tei/> (Viewed on 29 January 2001).

26. For more information on XML and SGML, see: "The XML Cover Pages." <http://www.oasis-open.org/cover/> (Viewed on 29 January 2001).

27. "Dublin Core Metadata Element Set, Version 1.1: Reference Description." <http://purl.oclc.org/dc/documents/rec-dces-19990702.htm> (Viewed on 29 January 2001).

28. Medeiros, Norm. "Making Room for MARC in a Dublin Core World." *Online* 23, no. 6 (November/December 1999): p. 58.

29. "AICPA Online." <http://www.aicpa.org/index.htm> (Viewed on 29 January 2001).

30. Morris, Dilys E. and Gregory Wool. "Cataloging: Librarianship's Best Bargain." *Library Journal* 124, no. 11 (15 June 1999): p. 45-46.

31. Ibid., p. 46.

The Library
and the Development of Online Courses

Mary G. Fraser
Shari Buxbaum
Amy Blair

SUMMARY. A survey of eight business faculty preparing online classes for a proposed distance education degree in international marketing was conducted by business librarians at Michigan State University. The results of the survey indicated that there were differences in faculty and librarian expectations as to the library support needed for the courses. *[Article copies available for a fee from The Haworth Document Delivery Service: 1-800-HAWORTH. E-mail address: <getinfo@haworthpressinc.com> Website: <http://www.HaworthPress.com> © 2002 by The Haworth Press, Inc. All rights reserved.]*

KEYWORDS. Distance learning, higher education, distance education, business, Michigan State University, faculty collaboration, library service

Mary G. Fraser is Assistant Business Librarian, Michigan State University. She has been the library liaison for many online courses in the College of Business and university-wide.

Shari Buxbaum is Head, Gast Business Library, Michigan State University.

Amy Blair is Head, Library Distance Learning Services Department, Michigan State University.

[Haworth co-indexing entry note]: "The Library and the Development of Online Courses." Fraser, Mary G., Shari Buxbaum, and Amy Blair. Co-published simultaneously in *Journal of Business & Finance Librarianship* (The Haworth Information Press, an imprint of The Haworth Press, Inc.) Vol. 7, No. 2/3, 2002, pp. 47-59; and: *Library Services for Business Students in Distance Education: Issues and Trends* (ed: Shari Buxbaum) The Haworth Information Press, an imprint of The Haworth Press, Inc., 2002, pp. 47-59. Single or multiple copies of this article are available for a fee from The Haworth Document Delivery Service [1-800-HAWORTH, 9:00 a.m. - 5:00 p.m. (EST). E-mail address: getinfo@haworthpressinc.com].

47

Is there a role for the library in the design and presentation of online courses? In response to a university-wide initiative to increase distance-learning opportunities, Michigan State University's Broad Graduate School is developing an "Internet-mediated program" for a Master of Science degree in International Business Studies (MIBS). This initiative has presented a unique opportunity for the business librarians to pose the question to the faculty who are developing the courses. This article summarizes the results of a survey done by the librarians, and the discussions that took place while conducting the survey. It also discusses the relationship of the new program to the library's previous experience in providing services to distance education students at MSU.

THE COLLEGE OF BUSINESS
DISTANCE LEARNING PROGRAMS

Michigan State University's Broad College of Business currently offers a Weekend MBA program and an off-campus Executive MBA program, in addition to the traditional MBA degree. Both of these programs have provided opportunities for the Gast Business Library staff to work with distance learning initiatives.

The Executive MBA program has been operating in the Metropolitan Detroit area for 36 years. It is located in Troy, MI, approximately one and a half hours driving time from Michigan State University, but within commuting distance of the "Big Three" automobile manufacturers, as well as other corporate headquarters located in southwest Michigan. Professors travel from the East Lansing, MI, campus to teach in Troy two evenings a week. In the pre-online era, the Executive MBA students did not use the Gast Business Library's resources or services, except for requesting books through a courier system. The physical distance, the ease of access offered by public and academic libraries in southwest Michigan, and the lack of free time in their busy lives made the option of visiting and using the on-campus Business Library unattractive. In recent years this has changed. The expanding availability of electronic resources through the MSU Libraries has brought the library onto the radar screen of the students in this program. Even though Executive MBA students are "using" the electronic library resources via the Web, the business librarians hear from the students in Troy infrequently. Perhaps five requests per semester from a population of 150 students are made via e-mail or telephone.

Several virtual classes have been offered to the on-campus Weekend MBA students over the past two years. In the fall semester of 2000, 180 Weekend MBA students were enrolled in six online courses. The idea for the MIBS degree program evolved out of the positive response from students enrolled in these initial online classes and the MIBS degree will include several of these courses as part of its curriculum. Electronic library resources for the courses are accessed through the Electronic Libraries Web page, on the MSU Center for International Business, Education, and Research (CIBER) Web site. These resources include electronic journals, databases purchased by the MSU Libraries, the library catalog, and an outstanding collection of Internet Web sites in the area of International Business collected and annotated by the College of Business CIBER staff.

The MSU CIBER program receives funding from the U.S. Department of Education to provide leadership in developing international business research and education programs. As part of its mission, MSU CIBER developed a platform to deliver a variety of online learning programs. The platform is called the Virtual International Business Academy or VIBA. The VIBA system is used to offer classes to MSU students and certificate programs for practitioners. The platform is used to conduct online meetings, seminars and workshops geared toward promoting international business education. Along with VIBA, the CIBER office is also currently overseeing efforts to launch the MIBS program. In the MIBS program description, the differences between this program and a traditional MBA program are outlined as follows:

- The MIBS target audience is working adults who want to study international business, whether employer-sponsored or independent.
- The program calls for an initial two-week on-campus, residential period, followed by a 15-week online study period. This module is repeated three times, for a total of 30 credit hours. The second and third residential sessions could potentially take place at sites in the Far East or Latin America, and Europe.

MICHIGAN STATE UNIVERSITY LIBRARY
DISTANCE LEARNING SERVICES UNIT

The MIBS degree will be the first online distance education degree offered through the College of Business, but not the first online program supported by the Gast Business Library. The business librarians currently support a Facilities Management certificate program for the Human Environmental Design department offered through MSU's Virtual University. The Virtual University is the umbrella unit on campus for all MSU distance-learning classes. Librarians throughout the MSU system have been involved with supporting various Virtual University programs for approximately four years.

The MSU Libraries' services to distance learners arc organized through the Library Distance Learning Services (LDLS) unit. This department was designed to provide research assistance and information delivery to all off-campus programs, units and online courses, including the MSU Executive MBA program, the Weekend MBA program and the future MIBS program. A full list of courses, programs and contact information can be found at: <http://www.VirtualUniversity.msu.edu>.

The proposed MIBS business degree is part of a burgeoning university-wide initiative to increase the Virtual University presence at Michigan State. Other full degrees at the Master's level are offered in Criminal Justice, Beam Physics, Packaging and Education. As this initiative grows so do the responsibilities and services offered through the LDLS office. Currently the LDLS office handles all off-campus requests from business students for specific research materials. These requests are shipped within 24-48 hours of receipt. Requests can be placed via e-mail, a Web form, an 800-number phone line, or fax. Articles are sent via first-class mail and books are sent via UPS or with the campus courier to off-campus sites, such as the Executive MBA site in Troy. When LDLS receives a business reference query it is forwarded to the appropriate business librarian.

In an effort to provide one stop shopping for off-campus students experiencing technical difficulties, the LDLS also manages the Libraries' Computing and Technology 24 hour HelpLine. This 800 line has greatly expanded from its original role as a request line for students in off-campus programs to order library materials and library cards. The HelpLine now provides access, technical and informational assistance to a wide variety of campus initiatives including Virtual University courses, on-campus courses with a Web-based component, and all aspects of library technology, assistance with software applications, e-mail, and a host of other areas. Information triage is the guiding principle of the unit, filtering the requests and making referrals to other units as needed. All calls are logged and tracked. This allows the LDLS office to determine areas needing improvement within courses, including technical problems within courses, and to pinpoint programs that are generating a great deal of interest.

The increase in electronic access to research materials has greatly altered the type of calls placed to the HelpLine. Many calls are now devoted to assisting users with their electronic access problems. Setting up the library proxy server to access e-journals and databases requiring IP recognition, discovering broken links to e-journals, and resolving software compatibility and printing issues are all frequent duties of the HelpLine staff.

The LDLS also develops guidelines for and coordinates the MSU librarians who serve as liaisons to distance education courses and/or programs. When a VIRTUAL UNIVERSITY course is proposed, the coordinator of the LDLS office appoints a librarian to assist and support the development and offering of the program. The LDLS unit defines the role of librarians involved with MSU virtual courses as follows:

- Assist faculty with locating supporting materials for the course under development, including appropriate databases, Web pages, full-text articles, etc.
- Provide online reference services and research assistance by phone, e-mail and Web-talk system to students enrolled in the VIRTUAL UNIVERSITY courses.
- Act as the copyright liaison between the VIRTUAL UNIVERSITY technical producer of the course, the faculty member teaching the course and the MSU Libraries' Digital Services Center, which secures permissions for inclusion of copyrighted materials in the online course material.

Past experiences working with the Facilities Management certificate program for the Human Environmental Design department demonstrates that it is the interests and needs of the MSU faculty member teaching the course that dictates the liaison librarian's actual level of involvement with VIRTUAL UNIVERSITY courses.

PLANNING FOR THE MIBS PROGRAM

In his article titled, *The Future of Library Services for Distance Education: What Are We Doing, Where Are We Heading, What Should We Be Doing?* Chris Adams of the University of Saskatchewan states,

The prevailing thinking of tomorrow will probably still be 'the library can absorb demands for materials and service for these new programs because they are already doing this for on-site users.' If this is the approach, then off-campus library services will remain reactionary and traditional, instead of being integrated creatively and thoughtfully into new technology initiatives. (Adams 1997, 1)

Motivated by the desire to integrate the library "creatively and thoughtfully" into this new program, and with the LDLS guidelines in place, the MSU business librarians are exploring how best to plan library services to support the MIBS program and other online College of Business coursework. The American College and Research Libraries' *Guidelines for Distance Learning Services* (http://www.ala.org/acrl/ guides/distlrng.html) provides guidance on what academic librarians should be doing regarding distance learning services. The goal, as interpreted by the MSU business librarians, is to offer the same opportunities and resources to faculty developing the MIBS courses and to the students enrolling in the online programs as are offered to the on-campus population. Traditionally, these services include collection development assistance, reference services, and research instruction. Challenges include utilizing "user-friendly and seamless information technology that will enable users to get the right information at the right time, in the right place, in the right format, and at the right cost, freeing them to go on with their jobs and their lives" (Grobler 1998, 170). Meeting these challenges requires new approaches and an understanding of how library services and information resources relate to the virtual course's content and development. It also involves developing methods for teaching off-campus students to effectively use the resources that are available to them.

INTERVIEWING BUSINESS FACULTY

With these goals and challenges in mind, the librarians at the Gast Business Library conducted a series of interviews with business faculty developing courses for the new VIBA program. To assist with the interview process the following questions were developed and distributed to the faculty before each interview:

- Do you know about the American College and Research Libraries' *Guidelines for Distance Learning Library Services*? If yes, how did you learn about them?

- Do you know about the MSU Libraries support for distance learning course development?
- Will the course you are developing involve library research? Other research? How will students access resources for your course?
- In your opinion, how could the librarians contribute to the success of a VIBA or MIBS course?
- Will your students have a need for reference services?
- As part of the VIBA or MIBS program orientation, should an introduction to the library be included?

A copy of the *ACRL Guidelines for Distance Learning Library Services* was also distributed to each faculty member with the interviewer placing emphasis on the "Resources" and "Services" portion of this document. Each faculty member was interviewed individually, with the interviews lasting from thirty to sixty minutes.

RESULTS OF FACULTY INTERVIEWS

Much information was acquired during the interview sessions. First, the two full-time staff members employed by MSU CIBER have largely taken on the responsibility of helping faculty locate and secure support materials for VIBA/MIBS course work, including information resources. The faculty within the College of Business ask one of these staff members for assistance, who in turn contacts a business librarian if there is difficulty locating a specific database, journal, or online article. This communication process is the result of the College of Business administration's desire to keep the process of developing online courses as simple as possible. Part of the simplicity includes creating one contact point for all faculty involved with the MIBS program. This includes utilizing the CIBER office and its staff for course development and resource assistance. The VIBA/MIBS explanatory material extends this single point of reference idea to their students by describing "VIBA's Digital Library" as "everything the students need, at their fingertips." There is no mention within the promotional material of the support offered through the MSU Libraries. The faculty appears to be satisfied with this arrangement. Their complaints about resources and research assistance revolve around frustration over accessibility and technical issues, such as not being able to create durable, full-text links to various publications and needing electronic access to journals that are not yet available online.

Second, the amount of actual research done for the current course work is very minimal. Case study analysis and pre-selected supplementary readings in the *Harvard Business Review, Wall Street Journal, New York Times* and some other e-journals make up the bulk of library material for these classes. Whenever possible, the majority of reading materials for the courses are being included as direct electronic links. These links are created and maintained by the MSU CIBER staff.

During the interviews, one faculty member explains: "(My) course emphasis is on content and analysis, not on information seeking skills. The course is totally self-contained and I don't want students to know about the library. I deliberately spoon feed to reduce their frustrations. Information seeking skills will come later." Another faculty member states, "There will be library research . . . but I am more interested in making them read and think, than search effectively." Only two faculty members are planning in-depth research projects for their classes, but both felt that their students would not require reference assistance to complete these projects. In fact, none of the faculty interviewed believe their students will require reference assistance.

Interestingly, despite the low level of research required of the program, many of the faculty members believe some type of training session covering the library resources will be useful to the students. Only one faculty member feels the instruction should be course-integrated, which is the methodology most often utilized within the Business Library's on-campus instruction program. All others believe a basic session covering database content and accessibility issues will suffice. Instructors are divided on whether this instruction should be Web-based or included in the first on-campus orientation session for the students.

It is the role of copyright liaison that evokes the greatest interest from several of the VIBA/MIBS faculty. Many of these faculty, especially those new to the world of online course development, were not aware of the need to secure permissions for all copyrighted materials included in their virtual course content. It should be mentioned that Michigan State University has chosen to take a very conservative stance on the issue of copyright permissions. Once made aware of this policy, many of the faculty are relieved that librarians are available to help them identify materials needing copyright clearance. Others are overwhelmed that this might be an issue for their course materials. Two faculty members believe that copyright issues are part of the MSU CIBER staff's responsibility. Another small group of faculty, mostly using their own textbooks and cases, dismiss these concerns as a non-issue for their courses.

Differing opinions regarding copyright issues appear to be commonplace in distance learning programs. Walsh, in the *Australian Library Journal,* states that . . .

> . . . as information is converted to, and increasingly created in, digital form the question of copyright protection has become vexed. We have seen in very recent times the emergence of polarized views. On one hand there are those who propose that copyright is irrelevant. On the other hand there are those who propose new and broader rights, increased protection and greater control for the owners of copyright. (Walsh 1996, 253)

IMPLICATIONS OF THE INTERVIEW RESULTS

The implications of the interviews are interesting. The faculty responses demonstrate that in their opinion traditional services such as resource support and collection development are being conducted in a satisfactory manner by non-library staff. The MSU CIBER staff has apparently met the needs of faculty in locating, securing and formatting course content. It should be noted that all of the courses, with the exception of one, are online adaptations of existing courses. Only one faculty member expressed interest in having the business librarians collect a list of appropriate Internet links to supplement her course content. Coincidently, she is also the only professor currently developing an original course for this program. The interviews did provide the librarians with a concrete list of items needed by the business faculty to make online course development easier, with durable links to *Wall Street Journal* articles and the *Harvard Business Review* topping the wish list.

One other collection issue, expressed by two faculty members, is the need to be aware of the geographical location of the students in this program. As one faculty member states, "Courses and information resources will need more global data and international focus as the program becomes global." The make-up of future MIBS students is unknown, but a large group of students from India, for example, might require collecting virtual resources for this specific geographic area.

The faculty predicts that research support and requests for reference service will be almost non-existent in the MIBS program. Questions remain about how faculty define reference services, since even the two professors requiring research projects do not believe their students will have a need for reference services. Perhaps the faculty defines reference services in terms of their own information needs. These are often for a specific citation, statistic, definition or data set, instead of the more general "help!" type research question. This discrepancy in expectations is not new to distance learning environments. In 1997, a group of British librarians reported on a survey of 1,000 distance learners, from 23 different UK universities. The results showed that there was a significant difference in expectations between students and course providers about the role of libraries in relation to the distance learning courses.

> Course providers interviewed generally regarded the role of libraries as irrelevant to their students or as a problem in their own institutional arrangements. And while 51% of the students responded *'No, It is not a clearly stated requirement of the course that I make use of libraries,'* 78% responded that they needed to supplement the course material with additional reading or research either *'to some extent, quite a lot, or a great deal.'* This survey suggests that students themselves are more aware of the extent to which they will need to use libraries than the course providers. (Unwin, Stephens, and Bolton 1998)

The lack of research projects demonstrates that the business librarians need to reconsider their dedication to course-integrated instruction and expand their methods for delivering instruction. Other than providing online resource guides, the MSU business librarians do not currently provide any type of virtual library instruction. The launching of the MIBS program provides a wonderful opportunity to develop online business tutorials on a variety of common topics. Potential audiences for the tutorials include both on-campus and off-campus students. Ideally, a combination of face-to-face instruction in the form of an initial orientation session, supported by virtual instruction available 24-7, will be best for the MIBS and VIBA students. This idea is supported by the philosophy behind the MIBS program, which emphasizes the value of on-site instruction as part of its core philosophy. Promotional material for the MIBS program states that there "is a value in the face-to-face interaction, and you just can't replicate that using technology." However, time during the on-campus components will be a valuable commodity. It remains to be seen whether there will be time granted for face-to-face library orientations.

One new opportunity for librarians appears to be that of copyright liaison. In order to address the differing opinions and reactions to this issue uncovered by the survey, the business librarians are launching an education initiative specifically for MIBS faculty in the form of an hour-long workshop on copyright issues in the electronic environment.

NEW CHALLENGES

It is apparent from the survey that the Gast Business "virtual library" and its Web presence need to be viewed with a more critical eye. Guidelines for creating user-friendly Web pages for distance learners are given in an article by Julie Linden. She points out that Webmasters do not always realize that for a distance learner, "the library's Web page is the library" (Linden 2000, 99). One faculty member offered this advice, " . . . for everything, librarians should focus on creating a friendly, intuitive, clear, simple interface to the library resources." It is necessary for the business librarians to organize the Web page to make it easy for distance learners to find the services they need, since this is the only library environment that the distance learner may encounter.

Another faculty member says, "VIBA course development is library driven. It is what is available electronically that builds course content and if we lose content, then how do we get it? And how do the students get it?" This theory was tested recently when ProQuest's ABI/Inform database lost full-text access to the *Harvard Business Review*. Multiple static links to articles from this resource, in multiple online classes suddenly became obsolete. Students and teachers panicked as case studies and assignments were immediately affected by this loss. Implications of "self-contained courses" other than possible inconveniences are discussed in the Stephens and Unwin article "The Heart of the Matter: Libraries, Distance Education and Independent Thinking":

> The self-contained course, where students study from packaged materials and are not expected to read or consult sources beyond supplied materials . . . available through electronic access might compound the trend towards narrowly prescribed reading, leading to even greater student isolation as teachers are pushed further into becoming designers of pre-packaged programmed learning. The self-contained package approach has the potential to deskill librarians as well as students, as does the illusion that a limited electronic reserve collection can fulfill the functions of an academic library. (Stephens and Unwin 1997, 2)

If the program is to be available globally, simple interfaces, dependability, and accessibility, which are not new issues for librarians dealing with electronic resources, become crucial in the distance-learning environment. One professor, who recently completed teaching a semester long VIBA course to a group of distance learners in Sweden, describes dealing with .pdf files as "a hassle." If this is true in Sweden, it is easy to imagine what technological challenges students from less developed nations might encounter. Databases such as ABI/Inform, FIS and Dow Jones that tout .pdf files as a benefit, will suddenly not be as useful in these situations.

CONCLUSION

The survey conducted by the MSU business librarians brought into focus two conflicting trends. First, professors developing an online course are very dependent on electronic resources and will almost instinctively create the coursework to match the availability of the online resources. Second, despite this dependency, the faculty we interviewed expressed little interest in seeking library participation in the process. This conclusion is validated by the literature review published by Beagle (Beagle, 2000) in which he surveys articles published by faculty on the topic of distance education. Results of a survey conducted by the ACRL Distance Learning Section Research Committee, during April-June 2000, identified collaboration with faculty as the number one research priority when designing the provision of library services for distance learners. Our interview experience here at MSU leads us to believe that the education of faculty regarding the origin, availability and copyright regulations of online resources will need to become a major outreach initiative as the MIBS program comes to fruition. Collection development choices, online reference services and research instruction are all dependent on collaboration with the faculty. If the faculty does not think of library access when developing distance education courses, then our goal of offering excellent service to our off-campus population is sure to fail.

Other opportunities revealed by the interview process include researching how faculty members define "reference service," creating a user-friendly portal for our information resources, and adding an online educational component to our current Web presence. As the new MIBS program is introduced, it will also be interesting to track through the Library Distance Learning Services unit questions concerning business reference and research, in addition to the requests for technical troubleshooting that are anticipated.

Librarians must redefine their roles and services, as they become partners in supporting distance education programs. Addressing the issues raised within this interview process is going to be crucial to the future success of distance education endeavors.

REFERENCES

Adams, Chris, "The Future of Library Services for Distance Education: What Are We Doing, Where Are We Heading, What Should We Be Doing?" *Journal of Library Services for Distance Education*, 1,1 (August 1997). <http://www.westga.edu/~library/jlsde/jisde1.1.html> [accessed 3/16/2001].

Beagle, Don. "Web-based learning environments: Do libraries matters?" *College and Research Libraries* 61, 4 (July 2000): 367-379.

Grobler, Lorraine M. "Towards the Virtual Library: Meeting Remote Business Students' Library and Information Needs." In *The Eighth Off-Campus Library Services Conference Proceedings: Providence, Rhode Island, April 22-24, 1998*, compiled by P. Steven Thomas and Maryhelen Jones. Mount Pleasant, MI: Central Michigan University, 1998, 165-173.

Linden, Julie, "The Library's Web Site Is the Library: Designing for Distance Learners" *College & Research Libraries News* 61, 2 (February 2000) 99,101.

Stephens, K., and Unwin, L., "The Heart of the Matter: Libraries, Distance Education and Independent Thinking" *Journal of Library Services for Distance Education*, 1, 1 (August 1997). <http://www.westga.edu/~library/jlsde/jlsde1.1.html> [accessed 3/16/2001].

Survey on research priorities in library services for distance learning, April-June 2000, Association of College and Research Libraries Distance Learning Section Research Committee. <http://gateway2.UVIC.ca/dls/summary.html> [accessed 3/16/2001].

Unwin, L., Stephens, K., and Bolton, N. *The Role of the Library in Distance Learning: A Study of Postgraduate Students, Course-Providers, and Libraries in the UK*. London: Bowker Saur, 1998.

Walsh, V. "The Future of the Library Profession," *Australian Library Journal* 4: 251-255.

The Role of Libraries
in Global Business Distance Education

Lisa Robinson

SUMMARY. This article examines the globalization of distance business education in the context of the provision of library services to such programs. It examines the multiple challenges faced by librarians when serving students in online business courses and programs, highlights some of the ways those challenges have been met in particular business programs, and delineates the challenges still to be met by business librarians. *[Article copies available for a fee from The Haworth Document Delivery Service: 1-800-HAWORTH. E-mail address: <getinfo@haworthpressinc.com> Website: <http://www.HaworthPress.com> © 2002 by The Haworth Press, Inc. All rights reserved.]*

KEYWORDS. Distance learning, globalization, digital library services, online instruction, virtual MBA, reference

This paper will examine the globalization of distance business education in the context of the provision of library services to these programs and courses. Distance business education is currently being provided by a variety of institutions–universities (both virtual and physical), col-

Lisa Robinson, MS, PhD, is Assistant Digital Services Librarian, Michigan State University. Her responsibilities include the digitization and description of audio recordings, copyright, and general reference.

[Haworth co-indexing entry note]: "The Role of Libraries in Global Business Distance Education." Robinson, Lisa. Co-published simultaneously in *Journal of Business & Finance Librarianship* (The Haworth Information Press, an imprint of The Haworth Press, Inc.) Vol. 7, No. 2/3, 2002, pp. 61-71; and: *Library Services for Business Students in Distance Education: Issues and Trends* (ed: Shari Buxbaum) The Haworth Information Press, an imprint of The Haworth Press, Inc., 2002, pp. 61-71. Single or multiple copies of this article are available for a fee from The Haworth Document Delivery Service [1-800-HAWORTH, 9:00 a.m. - 5:00 p.m. (EST). E-mail address: getinfo@haworthpressinc.com].

leges, corporate training programs–from around the world. It exists in a variety of formats–individual undergraduate and graduate courses, entire degree programs, executive and corporate training–and in a variety of media–print, satellite television, videocassette, online. Libraries are not necessarily deemed necessary for all these efforts. I have organized this paper around a series of questions: What is meant by distance business education? What is meant by the globalization of distance education for business? Where is the library and how are library services provided to distance education students? Do libraries in fact matter for distance education? The answers to these questions will highlight the multiple challenges faced by librarians when serving students in online business courses and programs, highlight some of the ways those challenges have been met in particular business programs, and delineate the challenges still to be met by business librarians.

WHAT IS DISTANCE BUSINESS EDUCATION?

Distance business education is a growing phenomenon in the United States and around the world. *BusinessWeek Online* lists thirty-nine universities with distance business degree programs, mostly in the United States but including those from overseas.[1] Not all of these programs make use of the Internet for distance education. But among universities, M.B.A. programs are often among the first to go online, since that relatively expensive tuition paid by students for that 1 degree enables institutions to recover quickly the cost of new program development. A number of major business schools, such as the Wharton School of the University of Pennsylvania, that already offer "executive M.B.A." programs for working professionals are now using technology to help them compete for students.[2]

The first M.B.A. program to go entirely online was the program at Athabasca University in Alberta, Canada in 1995. The AU Library provides "distance library service to AU students" and makes "reasonable attempts to provide library services to students outside of Canada."[3] Although both these types of students may appear in person to access the library's resources, they may also use telephone, fax, e-mail and the World Wide Web to contact the library for services. One of the most innovative distance library services is the capability to request books automatically from the library's online catalog using just a single on-screen button. In addition, students may request inter-library loan of journal articles and books using online forms, access electronic databases and reference tools through a proxy server, and seek reference assistance using an online form, e-mail, telephone, fax. And the library has not neglected bibliographic instruction. There is an online tutorial on how to use the online catalog and a Web page on how to search the World Wide Web.[4]

Yet in spite of the proliferation of online or partly online graduate degrees in business administration, most of the most highly ranked U.S. business schools, such as the University of Pennsylvania's Wharton School and MIT's Sloan School of Management, do not offer any of their M.B.A. courses online. The rationale may be that in such schools, students are looking for the chance to make personal contacts with their classmates and that such contacts are not as easily made online. However, this does not mean that the top business schools are not interested in promoting online interactions nor providing online library services. In 1998, Wharton launched an online community for students and faculty called WebCafé that allows teachers and students to exchange instructional materials and other documents online and creates a virtual "meeting space" for students and online clubs.[5] Wharton has also recently created a student intranet, called SPIKE, that provides a single, integrated interface for students' activities, such as e-mail, school announcements, coursework, group discussions. This interface can be customized and is accessible through a Palm device or integrated into Microsoft Outlook.[6] Librarians wishing to reach the faculty and students in these online environments will need to be prepared to effectively navigate this kind of technology.

In addition to print-based distance education and online business degree programs and courses, there are a wide variety of corporate-oriented training courses and certificate programs that are provided both by universities, often in partnership with corporations, as well as by "corporate universities." Corporations today are increasingly taking on responsibility for preparing their employees to compete in the global economy.[7] Colleges and universities are engaging in a variety of partnerships with corporations, including conducting onsite courses, sharing libraries and research, and creating custom-made degree programs. In one such example, the Hartford Financial Services Group collaborated with the University of Connecticut to develop a Business Mastery Certificate Program for the company, involving both face-to-face and online instruction of corporate leaders by university faculty. Such partnerships often involve sharing libraries and research between the corporation and the university. But some corporations are creating their own institutions of higher education, some of which offer courses to the general public as well as to their own direct constituencies. Motorola University has sites in thirteen countries and offers courses such as "Team Problem Solving" and "Applying Continuous Improvement Tools." They offer to design training classes that respond directly to employee needs by including "Subject Matter Experts from your organization and ours in the design and development phases."[8] Reference librarians could certainly be considered "subject matter experts." Such collaboration represents a new opportunity for business librarians to provide service to corporate and academic audiences simultaneously.

Corporations and universities often operate in very different cultures, ones in which the value of libraries and librarians may be seen quite differently. A growing number of cooperative educational ventures with corporations will be driven financially as universities and libraries of all kinds make agreements to underwrite the high cost of technology-oriented services.[9] Since higher education's institutional framework is changing, due in part to the versatility and perceived economy of networked learning, our most important future professional alliances as librarians may be with corporate virtual universities.[10]

WHAT IS GLOBALIZATION?

As the economic and telecommunication forces of globalization encourage business and social interaction with people from diverse cultures and places, global distance business education can help individuals have an informed and systematic approach to diversity and globalization in their work and to become more effective global business professionals.

The globalization of distance business education can mean the targeting of overseas students by universities or provision of distance education by overseas institutions. An example of the former is the Global University Alliance, which will soon begin offering graduate and professional courses, including business courses, online in Asia. Nine universities (Athabasca University in Canada, Auckland University of Technology in New Zealand, Chung Yuan Christian University in Taiwan, Hogeschool Brabant International Business School in the Netherlands, the Royal Melbourne Institute of Technology and the University of South Australia in Australia, the Rochester Institute of Technology in the United States, and the Universities of Derby and Glamorgan in

Great Britain) are collaborating with NextEd, an online-education technology company.[11]

A striking example of the latter type of globalization is The Open University of Hong Kong (OUHK), which offers distance education in a variety of subjects to the Hong Kong community and the rest of China and has recently graduated its first M.B.A.'s from mainland China. The university's School of Business and Administration has also just begun collaborating with the Hong Kong Productivity Council to develop educational and training programs in business administration.[12]

But one growing aspect of globalization is the idea that business education, whether at a distance or not, must increasingly focus on global business activity and issues of international diversity. The Internet provides an excellent means of bringing diverse and dispersed students together regardless of their location, and of exposing students to sources of information outside their country of origin through the use of hyperlinked Web pages. A new type of M.B.A. degree is emerging, a "global M.B.A."

The University of Cambridge's Judge Institute of Management in partnership with M.I.T. and F.T. Knowledge, a division of the London-based company that publishes the *Financial Times,* has created a new degree program, the "e-M.B.A." that admitted its first students in July 2001.[13] This program uses virtual learning technology combined with intensive residential periods in Cambridge to develop global business managers. Library and information services for this program are provided by the Institute's management library. The library holds core textbooks and journals, as well as electronic media, such as 600 full text titles on CD-Rom and the Web and a range of bibliographical, financial, and news databases.

In the executive education arena, the University of Michigan and F.T. Knowledge are also working together to offer two jointly-branded Web-based courses, "Developing the Manager in You" and "Finance for the Nonfinancial Manager." Each participant in these courses receives a "course map," which is a CD-ROM containing all the reading and background materials needed to complete the course. No library services are required for such a distance education course.

WHERE IS THE LIBRARY?

There was a time when this question had a straightforward answer. For universities, a library was a building on campus where students went to consult print books and journals. As universities started to engage in distance education, through correspondence courses, telecourses, and remote classrooms, the university library has stretched itself by sending its items (or photocopies of its items) by mail to distance education students. This model, that "the library" is located in one physical place and reaches remote students by mail, is one which appears to inform a number of distance education programs.

The Off Campus Library Service (OCLS) of Central Michigan University (CMU) is comprised of reference and document delivery services. Started in 1976, OCLS is nationally recognized as a learner-centered model program among academic institutions. The Document Delivery component of this service is located on the main campus and handles requests for print materials from all students enrolled in CMU's College of Extended Learning courses regardless of location or course format. The librarians provide copies of articles from journals owned by CMU and of course materials, and will mail books from the CMU Libraries.[14] For the off-campus students of Central Michigan, the library is still the one located on campus.

Similarly, at Deakin University in Australia, which maintains multiple campuses and offers part of its Bachelor of Commerce degree through distance education, the campus libraries form the support for off-campus study. Off-campus students can request books and other materials from the Library by mail, fax, telephone, e-mail and through the Web-accessible catalog, and the requested items will be mailed to the student. However, off-campus students are also encouraged to borrow in person from any of the campus libraries or to make use of interstate university and college libraries.[15]

Librarians cannot even be certain that the participants in distance education courses are located off-campus. Holly Heller-Ross, in her survey of library support for distance learning programs, found that "online courses are offered to both on-campus and distance-learning students, on-campus faculty are creating World Wide Web pages with course materials, and e-mail is ubiquitous. The lines between on and off-campus students and courses are indeed blurring as technology is incorporated into all aspects of education."[16] We can see this blurring quite clearly in the move of university libraries increasingly into the realm of online library catalogs, electronic databases and full-text resources. It has become commonplace for an academic library to offer at least some online resources, whether or not that university offers distance education or online courses. It is therefore sometimes assumed by administrators and faculty that such digital libraries will be compatible with any Web-based learning environment and therefore easily provide online resources to supplement online course materials.[17]

The Association of College and Research Libraries in its *Guidelines for Distance Learning Library Services* defines distance learning library services as "those library services in support of college, university, or other post-secondary courses and programs offered away from a main campus, or in the absence of a traditional campus, and regardless of where credit is given. These courses may be taught in traditional or non-traditional formats or media, may or may not require physical facilities, and may or may not involve live interaction of teachers and students. The phrase is inclusive of courses in all post-secondary programs designated as extension, extended, off-campus, extended campus, distance, distributed, open, flexible, franchising, virtual, synchronous, or asynchronous."[18]

But such a conception is not without its problems. Some of these problems, such as having the technical infrastructure necessary to supply digital materials and authenticate user access, may not be under library control. Other problems, such as the conversion of print materials to digital format and the resultant need to protect authors' and publishers' intellectual property rights, may require collaboration with other institutions. But some problems, such as staff familiarity with computer technologies and willingness to work in an online environment, are matters that only the librarians themselves can address.

DO LIBRARIES MATTER TO DISTANCE EDUCATION?

Donald Beagle, in his recent article in *College and Research Libraries,* reviewed articles in a number of leading journals devoted to Web-based education, and found that most discussions of online education do not even mention libraries. He concluded that "Web-based learning environments have emerged from a distance education tradition that . . . exhibits a tendency to assume minimal access to library services."[19] There are indeed serious challenges to the provision of library services to distance learners. One major challenge is that most library collections (books, journals, and media) are usually selected for on-campus use, and most library services (instructional classes, print reserve services, research indexes or databases and library tours) are designed for on-campus programs. These collections and services often do not serve the needs of off-campus students well. Publishers of online journals may also erect barriers to remote access, for no apparent reason. One such example at Michigan State University is the online journals provided by Ingenta. These 128 journals, covering the sciences, medicine, social sciences, and business, are not accessible through a proxy server, and therefore are not available off-campus. This is a severe limitation to distance education students who cannot be assumed to be able to come into the library building for journal access.

There can often be "a significant mismatch of expectations between students and course providers about the role of libraries in the distance learning mode." In a survey of a thousand students and faculty participating in distance education in the United Kingdom, Kate Stephens and Lorna Unwin discovered that faculty viewed library services as irrelevant to their students, while students believed that a library was necessary to supplement course material with additional reading.[20] The authors describe two types of distance education programs. In the first type, there are fully self-contained courses where students are provided a packet of materials that includes all the necessary reading and research sources for the course. A library, online or otherwise, is assumed to be irrelevant to the educational experience. In the second type, there are courses in which students are expected to study largely from packaged materials, but provision is made for wider reading and research. In this type, libraries, particularly ones with online resources, are invaluable. The first type of course is often designed in that way in the belief that it is more equitable to students, in that everyone has the same access to the same materials. The designers of the second type, however, believed it was more important to develop students' autonomous learning skills that include being able to search for and retrieve information from a variety of sources and in a variety of formats.

Students in distance education courses of the second type certainly require remote access to the full range of library services, including reference assistance and bibliographic instruction, interlibrary loan, course reserves, circulation, and database access. The Electronic Library of the Open University of Hong Kong (OUHK)[21] is an excellent example of such comprehensive provision of library services. This initiative began in 1997 and was recently named best of its type for international education in a European Commission-sponsored competition.[22] It provides round-the-clock, free, remote access to library services from home and expanded the library collection to about 500,000 volumes of equivalent electronic collections. It also offers access to library catalogs of the higher education institutions in Hong Kong and overseas, as well as to previous OUHK examination papers and additional readings. All electronic library services, including online catalog, electronic reserve collection, the electronic databases and resources, and distance education institutions, were integrated through a single Web-based common user interface, which is provided to students in the form of free dial-up kits by the Library. A built-in English/Chinese search engine enables user queries in both languages. There is also a video server providing on-demand instructional videos to teach users on how to use the electronic library services at their own time and pace. The bilingual online public access catalogue has been made available to users since late 1992 and supports both English and Chinese. Since not all students know the Chinese inputting method from the keyboard, a special device known as "hand writing pad" was installed and interfaced with the DYNIX library system. The pad could recognize the handwriting of users and transform it into computer-recognized form.[23]

CONCLUSION: CHALLENGES TO BE MET

Unless libraries are encouraged to play a central role in the distance and online education process, and are supported in that effort, both financially and technologically, students in distance education programs will face an environment where their learning experiences will be tightly bounded and controlled. Although advances in network and communication technology make it increasingly possible for students to become more autonomous learners and to more easily reach beyond the confines of a single campus, the assumptions that administrators, faculty, and librarians make about such education will limit the effects of that technology. The assumption that everything a student needs to know in a course can be put on a CD-ROM will thwart the involvement of libraries in distance education.

But librarians themselves must look at what they do differently. Collection development, for example, needs to be done with remote users in mind. Collection managers must become familiar with works in all formats, not just print, and be willing to order and manage those formats. They must become conversant with digital technology and the mechanisms for the delivery of content over the Internet.

Reference will require more familiarity with Internet communications software technologies also. Reference librarians will need to develop their abilities to conduct reference interviews through technological mediation, not just through the traditional face-to-face reference interview. They must also become increasingly aware of global information resources, and bear in mind that time zone differences may complicate their reference interactions.

Bibliographic instruction librarians must develop Web-based modules and research guides to materials. We can no longer assume that patrons will be able or willing to come into the library in person to receive such instruction. And all librarians will need an increased sensitivity to cultural differences and proficiency with foreign languages to facilitate the delivery of library services to globally-located distance education students.

As Web-based learning environments become more common, libraries and librarians run the risk of being marginalized. Averting that fate will require action on the part of librarians. Librarians will need to advocate for the financial and technological support needed to develop tools for serving distance learning populations, whether it be the creation of Web interfaces or the licensing of electronic resources. Librarians will also need to break down limiting assumptions about what constitutes library services to distance education and discourage a reliance on a pre-packaged, limited class readings model. And finally, librarians will need to actively embrace collaborations with the designers of distance education programs to ensure that information technology is not used in an unnecessarily limiting way and that the wealth of global information resources remains available for students, whether on campus or off.

NOTES

1. *BusinessWeek Online* (February 9, 2001). <http://www.businessweek.com/bschools/00pt/index.html#dist>.

2. Jennifer Lewington. "Canada's On-Line MBA: Program at Athabasca U. is viewed as a model for postsecondary education." *The Chronicle of Higher Education* (March 17, 1995).

3. Athabasca University. *Library @ Athabasca University.* <http://library.athabascau.ca/> Last accessed February 8, 2001.

4. Athabasca University Library. *How to Search AUCAT.* <http://library.athabascau.ca/help/aucat/page1.htm>. Last accessed February 8, 2001.

5. Marion Agnew. "Collaboration on the Desktop." *Information Week Online.* (July 10, 2000) <http://www.informationweek.com/794/collab.htm>. Last accessed February 8, 2001; The Wharton School of the University of Pennsylvania. *WebCafé: a collaboration and teaching tool at Wharton.* <http://webcafe.wharton.upenn.edu/pages/overview.html>. Last accessed February 8, 2001.

6. The Wharton School of the University of Pennsylvania. *Wharton's SPIKE: Overview of SPIKE 6.* <http://www.wharton.upenn.edu/spike/>. Last accessed February 8, 2001.

7. Jeanne C. Meister. "The Brave New World of Corporate Education" The *Chronicle of Higher Education* (February 9, 2001). <http://chronicle.com/weekly/v4/i22/22b01001.htm>. Last accessed February 6, 2001.

8. Motorola University. *Custom Learning Design.* <http://mu.motorola.com/CLD/index.html>. Last accessed February 9, 2001.

9. Chris Adams. "The Future of Library Services for Distance Education: What Are We Doing, Where Are We Heading, What Should We Be Doing?" *Journal of Library Services for Distance Education* 1 #1 (August 1997) <http://www.westga.edu/~library/jlsde/jlsde1.1.html>. Last accessed December 5, 2000.

10. Maryhelen Jones, "High Five for the Next Five: Librarians and Distance Education." *Journal of Library Services for Distance Education* 1 #1 (August 1997). <http://www.westga.edu/~library/jlsde/jlsde1.1.html>. Last accessed December 5, 2000.

11. Geoffrey Maslen. "Universities Collaborate on Online Instruction in Asia." *The Chronicle of Higher Education* (June 16, 2000). <http://chronicle.com/free/2000/06/200006160u.htm>. Last accessed June 16, 2000.

12. Open University of Hong Kong. *HKPC and OUHK form partnership to provide professional business training.* <http://www.ouhk.edu.hk/~oliwww/whatnew/PressRelease/2000news/pr001218/pr001218.htm>. Last accessed February 7, 2001.

13. Goldie Blumenstyk. "U. of Cambridge to Collaborate with a Media Giant on an Online M.B.A." *The Chronicle of Higher Education* (July 17, 2000). <http://chronicle.com/free/2000/07/20000071701u.htm>. Last accessed July 17, 2000; Judge Institute of Management Studies. *JIMS Programmes–eMBA* <http://www.jims.cam.ac.uk/programmes/mba/emba_f.html>. Last accessed February 9, 2001.

14. Central Michigan University. *Off Campus Library Services.* <http://ocls.cmich.edu/index.html>. Last accessed February 9, 2001.

15. Deakin University. *Off Campus Course Guide: Library Services.* <http://www.deakin.edu.au/home/courses/2001occg/study_services/library.htm>. Last accessed February 9, 2001.

16. Holly Heller-Ross, "Library Support for Distance Learning Programs: A Distributed Model" *Journal of Library Services for Distance Education* 2 #1 (July 1999). <http://www.westga.edu/~library/jlsde/vol2/1/HHeller-Ross.html>. Last accessed February 7, 2001.

17. J.R. Bourne, A.J. Borderson, & J.O. Cambell. "A Model for On-Line Learning Networks in Engineering Education." *Journal of Asynchronous Learning Networks* 1 #1 (March 1977). <http:///www.aln.org/alnwev/journal/issue1/bourne.htm>.

18. Association of College and Research Libraries, *Guidelines for Distance Learning Library Services.* <http://www.ala.org/acrl/guides/distlrng.html>. Last accessed February 6, 2001.

19. Donald Beagle. "Web-based Learning Environments: Do Libraries Matter?" *College and Research Libraries* 61 #4 (July 2000):367-379.

20. Kate Stephens and Lorna Unwin. "The Heart of the Matter: Libraries, Distance Education and Independent Thinking." *Journal of Library Services for Distance Education* 1 #1 (August 1997). <http://www.westga.edu/~library/jlsde/jlsde1.1.html>. Last accessed May 16, 2001.

21. The Open University of Hong Kong. *Electronic Library.* <http://www.lib.ouhk.edu.hk/>. Last accessed February 7, 2001.

22. David Cohen. "Hong Kong's Boom in Distance Education May Be a Sign of What's to Come in Asia." *The Chronicle of Higher Education* (July 14, 2000). <http://chronicle.com/weekly/v46/i45/45a05001.htm>. Last accessed January 31, 2001.

23. Wai-man Wong. "Library Services for Distance Learners in the Open University of Hong Kong." *AAOU '98–Asian Librarians' Roundtable* (Sept 1998). <http://www.ouhk.edu.hk/~AAOUNet/round/waiman.pdf>. Last accessed February 7, 2001.

Library Services
for Off-Campus Business Professionals

Anne Marie Casey

SUMMARY. Central Michigan University has been offering degree programs to business professionals off-campus since 1971 through the College of Extended Learning. In 1976, Off-Campus Library Services was formed to provide library services exclusively for students enrolled in off-campus courses. This article describes the off-campus administration degree programs and the reference, instruction, and document delivery services that Off-Campus Library Services provides to these students. *[Article copies available for a fee from The Haworth Document Delivery Service: 1-800-HAWORTH. E-mail address: <getinfo@haworthpressinc.com> Website: <http://www.HaworthPress.com> © 2002 by The Haworth Press, Inc. All rights reserved.]*

KEYWORDS. Off-campus library services, distance learning library services, library instruction, reference services, document delivery, library partnerships, off-campus students, distance learning students

---

Anne Marie Casey, BA, MA, AMLS, is Director of Off-Campus Library Services, Central Michigan University. Prior to this position, she served as Off-Campus Librarian for the West Region and Off-Campus Librarian for the South Region at Central Michigan University.

[Haworth co-indexing entry note]: "Library Services for Off-Campus Business Professionals." Casey, Anne Marie. Co-published simultaneously in *Journal of Business & Finance Librarianship* (The Haworth Information Press, an imprint of The Haworth Press, Inc.) Vol. 7, No. 2/3, 2002, pp. 73-85; and: *Library Services for Business Students in Distance Education: Issues and Trends* (ed: Shari Buxbaum) The Haworth Information Press, an imprint of The Haworth Press, Inc., 2002, pp. 73-85. Single or multiple copies of this article are available for a fee from The Haworth Document Delivery Service [1-800-HAWORTH, 9:00 a.m. - 5:00 p.m. (EST). E-mail address: getinfo@haworthpressinc.com].

INTRODUCTION

Central Michigan University started teaching off-campus courses in the early 1900s and has been offering entire degree programs off-campus since 1971. Beginning in 1976, library services for off-campus students have been provided by Off-Campus Library Services (OCLS). OCLS provides library services for all off-campus students regardless of degree program. However, over the years that OCLS has been in existence, the majority of students taking off-campus classes have been business professionals in the Master of Science in Administration degree program. The services described here are available to all off-campus students but because of the high numbers of students taking courses or working on degree programs in administration, most have been tailored to research in business. Most of the OCLS annual acquisitions budget is dedicated to purchasing business monographs and sustaining subscriptions to business periodicals and databases. The OCLS Web site places a strong emphasis on business topics and many of the handouts developed for instruction are also geared to administration classes.

BRIEF HISTORY OF CEL AND OCLS

Central Michigan University has been offering degrees to business professionals at a distance through the Extended Degree Programs of the College of Extended Learning (CEL) since 1971. Degree programs are available at over 60 centers and cohort locations throughout the United States, Canada, and Mexico. In addition, online and print-based learning package courses and degrees are available nationally and internationally through the Distance and Distributed Learning (DDL) division of CEL.

Courses offered at program centers and in cohorts are taught in classrooms by campus or adjunct faculty. All of the classroom courses are offered in a compressed format. Many are taught on weekends over a six-week period. Others are taught on weeknights over six, eight or nine weeks. DDL courses are taught through the World Wide Web and through print-based learning packages.

Program Centers offer one or more courses per term on an open enrollment basis. As soon as students are admitted to the program, they may start taking courses in the next term. Classes are offered year round so students are not required to wait until September or January to start their degree programs. Cohorts are groups of 25-30 students pursuing the same degree program, who take all of their courses together in a predetermined sequence.

Over 12,000 students are enrolled annually in the College of Extended Learning, which delivers over 2,000 courses per year. The average age of the CEL student is 37. Approximately 55% are graduate students and 45% are undergraduates. Most CEL students work full time while they are pursuing a degree through CMU that normally takes about two years to complete. Students in program centers and cohorts are generally not required to have personal access to computers although most have access at work or at home. In courses where the use of a computer is required in the classroom, it is supplied by CMU.

Library services for students registered for courses through the College of Extended Learning are provided exclusively by OCLS. Established in 1976, OCLS is comprised of reference, instructional services and document delivery services. The operating budget for OCLS comes from the College of Extended Learning. OCLS has developed and maintains a Web site separate from the main library Web site, which focuses more on the needs of students taking classes at a distance. The OCLS staff consists of seven librarians, seven FTE support staff and up to 15 student assistants per semester. The director and two of the off-campus librarians are based in Park Library on the campus of Central Michigan University. One off-campus librarian is responsible for library instruction to students in Canada and Mexico, the other is responsible for library instruction to students in DDL and in Michigan outside the metropolitan Detroit area. The librarian responsible for instruction in the Metro Detroit area is housed in the CMU regional office in suburban Detroit. The librarian who handles instruction for students in the northeastern U.S. is located in the CMU regional office in suburban Washington, DC. The librarian responsible for instruction to students in the Western U.S. is located in Kansas City. The librarian who handles instruction for students in the southeastern U.S. is housed in the CMU regional office in Atlanta.

Six of the support staff are located at the main campus. Five work with document delivery and the sixth handles copyright clearance for faculty teaching off-campus courses. Half time reference assistants are located in two of the field offices. All of the student assistants are employed in the Document Delivery Office or for the copyright service.

MASTER OF SCIENCE IN ADMINISTRATION PROGRAM AND UNDERGRADUATE ADMINISTRATION DEGREES

"The 36-semester-hour Master of Science in Administration degree program provides the knowledge and skills required for managers, administrators, and supervisors to function more effectively in all types of organizations, plus the specialized managerial expertise needed for a particular professional field" (Central Michigan University 1999, 52). The MSA degree is offered in program centers and cohorts throughout the U.S., Canada, and Mexico. Most of the MSA core courses and the general administration concentration courses are available online.

All MSA students are required to take four core courses: MSA 600–Administrative Research and Report Methods, MSA 640–Quantitative Applications in Administrative Decision-Making, MSA 685–Integrative Analysis of Administration, and either MSA 634–Managerial Accounting Concepts or MSA 635–Financial Management. Additional classes are chosen from a list of concentration courses depending on the student's concentration.

The ten MSA concentrations are general administration, health services administration, hospitality and tourism administration, human resources administration, information resource administration, international administration, leadership, public administration, software engineering administration, and sport administration. All concentrations are not available at every program center. Cohorts normally offer only one concentration because they are formed in conjunction with a particular organization such as a hospital or police department. Additionally, graduate certificate programs consisting of 15-18 credit hours are available in all of the concentrations except for sport administration.

Central Michigan University also offers undergraduate degrees and courses targeted to business professionals in program centers in the state of Michigan and through the World Wide Web. The degrees that are currently available are the Bachelor of Applied Arts Degree with a Major in Administration and the Bachelor of Science Degree with a Major in Administration. The Major in Administration has four concentrations: guest services administration, industrial administration, organization administration, and service sector administration.

OCLS SERVICES

Instruction

Librarians provide instruction formally for two of the classes required of all students in the MSA degree program, MSA 600–Administrative Research and Report Methods and MSA 685–Integrative Analysis of Administration. For the latter class, which is considered the capstone class and taken last in the sequence, packets are sent to the professors for distribution at the first class or mailed to the students before class begins. The packets normally consist of current handouts detailing OCLS services and information on the OCLS Web site. In addition, a letter from the librarians is included, which contains contact information and reminds the students to contact OCLS if they need assistance with the literature review section of the final project. Wherever possible, librarians provide on-site library instruction sessions in the MSA 685 classes.

Samples of MSA 685 projects are available through OCLS. These are examples of high quality papers, chosen by faculty committees to serve as examples to the students. Part of the MSA 685 packet is a list of the current samples and instructions on how to obtain them.

The MSA 600 course has been targeted by OCLS for library instruction because it is the research class. Students are required to write a proposal for the final project in which they will explore solutions to workplace problems or write business plans. This is often the basis for the final MSA 685 project. They are also required to do a literature review. The library instruction classes are centered on teaching the students how to obtain materials for the literature review from among the resources available through OCLS or in other places. One of the required texts for this class is the *Off-Campus Library Services Guide,* a booklet that describes OCLS services as well as conducting research.

Librarians travel to most of the MSA 600 classes to deliver an on-site library instruction session. In the major metropolitan areas, the librarians may speak to classes meeting in their own buildings or drive to other classrooms located in the metropolitan area. When MSA 600 courses are taught in other areas, librarians will drive or fly to centers, depending on the distance. In most cases an OCLS librarian delivers a one and one half to three hour library instruction session for the MSA 600 class. MSA 600 faculty members expect a librarian to present a library instruction session generally in the first or second class meeting. On the rare occasions where a librarian does not present in an MSA 600 class, the professors generally request packets and PowerPoint presentations to help teach the students about OCLS. (Generally the only time a librarian does not teach a library instruction session in MSA 600 is in a cohort where the library instruction session was presented in the first course.)

Library instruction classes vary in length of time depending on whether computers are available and on the amount of time that professors are able to give to the librarian. Regardless of the duration of the library instruction session, all librarians cover the same basic items: OCLS services, accessing databases and full text articles available from the OCLS Web site, and searching for references and articles in a database most appropriate to the concentration of the majority of students in the class. Depending on the length of time allotted and the availability of computers, librarians also may teach students how to do specific research projects required, may teach advanced search techniques in a particular database, such as *ABI/Inform,* or may conduct hands-on exercises.

The regional offices in Atlanta and Detroit have computer classrooms that the librarians can use for the MSA 600 instruction sessions. These are ideal because the students can actually get some hands-on experience and some one-on-one help from the librarians with their individual topics. In other areas, computer classrooms may be available from a military education office or cohort sponsor and are borrowed as often as possible. Otherwise, library instruction is done in the classroom. In some classrooms, where phone connections are available, the librarians do live demonstrations. Where live connections are not an option, the librarians do PowerPoint presentations, with screen captures of Web pages. Instruction classes are held occasionally in base libraries or libraries in cohort locations such as hospitals, and librarians use the online and print resources in these libraries in their instruction.

Class schedules come out on a quarterly or semi-annual basis in most of the program areas, so the librarians normally have time to read the syllabus and discuss assignments with the professor so they can tailor the instruction to specific class assignments and to the concentration of the majority of the students. Most of the time, the *ABI/Inform* database is introduced to the students because they are all working on some type of administrative topic. Other databases are often demonstrated to classes with strong concentrations of health services administration students or software engineering administration students. Special attention is paid to specific class assignments so if the students are required to find ten scholarly articles on an administrative topic, the librarians teach the class how to search in *ABI/Inform* using the class descriptor code for experimental or theoretical treatments. If a class is assigned to find financial information on companies, the librarians include instruction on SIC Codes, common sources of company financial information and finding that information on the World Wide Web or through the OCLS resources.

Most program centers offer two to four courses per term. Whenever the librarians visit a program center to conduct a library instruction session for MSA 600, they also attempt to do mini sessions in each of the other classes being offered at the same time. These mini sessions generally last for about 30 minutes and are made up of a brief description of OCLS services plus information on databases specific to the particular course and assignments.

MSA 600 is taught in many of the open enrollment program centers once a year. If the program center requires air travel or a long drive for the regional librarian, he/she may visit that center only when the MSA 600 class is offered. The result is that some students may be halfway through the degree program before they meet a librarian in person. To address the challenge this presents, print information on OCLS, such as the *Off-Campus Library Services Guide,* welcome letters from the regional librarian, and bookmarks or post-it notes with the OCLS phone and fax numbers and Web site URL are given to all students upon admission. In addition, OCLS is developing new forms of instruction such as chat sessions and interactive guides to services for new students who may not have a formal library instruction session until they are part way through the program or who need instruction on new services.

Online classes were first developed for the MSA core courses in the late 1990s. The first MSA 600 online class was offered in 2000. Since students who take the Web-based classes do not meet in person, OCLS provides instruction through chat sessions. Formal library instruction chat sessions are held in online MSA 600 and MSA 685 classes and in other online classes at the invitation of the instructors.

Library instruction to undergraduate students in administration classes has been minimal until the late 1990s because traditionally undergraduate classes made up a small percentage of the overall classes taught through CEL and there is no required research class for all undergraduate students. By the fall of 2000, undergraduate classes made up approximately 45% of the classes taught in Michigan. The undergraduate degree programs do not have a research course similar to MSA 600. However, one course, MGT 312–Introduction to Management, has been chosen as a course to target for library instruction because it is the first management class that most undergraduates take. In addition, the regional librarians in Michigan read course syllabi in search of research assignments in the undergraduate classes. For many with research assignments, librarians offer to do instruction sessions that cover the basics about OCLS and include a specific instruction component related to the research assignment. Also, because the two librarians responsible for instruction in Michigan are within driving distance of their centers, they are able to respond to occasional requests from faculty and from program administrators to offer instruction sessions in undergraduate classes in which many of the students are new to the program.

Reference

OCLS reference services have evolved considerably over the years due to ever-changing technologies. The reference philosophy has not changed. From the beginning OCLS librarians have always attempted to assist CMU off-campus students with their research as effectively as possible.

In 1976, two librarians were hired to provide reference and instructional services exclusively to off-campus students. One was based in Park Library on campus and the other at Wright Patterson Air Force Base in Dayton, Ohio. In the early days of the service, requests came in by telephone and mail. Librarians did literature searches for students in print indexes or in online databases and mailed the results generally within 24 hours of the request. Alternately, they assisted students in conducting research in libraries in their own areas. This was accomplished by suggesting search strategies, controlled vocabulary, and indexes or databases available in particular local libraries. In the early days, OCLS librarians visited all major libraries in the vicinity of program centers annually and compiled lists of resources available in these libraries.

In 1996, a significant change in reference requests began to appear. In the early part of that year, the basic FirstSearch databases, including a subscription to *ABI/Inform,* was made available to off-campus students first by Telnet, and later that year through the CMU Libraries' Web site. Students were encouraged to do their own research in the databases, assisted by the OCLS librarians. Rather than calling to request mediated searches, students were asking for assistance with their own research through the new databases made available through the Web site.

OCLS received 7,535 reference requests in FY 1999-2000. More than half were telephone requests. A very small percentage was walk-in customers. Most of the remainder came in through e-mail. The e-mail requests are divided into two categories. The first are free form requests that may come into the document delivery e-mail address, the reference e-mail address, the main libraries' Web site or individual librarians' e-mail addresses. The other group of requests comes into the *Ask an OCLS Librarian* link on the Web site. This link provides a form for students to fill out and enter a request. These are generally much more specific than the free form requests in the other category.

Until January 2000, the librarians in regional offices only assisted students who received instruction from that regional office. At the start of the 2000-year, all references calls began coming into a central toll-free number. From there they are transferred to the reference librarian on duty.

Currently, reference requests fall primarily into three basic categories: technical assistance, literature searches, and research assistance. The first category is substantial because many students have trouble reconfiguring their browsers to use the proxy server that CMU has set up or run into trouble with firewalls and browsers that are not compatible with the proxy server.

The second category of reference requests is for literature searches. At the request of the student, OCLS librarians will research a topic in one of the business, health care administration or other databases such as *ABI/Inform, Wilson Business Abstracts,* or *HealthStar* and e-mail, fax or mail a list of references on the topic within 24 hours. When performing literature searches, librarians tend to send broad topic searches to give the students some choice on the information they get. OCLS librarians do not choose articles or books for the students.

The third category of reference is much closer to traditional academic library reference. Students, who are using the databases CMU provides through the Web site, call or e-mail for assistance with the search process. In these transactions, librarians work with the students to refine their topics, choose appropriate databases and controlled vocabulary, and set up search strategies. Ideally, if students can be online and on the telephone simultaneously, librarians are able to be online and do the searches with the students and can assist when problems come up in the search. If students are not online when they call, they are encouraged to call back if they run into problems with the search following the directions the librarian has given them. OCLS is investigating reference chat software, which will allow the librarian and student to communicate while working through a database search together regardless of whether the student has a second phone line.

Some reference questions come up over and over again and OCLS develops tools and collections to answer these questions quickly and assist students to find the information easily. Among the most common requests are those for information about developing a business plan and research on small business startups. A significant number of students develop a business plan for the MSA 685 project and contact OCLS in both MSA 600 and MSA 685 for research assistance. OCLS has developed a number of resources for these topics:

- Multiple copies of books on new business startups and developing a business plan have been purchased with OCLS funds for both the general library collection as well as an OCLS office collection.
- Small business and business plans bibliographies are available on the OCLS Web site and in print.
- One area on the OCLS Web site links to relevant Web sites with information on business plans and starting a new business.
- Sample business plans that can be copied and mailed to the students are housed in each of the reference offices.
- Data is gathered about local business collections in the public and other libraries in the vicinity of each of the program centers and cohorts for referrals.
- Referrals are made to associations for further information on a particular type of business.

Document Delivery

In March of 1977, a toll-free number was established for students in Ohio to contact OCLS to request copies of articles and book loans. In late 1977, toll-free access was extended to students in the 48 contiguous states and by 1979 to students in Hawaii. Today, students in Canada and Mexico also have toll-free access. In the first six months of the service, 545 requests were taken. At its highest point in FY 1993-94, OCLS processed 110,046 requests. In the latter half of the 1990s requests began to drop off as more full text articles became available through the Web site.

Located in the main library on the Mt. Pleasant campus, Document Delivery is open seven days a week to take requests for books and articles and other library materials from students. Students can submit requests through a toll-free phone number, toll-free fax number, a departmental e-mail address or through a request form on the Web site. Students and faculty may request up to 20 items per week per course. The OCLS staff processes and sends out anything available in the CMU

Libraries within 48 hours of the request. Most materials are sent out by mail or other postal delivery services to students' home or work addresses. In 2000, Document Delivery began to e-mail electronically available items to students.

Books are loaned to off-campus students for periods of 30 or 42 days depending on their geographic location. Off-campus students' library cards are maintained in the Document Delivery Office. Copies of articles, annual reports, and financial data copied from reference books are the students' to keep.

In the late 1990s, OCLS noticed a significant annual decline in the fill rate for article requests. This was attributed to the fact that students were able to obtain a significant number of articles from the online databases available to them through the OCLS Web site. In a successful attempt to fill more orders, Document Delivery began to send any requests for items not owned by the CMU Libraries to the Document Access Department (Inter-Library Loan) provided the requestor had a minimum of three weeks in which to obtain the article. This has been a very successful venture and improved the fill rate by almost 12% in the first year.

OCLS Web Site

OCLS provided access to the FirstSearch databases through the CMU Libraries' Web site beginning in 1996. In 1997, OCLS developed it's own Web site (www.lib.cmich.edu/ocls), geared to the needs of off-campus students and faculty. From it students can be validated through a proxy server so that they can have access to over 70 databases, including nine business databases. Other links on the OCLS Web site include the Libraries' online catalog, CENTRA II, and links to other Web sites under categories such as business plans, starting new businesses, company information, human resources and training and health care administration. Bibliographies for most subjects taught through CEL are available as well as electronic request forms for reference and document delivery assistance. Formal instruction in classes concentrates on introducing students to the Web site as a powerful tool for research that they always have at their fingertips.

The OCLS Web site has been under constant revision since its inception. Since it truly functions as a virtual library to the thousands of CMU students who will never visit Mt. Pleasant, Michigan, the OCLS staff has been active in soliciting ideas for improvements from faculty and students and in making those improvements. In 2001, a completely revamped Web site was introduced with a new URL (ocls.cmich.edu). New information was added to the site and links were reorganized and presented in a format that is much easier to navigate.

Partnerships

Unlike many libraries that provide services to distance students, CMU neither has reciprocal agreements with other libraries nor pays for services from other libraries. However, informal partnerships have evolved over the years with libraries in some areas.

Many of the military bases where CMU maintains program centers have strong base libraries that reach out to the higher education students among their populations. Many base librarians have worked closely with OCLS over the years to assist with library instruction. Either part or all of the library instruction is done in some base libraries. In these situations, students can learn about the OCLS resources, get some hands-on experience in the library and learn about the resources available to them from the base library. In turn, OCLS has donated subscriptions to *Business Periodicals Index* and other indexes to many of the base libraries, has invited base library staff to become guest users of OCLS services, and has assisted with collection development of graduate level business materials for some of the libraries. Among the benefits to CMU of the partnerships with military libraries is the accessibility to CMU students of military resources that OCLS would have difficulty supplying and the ability to teach library instruction classes in an actual library. Benefits to the military libraries include stronger business collections for graduate level students and the marketing of their services to graduate students on the installations.

For many years libraries in the metropolitan Detroit area maintained collections of MSA 685 samples for students in that region. Initially, the MSA 685 projects were only available in microfiche so students normally had to go to a library to read them. By having sets in local libraries, students did not have to wait to receive the fiche from Document Delivery.

Libraries in cohort locations have been very helpful. Many cohorts in the U.S. are in hospitals. Often the hospital library has participated in bibliographic instruction and worked with CMU staff to anticipate assignments that may bring students into their libraries. In Canada and Mexico, cohorts often meet on college or university campuses. The libraries on the campuses have allowed OCLS to do library instruction, loaned computer labs and set up reserve collections for CMU.

ONGOING CHALLENGES AND THE FUTURE

Since the beginning, OCLS has constantly faced a major challenge in promoting the service. Throughout the years that OCLS has been in existence, the most common complaint from students is that they do not know about the library services early enough in their degree programs. In 1979, a Library Student Questionnaire was mailed out to a random sample of off-campus students. Publicity and promotion of the service were listed by those who responded as the areas most in need of improvement (Doyle and Somers 1980, 6). The most common complaints received currently are from students who do not learn about OCLS services until they are nearly finished with their degree programs. OCLS distributes print materials on its services to newly registered students through program administrators and works closely with instructors to get the message about OCLS across. These methods have not always been effective because many students do not seem to recognize the benefits of OCLS until they need to do research. If they take MSA 600 or MGT 312 in the early part of their programs, they learn to use OCLS services effectively.

In order to promote the service more effectively, OCLS embarked on a study of other forms of instruction in 2000. Some of the areas being explored are regular instruction chat sessions, point-of-use instruction on the Web site, and e-mail distribution lists for selected instruction topics.

Since 1976, OCLS has successfully delivered library services to business professionals taking administration classes all over North America in a timely fashion. The goal for the near future is to promote the service more effectively to reach all students early in their programs and to continue to educate students so they can retrieve the information they need effectively and easily as soon as they need it.

REFERENCES

Central Michigan University. 1999. *College of Extended Learning Bulletin 1999-2000.* Mt. Pleasant, Mich., 1999.

Doyle, Richard and C. Norman Somers. 1980. "Central Michigan University's External Library Program." Institute for Personal and Career Development, Central Michigan University. Photocopy.

Bridging the Distance:
Pace University Library and Remote Users

Medaline Philbert

SUMMARY. This article outlines Pace University Library's commitment to address the needs of the university distance education populace. Discussion focuses on one of the programs offered by Pace University, e.MBA (Executive MBA). Pace University Library offers many services to meet the research needs of its remote users. These include remote access to electronic resources, Interlibrary Loan, a toll-free number, and an online form for submission of reference queries. To improve document delivery services, the library subsidizes SUMO Uncover, and also uses Digital Sender to e-mail or fax documents to students. Pace University Library continuously looks at new methods to effectively serve its distance education populace. *[Article copies available for a fee from The Haworth Document Delivery Service: 1-800-HAWORTH. E-mail address: <getinfo@haworth pressinc.com> Website: <http://www.HaworthPress.com> © 2002 by The Haworth Press, Inc. All rights reserved.]*

KEYWORDS. Distance education, e.MBA, library, remote access, interlibrary loan

Medaline Philbert, BBA, MLS, is Assistant University Librarian for Distributive Learning, Pace University. She worked as an Adjunct Instructor at Baruch College, and as Information Services Librarian at the Science, Industry and Business Library of the New York Public Library. She is a member of ALA, ACRL, ASCLA, DLS, NYBLC, and LITA.

[Haworth co-indexing entry note]: "Bridging the Distance: Pace University Library and Remote Users." Philbert, Medaline. Co-published simultaneously in *Journal of Business & Finance Librarianship* (The Haworth Information Press, an imprint of The Haworth Press, Inc.) Vol. 7, No. 2/3, 2002, pp. 87-98; and: *Library Services for Business Students in Distance Education: Issues and Trends* (ed: Shari Buxbaum) The Haworth Information Press, an imprint of The Haworth Press, Inc., 2002, pp. 87-98. Single or multiple copies of this article are available for a fee from The Haworth Document Delivery Service [1-800-HAWORTH, 9:00 a.m. - 5:00 p.m. (EST). E-mail address: getinfo@haworthpressinc.com].

INTRODUCTION

While universities across the United States are increasingly providing courses and awarding degrees in distance education, libraries are feeling more and more pressure to apply new methods to serve this new group of students in non-traditional settings. The buzz of distance learning/education, distributive learning, or other similar terms, is zapping through academe. Pace University <http://www.pace.edu> is participating in this phenomenon, providing courses and degrees through its distance education program.

This article describes the process I used to respond to a last-minute request for library service for a business class. It also discusses the procedures the library put in place to meet faculty needs for library service in the distance education programs, with an emphasis on building lines of communication between faculty and the library.

Pace University currently offers two online programs, the e.MBA (Executive MBA) and the National Coalition for Telecommunications Education and Learning (NACTEL). Pace University Library promotes and supports distance learning programs and services. The mission of the library has been modified to extend that of the university to meet the unfolding educational needs of its populace. Services provided to students in the traditional setting are equally available to distance education students. Adjustment of service has been made in order to effectively serve faculty and students in distance education programs.

To accomplish such challenges, Pace University Library formed a Distance Education Committee in the Fall of 1999. The Distance Education Committee is comprised of members from each department of the library. Through the committee, policies, procedures, and resources are discussed to determine how best the needs and services of students can be met. At the university level, the Provost's Council on Distance Education is comprised of deans, faculty, librarians and representatives from the Division of Information and Technology. To fully serve and coordinate the needs of distance education programs for the library, a full-time librarian has been appointed. Similarly, other institutions such as SUNY-Plattsburg and John Hopkins, offer full service to their distance education programs, and have appointed a full-time person as a point of contact to ensure that the library receives support to carry out the task of serving distance education programs (Kirk and Bartelstein, 1999).

MEETING THE NEEDS OF THE e.MBA–
EXECUTIVE MBA PROGRAM

The e.MBA Distance Education program was launched in Spring 2000. Although Pace University Library has the infrastructure to support new methods of delivering library services, the library needed to decide how best to reach distance education students and provide them effective services without making compromises. Challenges the Pace University Library faced at the time centered on registration of users and authentication (for example providing library barcodes to distance education students for remote access to the electronic resources, and the identification of students as distance education students for Interlibrary Loan services). Additional issues such as reference services to distance education students were also addressed.

e.MBA Faculty Request

The faculty involved with the program contacted the Head of Information Services and Resources requesting library orientation to the resources available to distance education students in the e.MBA program. The faculty was in dire need, as the students were soon arriving for their eight-day residency orientation. I was given this assignment, and I had no more than two weeks to work on this project and create a Web page.

How the Library Met the Faculty Needs

In any institution, organization, or corporation, success is obtained through collaboration. I met with various department heads, Reference, Interlibrary Loan, Circulation, and Systems and members of the Library Distance Education Committee, to obtain information on policies, and how these policies could be adjusted to meet the needs of students in the distance education programs. Students from New York, New Jersey, California, Connecticut and other parts of the United States were to visit Pace University for an eight-day orientation. The library component was only one aspect (two hours) of that orientation. I met with the faculty before the orientation to discuss how the orientation was going to be conducted, indicated why business information was pooled into a separate Web page rather than accessing it from the library's home page, and most important, to obtain feedback and additional information about the research needs of the students. At the beginning of our meeting, the faculty requested that I use two companies, Cisco Systems and Qwest, in my examples, as students will be concentrating on these two companies in the program. I demonstrated to the faculty the Web page I put together "e.MBA@PACE" that is accessible at <http://www. pace.edu/library/instruct/emba/>, to the faculty. Unanimously, they were very pleased and excited about it, making only minor suggestions in the layout.

Rather than directing the e.MBA students to the library home page and attempting to give instructions on how and where they could access business information and resources available at Pace University, I took a different approach. The resources available at Pace University Library and at other sites were pooled together under one umbrella, e.MBA@PACE. At the time, only one thought crossed my mind, and that was easy access. Distance Education students are not like the traditional students. They do not have the privilege to seek assistance at the Reference Desk and participate in a reference interview. Therefore, performing library orientation only through the library's home page, which covers information for all the disciplines, would not have been as effective as performing an orientation to library resources through a Web page channeling only business resources. Another important aspect that I took into consideration was the fact that I had only two hours of physical contact with them. Eventually, the students would return to their place of residence and begin their intensive program. The e.MBA students needed to have a certain level of independence in accessing information relevant to their research needs. To increase that level of independence, the library orientation was not conducted in the library using the Electronic Classroom. The faculty specifically wanted the students to feel comfortable using their laptops (each student was given a laptop), and to use the opportunity during their eight-day orientation to seek assistance with any technology problems they may encounter.

During the meeting with faculty, while the Web page was being demonstrated, I mentioned to them what was available to distance education students, what was being discussed at the Library Distance Education Committee, and what would be implemented soon. They were quite thrilled that the library had taken such an active role, and immediately indicated that they wanted me to be the liaison to the program. From that point forward, I have passed on any new information to the faculty. For example, the toll-free telephone number for students to use for reference questions, and responses to remote connection queries, has been passed on to the faculty members who, in turn, inform their students. Students have called and e-mailed me directly with research questions and remote connection issues. Many remote issues concerned connection from AOL. Communication went on with faculty via e-mail and some of their concerns were about interlibrary loan services and the issuing of barcodes.

Providing Library Barcodes

The issue of providing library barcodes to students as quickly as possible was one of the faculty concerns. This was resolved by having a graduate assistant from the Lubin School of Business (who also assisted students during their orientation) collect the students' identification cards after they were issued, and bring them to the library with the information slips (indicating name, address, social security number, telephone, and e-mail address) already filled out by the students. This worked as a stopgap measure for the first class. The system has been refined so that now distance education students, including the new class of e.MBA students for spring 2001, can obtain their library barcodes by sending an e-mail to barcodes@pace.edu.

Meeting the Need for Interlibrary Loan Services

The Library Committee decided that distance education students would have Interlibrary Loan services. To determine the most cost effective means, taking into account delivery time, a comparison of three delivery services was made. It has been decided to use United Parcel Service (UPS). FedEx will be used only if an emergency has been determined.

The library needs to know how to distinguish distance education students from the rest of the student body. At the time, it was decided that students could identify themselves by writing e.MBA@PACE after their name when placing an Interlibrary Loan request.

An ideal situation would make it possible to identify students utilizing a unique identification code that is universal to the Registrar's Office, the library and other pertinent offices. The university personnel are looking into the matter, and we are hoping it can be resolved. Then students do not have to identify themselves in the "Other Information" box, mentioned below, as distance education students; they would be identified as such in the Innopac system itself.

At the moment, students identify themselves as distance education students in the "Other Information" box when filling out the Interlibrary Loan form, and must also include information about the courses they are enrolled in, their social security number, e-mail addresses, mailing addresses, and telephone numbers. Books, articles, or other sources owned by the Pace University Library can be requested through the library's online catalog. The materials are sent directly to students' home addresses. Articles, regardless of length, are scanned and e-mailed to students through the use of the Digital Sender.

However, for sources that Pace University Library does not own, students will use the Interlibrary Loan service to request the materials. As mentioned above, students identify themselves as distance education students, and Pace University Library will mail requested materials from other libraries to students' home addresses. When books are borrowed from the Pace University Library collection as well as from other universities or colleges, students are required to insure the book for one hundred dollars ($100). All the necessary forms to return the material are included.

Interlibrary Loan Service can take up to ten (10) business days. As a result, students are encouraged to use their local public libraries or other libraries in their neighborhood that will grant them access to their resources. Moreover, students are advised to start their research early to ensure that they will receive needed sources in a timely manner.

Full-text articles to citations that students have can be e-mailed directly to them if e-mail addresses have been provided. This in itself will minimize cost to the library if these articles are obtained online through the databases. Articles from other media, microfilm for example, will also be faxed to students utilizing the Digital Sender. Students requiring a few pages of a book can also receive these via fax as well.

Besides sending articles through e-mail and fax, Pace University Library recently purchased another service, SUMO Uncover (Subsidized Unmediated Ordering of Research Documents) that delivers documents. Through SUMO, research documents from scholarly articles and research journals that are not available at Pace University Library's print serials collection or its full text online databases can be ordered. Currently, this delivery service is subsidized by the library and made available only to faculty, graduate students, distance education students and staff. Traditional students do not have access to this service. A user profile has to be created in order to use the service. This enables the provider, Uncover, to send the requested articles or documents directly to the patron via fax. Rather than having students read through two pages of instructions, the library will create accounts for users when the initial request is made. Of course, it is expected that requests made through the SUMO Uncover service be limited to a reasonable number.

Pace users who are not entitled to the current subsidized arrangement can still use the service with the option of using their credit cards to pay for the documents. SUMO Uncover provides another means for faculty, graduate students, and distance education students to obtain research documents that are not available in Pace University Library, and are usually obtainable mainly through Interlibrary Loan Services. However, the service has been programmed to abort if users attempt to request research documents or articles through SUMO Uncover which are available through Pace University Library databases.

REMOTE ACCESS

Access to Pace University Library electronic resources is restricted to current Pace students, faculty and staff. Traditional students have access to these databases on campus without the need of authentication. However, to ensure that access to these online resources is equally available to traditional and distance education students, remote access has been provided. Kirk and Bartelstein indicated that less than half of institutions surveyed do not have a plan for information technology, and less than one third have a plan to utilize the Internet for distance learning (Kirk and Bartelstein, 1999). Institutions have to keep abreast of the information age and be proactive rather than reactive. Pace University Library has set up an easy and simple system where students, faculty and staff need only enter the last six digits of their library barcode to access the databases remotely. To access, students will enter the library's home page, <http://www.pace.edu/library>, click on the button Databases, and then will be prompted to enter the last six digits of their library barcode on the Remote Database Access authentication screen.

The procedure to obtain a library bar code is also very simple. The library bar code is provided online to distance education students by students sending an e-mail request to barcodes@pace.edu. Students identify themselves as distance education students by providing their names, addresses, social security numbers and the courses in which they are enrolled. Students will receive their barcodes within 48 hours. Students in the e.MBA program obtained their library barcodes in person during their eight days of orientation, in April 2000. At that time, the e-mail barcode request system was not yet in place. Traditional students, faculty and staff request their library barcodes at the Circulation Desk and show their Pace University identification cards that verify that they are current Pace members. A small registration form requesting name, address, social security number and telephone number is completed and within three minutes a library bar code is issued. The goal was to create a parallel system for remote users that would be simple and speedy.

Solving Remote Problems

Students need to learn how to login to gain access to electronic resources. Unfortunately, students do come across authentication problems. When this happens, students, faculty or staff are provided guidance. A link to solutions has been provided in the Remote Database Access page. Students in the e.MBA program who used the Internet Provider AOL frequently encountered remote access problems. The system librarian has informed librarians of the various scenarios and how they can be rectified. Authentication problems can stem from a number of reasons such as, (a) the barcode is not yet entered into the system and as a result, the patron record server does not have the barcode; (b) if the barcode has been entered into the system, the expiration date has to be checked for currency–authorized remote access is for current students only; (c) a delinquent borrowing record will affect access even if the students' barcodes and records are current. Any of the three problems can occur. However, another dilemma can occur as well, and that relates to *cookies*.

Access to the databases remotely may be successful, but upon the selection of a database, students, faculty or staff may be prompted to enter user identification and password. When this happens, users may have to change the settings of their browser preferences/options (if they are using Netscape or Internet Explorer) by enabling "cookies." By enabling cookies through preferences/options, the authentication requirement from the vendor side will be removed. This vendor authentication occurs on campus as well as remotely, and will be resolved by checking the browser setup through preferences/options.

There are instances when a vendor's server is down. In these situations, systems and technical support in the library will contact the vendor to find out how soon it will be rectified. If the problem stems from Pace University servers, the system librarian and technical support, together with The Division of Information and Technology, collaborate to rectify the situation in a timely manner. When this happens, students, both on site and remotely (students phone in), are brought up-to-date and are encouraged to attempt connection to the databases later.

RESEARCH ASSISTANCE
TO DISTANCE EDUCATION STUDENTS

How would students' research questions be addressed? Students need help in making database selections, searching databases, and in deciding which resources are relevant to their research needs. "They do not want to read manuals" (Niemi, Ehrhard, and Neeley, 1998). Before the design of the Distance Education Services Web page, students in the e.MBA (Executive MBA) program had direct contact with the librarian liaison. Questions were asked about troubleshooting remote access, and providing research assistance for specific information, as well as refining search strategies. However, distance education students who had research queries sometimes needed to reach a business reference librarian.

Pace University Library resolved this problem by making available a toll-free telephone number that distance education students could use to call for assistance. To speak with a business librarian during normal library hours, a student can call 1-877-974-BOOK (2665) with questions regarding research assistance, library services or any other library issues. An online form, RefQuery, is also available that students can use to e-mail research questions to the library at any time of the day. Response time to answer queries through the toll-free telephone number and the online form will be immediate during normal working hours. However, during weekends and holidays, response time will be 24 hours to 48 hours. A Web page specifically designed for the distance education population, both students and faculty, includes information about library services. Access is at <http://www.pace.edu/library/links/disted/>, or from the library's home page, <http://www.pace.edu/library>; click Distance Education Services in the left blue column.

Research queries from students, via the toll-free telephone number, will be shared between the two major libraries at Pace University. Days of shared responsibilities are alternated between libraries, and librarians from the designated library will be responsible to answer students' queries for a specific time.

Currently, public relations of the library services are done through direct contact with distance education faculty, and *Information Edge: A Newsletter of the Pace University Library* that is published semi-annually. The most effective public relations efforts have been through direct contact to distance education faculty via e-mail and telephone. Faculty channels the information to students either through e-mail, CourseInfo, or WebBoard, whichever is appropriate. Any changes or additions to services are immediately passed along to faculty who always indicate high levels of appreciation.

Pace University Library Instructional Services Team has developed many online guides to assist the general student population with their research needs. Research guides have been created for specific classes and subject areas and these are accessible online through "Research Assistance" from the library's home page. In addition, database guides for most of the databases have also been created and have been made available online.

ReVeaL: Research in the Virtual Library, is a step-by-step research guide that has been developed specifically for distance education students at Pace University. The purpose of ReVeaL goes beyond assisting students to complete class assignments. ReVeaL is designed to enable students to develop research skills that they will apply beyond the classroom setting. The goal is for students to acquire a life-long learning tool. An Instructional Services Librarian is in the process of completing an interactive research guide, Apollo, which will replace ReVeaL. ReVeaL is accessible through "Research Assistance" from the library's home page.

OTHER REMOTE USERS

Pace University Library faced similar requests to that of the e.MBA request: to create Web pages that identify library resources for the NACTEL (National Coalition for Telecommunications Education and Learning) program and the DPS (Doctorate in Professional Studies program). Students in the NACTEL program are one hundred per cent remote. That is, they do not physically have to come to Pace University for orientation or for any other matter. Associate Degrees are obtained through this program. Students in the DPS program come to campus on weekends to attend class. I met with the Associate Director of the program and other members involved with the NACTEL program to discuss the creation of a Web page. Another librarian developed the DPS Web page. In this way, pages about library resources aimed at specific programs are created, rather than sending remote students to the entire collection of electronic resources available from the library.

Pace University and especially, Pace University Library, is looking into the future to provide access to information beyond the normal scope of distance education students to include remote access to information to physically challenged students. This is another type of student population who will benefit greatly from distance education programs and remote access to information.

CONCLUSION

Many institutions are gravitating to distributive learning. Some will encounter problems; others will be successful from the start, due perhaps, to careful planning. Librarians who are in the process of developing distributive learning services, or who have encountered similar problems in providing distributive learning services, may find the procedures and solutions mentioned above serve as a guide to help them get started in this exciting area.

Pace University Library took a proactive role and approached faculty and deans involved with distance education programs, thus demonstrating and reinforcing the library's ongoing usefulness and relevance in distance education. By offering access to resources and information remotely, and indicating willingness to continue to meet the various program needs, the library remains central to the educational process. This is an excellent opportunity to have the rest of the institution see the value of the library. To date, besides the general information to library resources for remote users, the library has developed Web pages specifically for certain distance education programs, namely e.MBA (Executive MBA) and NACTEL (National Coalition for Telecommunications Education and Learning).

The library will continue to work with the Center for Instructional Technologies and the Pforzheimer Center for Faculty Development, with the Assistant University Librarian for Distributive Learning as liaison, to improve services to faculty and students. This will open avenues to exchange ideas and initiate new programs.

The Library Committee for Distance Learning meets after the University Distance Education Committee has met, to discuss policies, issues and new services. Representatives on the library committee, who are also members of the Pace University Distance Learning Committee, bring to the library committee concerns, ideas, and needs the institution's committee has raised. The committee met often over a short period of time, because of an impending deadline, to have certain services in place before the beginning of the distance learning programs.

Pace University Library concentrates first on providing necessary services to distance education students, as well as to its other students.

Effective ways of implementing new ideas and meeting new needs as they arise are examined regardless of budgetary constraints. If money becomes the primary concern, then many great ideas may not come to the table.

The future of distributive learning lies in the creation of partnerships "among academic and public librarians, computing professionals, college and university administrators, faculty, publishers, and vendors" (Kirk and Bartelstein, 1999).

REFERENCES

Information Edge: A Newsletter of the Pace University Library. Vol 5, No. 1 Fall 2000.

Kirk, Elizabeth E. and Andrea M. Bartelstein (1999). "Libraries Close in on Distance Education." *Library Journal* 124 (6), pp 40-42. Retrieved November 12, 2000 from UMI Database (Proquest) on the World Wide Web <http://proquest.umi.com/>.

Niemi, John A. and Barbara J. Ehrhard; Lynn Neeley (1998) "Off-Campus Library Support for Distance Adult Learners." *Library Trends* 47 (1), pp 65-74. Retrieved November 12, 2000 from UMI Database (Proquest) on the World Wide Web <http://proquest.umi.com/>.

Providing Library Service
to Off-Campus Business Students:
Access, Resources and Instruction

Jill S. Markgraf
Robert C. Erffmeyer

SUMMARY. The conversion of a traditionally research-intensive graduate marketing course to an online environment at the University of Wisconsin-Eau Claire posed challenges for the library. In providing services to a new population of off-campus graduate marketing students, the library faced issues in three categories: availability of library resources, access to resources and services, and instruction in an asynchronous environment. This paper looks at how the course instructor and the library collaborated to address these issues, discusses what was learned, and offers recommendations for those facing similar challenges. *[Article copies available for a fee from The Haworth Document Delivery Service: 1-800-HAWORTH. E-mail address: <getinfo@haworthpressinc.com> Website: <http://www.HaworthPress.com> © 2002 by The Haworth Press, Inc. All rights reserved.]*

KEYWORDS. Distance education, business students, marketing students, off-campus library service

---

Jill S. Markgraf is Distance Education Librarian, McIntyre Library, University of Wisconsin-Eau Claire, Eau Claire, WI (E-mail: markgrjs@uwec.edu).

Robert C. Erffmeyer is Professor of Marketing, College of Business, University of Wisconsin-Eau Claire, Eau Claire, WI (E-mail: erffmerc@uwec.edu).

[Haworth co-indexing entry note]: "Providing Library Service to Off-Campus Business Students: Access, Resources and Instruction." Markgraf, Jill S., and Robert C. Erffmeyer. Co-published simultaneously in *Journal of Business & Finance Librarianship* (The Haworth Information Press, an imprint of The Haworth Press, Inc.) Vol. 7, No. 2/3, 2002, pp. 99-114; and: *Library Services for Business Students in Distance Education: Issues and Trends* (ed: Shari Buxbaum) The Haworth Information Press, an imprint of The Haworth Press, Inc., 2002, pp. 99-114. Single or multiple copies of this article are available for a fee from The Haworth Document Delivery Service [1-800-HAWORTH, 9:00 a.m. - 5:00 p.m. (EST). E-mail address: getinfo@haworthpressinc.com].

INTRODUCTION

The unique nature of distance education (DE) combined with the unique needs of business students combine to pose challenges to libraries attempting to serve them. This paper describes one library's experience in providing service for a new online marketing course and offers recommendations based on the results.

McIntyre Library serves the University of Wisconsin-Eau Claire, a regional four-year public university with 10,395 students. As is typical at such institutions, McIntyre Library is the only library on campus, and among its faculty of 14 librarians there is no designated business librarian.

At UW-Eau Claire, as with most other universities, distance education (DE) has been around for decades in its various incarnations. And for decades, the library has been serving DE students in some capacity. In recent years McIntyre Library stepped up its efforts in serving the bourgeoning population of DE students by hiring a half-time DE librarian, developing a DE library services Web site (http://www.uwec.edu/admin/library/Exlibra/index.htm), and establishing services specifically for DE students. Until the summer of 2000, most of the university's DE courses were offered synchronously, that is with students and instructors communicating in real time, via technologies such as interactive television and audiographics. Library services put in place to serve these students included home delivery of library materials, e-mail and toll-free reference service, and remote access to library databases. Library instruction for DE students was offered much the same as for on-campus students, albeit using the mode of delivery apropos to the course and, by necessity, placing more emphasis on the technical details of connecting to library resources remotely.

In summer of 2000, the University of Wisconsin-Eau Claire launched five completely Web-based courses, and as a result, the library was contending with an asynchronous learning environment where students were no longer available at a set time or place for instruction. Of the five online courses, from disciplines including Education, Psychology, History and Business, it was the College of Business' Marketing course that relied most heavily on library resources and consequently put to the test DE library services. This paper will focus on that course.

The UW-Eau Claire's College of Business launched its online course as part of a four campus collaborative effort to convert nine MBA foundations courses for delivery on the Internet. The 2-credit graduate course, Marketing Analysis Foundation, had previously been offered on-campus as well as via interactive television, and was a library research-intensive course. A major requirement of the course was the preparation of a Situation Analysis for an established brand name product. Sections of the Situation Analysis that students were asked to research and write included a brief history of the company, a description of the product category and the specific brand, identification and analysis of competitors, a discussion of environmental variables affecting the industry and the product, an evaluation of existing consumers of the brand, marketing mix, i.e., an analysis of the "four Ps"–product, place (distribution), promotion and price, a discussion of international ramifications, and a conclusion offering comparisons and recommendations.

In the past, library faculty had provided library instruction sessions onsite or via interactive television. The sessions covered the use and selection of indexes, databases, reference tools and other resources for students doing their Situation Analysis research. A *Marketing Information Guide* (http://www.uwec.edu/Admin/Library/Guides/sit_anal. html), initially a print-based library research handout developed specifically for this assignment, was distributed to all students in the course during their library instruction. It suggested resources–many in print–to use in researching each section of the analysis. Reference librarians were accustomed to providing hours of individual attention assisting students in their research efforts for the course. Because of the library-intensive nature of the course, the untold hours of individual assistance and consultation, and the reliance on reference materials–including print non-circulating titles–there was some skepticism on the part of library faculty upon learning that the course and the research project were going to be taken online and offered at a distance.

A variety of sources provided input in the development of this paper. E-mail, telephone conversations and in-person interviews from both semesters were drawn upon. At this juncture the course has been offered at two different times to a total of 45 students. At the conclusion of the second course student input was solicited using an online survey on a variety of issues. The questions are contained in Table 1. Student participation was anonymous and voluntary. A total of 16 of the 18 students responded for a response rate of 88.9 percent. Where appropriate we have used their survey responses to substantiate our observations and recommendations.

Of concern to librarians were challenges that fell into three categories: availability of resources, access to resources and services, and instruction in an asynchronous environment.

TABLE 1. Post-Course Student Assessment of Library Resources

1. Did you experience problems using the password-protected databases?
   - If yes, did you consider them major or minor problems?
   - Were your problems resolved?
   - Please describe the problems you encountered.

2. Please indicate what percentage of your research was drawn from
   - Online library databases
   - Online free Internet sites
   - Resources available through your place of employment
   - Paying for other online information sources
   - Other

3. What other resources did you use?

4. Had they been available, how likely (very, somewhat or not) is it that you would have used these forms of additional library research?
   - Online chat with librarian
   - Tutorial on searching specific databases
   - Tutorial on using the library's online catalog
   - Tutorial on database searching in general
   - Tutorial on remote access to library
   - Online lecture on library research
   - 24-hour e-mail or fax delivery of materials

5. Do you feel this was an appropriate assignment for this course?

6. How likely (very, somewhat or not) do you think you will be able to utilize research skills used in this course in future courses or work assignments?

AVAILABILITY OF RESOURCES

The *Guidelines for Distance Learning Library Services,* developed by the Distance Learning Section of the Association of College and Research Libraries, states:

Access to adequate library services and resources is essential for the attainment of superior academic skills in post-secondary education, regardless of where students, faculty, and programs are located. Members of the distance learning community are entitled to library services and resources equivalent to those provided for students and faculty in traditional campus settings. (Association of College and Research Libraries [ACRL], 1998)

Students in the on-campus course had relied heavily on print resources in the library's reference collection. When the course was offered via interactive television to students at a 2-year college an hour away, the students did some of their research online and some at the college's library, but they were expected to make at least one trip to McIntyre Library to do research as well. Because an on-campus visit was *not* an expectation of the online course, librarians were concerned that students might not have access to the resources necessary to complete the Situation Analysis. While the increasing availability of online resources in the areas of business and marketing made our business DE students better served electronically than our students in most other disciplines, many of the key resources traditionally used to complete the Situation Analysis were in print format only. Sources such as the *International Directory of Company Histories,* the *Encyclopedia of Consumer Brands,* and *Brands and Their Companies* had been popular resources in gathering company and product information. Students relied heavily on the print-based *Market Share Reporter, Mediamark Research,* and *Simmons Study of Media and Markets* for the competitive analysis portion of their projects. Sources such as *Lifestyle Market Analyst* and the *Official Guide to Household Spending* provided valuable consumer information.

In an effort to address this concern, librarians reviewed the Situation Analysis assignment, consulted with the professor, and revisited the *Marketing Information Guide*. It was clear that some of the students' reliance on print resources was driven by the *Guide's* emphasis on them. By revising the *Guide* to emphasize online resources of information, the playing field had begun to level. However, some sections of the Situation Analysis were not well served by available online resources. Without access to costly consumer databases (e.g., *Mediamark*), consumer behavior/demographic data was especially difficult to cull from the selection of databases available. This difficulty was acknowledged by the instructor, who modified the assignment somewhat to place less emphasis on those sections difficult to research given the available resources.

Unless these modifications are viewed as undesirable compromises, it can be argued that some of the resulting changes increased the information literacy value of the assignment. According to Dewald, Scholz-Crane, Booth and Levine (2000, p. 33), "Information literacy is a fundamental component of the education process, at the basic and advanced level in which a student learns how to think actively and critically about information rather than to passively receive prepackaged facts or materials." Whereas the print *Guide* used by the on-campus students suggested very specific print resources for very specific pieces of information, off-campus students were required to select from a number of suggested databases, and extract, interpret and draw inferences from information found therein. By having the students select among possible resources, the assignment is in keeping with ACRL's *Information Literacy Competency Standards for Higher Education* (ACRL, 2000, p. 9), which states, "The information literate student selects the most appropriate investigative methods or information retrieval systems for accessing the needed information."

ACCESS TO RESOURCES AND SERVICES

Unique features of the MBA program illuminated the successes as well as the limitations of existing library services in place for DE students, including remote access to library databases, document delivery and reference assistance.

Remote Access

With the emphasis on online resources, the issue of access to electronic databases was paramount. The library provided off-campus access to its online indexes and databases through a proxy server, which identified and authenticated students by requiring them to enter their campus usernames and passwords.

While the proxy server had been adequate in the past, the marketing course posed new challenges. Students in the collaborative MBA Foundations program were registered at their home campus. As a result, students enrolled in the marketing course might in fact be registered at any one of the four participating state universities, and only those registered at UW-Eau Claire would have the campus username and password required by the proxy server. As the *ACRL Guidelines* state, the originating institution–i.e., that which offers the DE course–is responsible for "meeting the information needs of its distance learning programs in support of their teaching, learning, and research. This support should provide ready and equivalent library service and learning resources to all its students, regardless of location" (ACRL, 1998).

While the students all had access to library resources and databases through their home institutions, not all institutions provided the same resources. In order to provide equitable access to all students in the UW-Eau Claire course, it was clear that they would need access to UW-Eau Claire resources. How would we provide access to proprietary databases to those students enrolled in the UW-Eau Claire course but registered elsewhere? As a solution to this access problem, the library created a temporary generic campus username and password that could be used by students registered at other campuses in logging onto the proxy server. The username and password were distributed by the professor and expired at the end of the term.

Providing access to databases for students registered at several universities turned out to be only the beginning of proxy-related technical challenges. About one-third of our students indicated they had major problems using the password-protected databases. One third indicated they had minor problems and only one third responded that they had no problems. The process of setting up a browser to connect to the proxy server was awkward to implement and equally awkward to explain at a distance. While the students were provided with both print and online instructions for using the proxy, there were no guarantees that they would read the information, understand it, or that it would work as intended. Students tended to avoid using those databases requiring proxy access in favor of the seemingly less complex, but also less valuable, free Internet sites.

The post-course evaluation asked students to estimate the percentage of research that came from various sources. The range of estimated use of library online databases ranged from zero percent to 100 percent with a median of 70 percent. The range of estimated use of free Internet sites ranged from zero percent to 99 percent with a median of 30 percent. Three respondents indicated they utilized their company's online resources to some degree, ranging from 10 to 30 percent. Surprisingly, one-third of the respondents also indicated that they augmented their research work by visiting their local university library.

It was only toward the crucial deadline that it appeared that the students realized that free Internet sites were not going to provide them with all, or even most, of the information they were going to need. As a result, the library received many a frantic phone call and e-mail message days before the Situation Analysis was due, asking how to connect to the databases. Of a documented 35 questions posed to the DE librarian by 12 students in the course, 20–or 57%–were regarding proxy issues. In some cases the solution was straightforward; simply being made aware of the proxy instructions, or entering a username in the correct format. In other cases, the problems were more complex; incompatibilities with Internet service providers or Web browsers, or interference due to firewalls at the place of employment from which the student was attempting to connect. Regardless of the solution, the inconvenience and frustration of not being able to connect to the databases at a crucial time in the course was something that had to be remedied.

It would be preferable to have students confront the proxy hurdle early in the course so that any problems, questions or misconceptions could be addressed before the assignment due date was pending. To this end, a change in the curriculum was implemented when the course was offered a second time in September 2000. During the first week of class, students were asked to retrieve an article from one of the library's proprietary databases requiring use of the proxy server from off-campus. As expected, the library received several questions during that first week related to setting up and using the proxy server. The expectation was that once these problems were addressed, students could concentrate on their research rather than on the technicalities of getting connected to databases. In addition, it was hoped that having the students use the proxy during the first week would lessen their intimidation of the proprietary or restricted databases and thereby decrease their tendency to rely on free Internet sites. To some extent, these expectations were met, but not entirely. Several students failed to complete this first assignment, and others obtained articles by other means. As a result, they still encountered last-minute proxy problems. To further improve this situation in future offerings of the course, the professor and the DE librarian plan to add additional structure to the assignment, asking for specific information from a specific proprietary database, and the professor plans to place greater emphasis on the completion of this assignment.

While the change in curriculum eased some of the problems associated with using the proxy, it didn't make the proxy server any easier or less cumbersome to use or explain–especially at a distance. As stated by Bob Mordan, an online instructor at UW-Superior, "Try to simplify steps which frustrate students when using the Internet. The statement, 'never frustrate the student,' is a good motto to follow" (Mordan, 2000).

Even better than figuring out a clear and concise way to explain setting up a browser to connect to a proxy server, therefore, would be to eliminate that step all together. To that end, the library is implementing an alternative technology, EZproxy, a URL rewriting proxy server which requires the library to edit URLs for which it wants to provide validation, but requires no browser configuration on the user's end and is therefore a more seamless interface for the user.

Document Delivery

Increasingly, the full text of financial and business information is available online. For that information that is not available electronically, the library provided document delivery services, through which students could request books in the McIntyre Library collection and photocopies of journal articles to be mailed directly to their homes. The turn-around time for this service ranged from several days to a week.

Inadequacies in these existing document delivery procedures became apparent during the marketing course, which–in contrast to our previous DE semester-long offerings–was only 8 weeks in duration. Whereas a week's turn-around time for home delivery of a journal article or book is workable in a semester-long course with some advanced planning, it is not adequate in a course that is compressed to a few weeks. While the students were relatively well-served by online full text materials, some print-only resources were requested, and probably would have been requested in many more instances if they could have been retrieved in a more timely manner.

About two-thirds of students responding to the post-course assessment indicated they would be very likely to use a 24-hour document delivery service. As a result, the library is looking into alternatives for digitizing and delivering print materials electronically. Solutions to urgent requests–such as immediate faxing of articles or pages from reference books, for which the library had no established procedures–were offered on an ad hoc basis to meet the pressing and sometimes unanticipated needs of DE students. As the *ACRL Guidelines* state, "Because students and faculty in distance learning programs frequently do not have direct access to a full range of library services and materials, equitable distance learning library services are more personalized than might be expected on campus" (ACRL 1998).

Reference

The increased personalized service manifested itself in ways other than document delivery. The nature of reference assistance was much more personalized, ironically, than most face-to-face encounters at the reference desk. While students were provided with the general Reference Desk e-mail address, phone number and hours as well as the DE librarian's name, contact information and schedule, most directed their questions to the DE librarian. Unlike on-campus students who interacted with whichever reference librarian was on duty at the time of need, off-campus students tended to seek out and work with the same person whenever help was needed. There were advantages as well as disadvantages to this behavior. Questions came in batches, around various due dates, and usually on weekends when DE students devoted the most time to their studies. Most questions were sent to the DE librarian's personal e-mail address rather than to the general reference e-mail address, which was monitored by librarians on weekend duty. In many cases, a more timely response to a question would have been possible had the question been directed to the reference desk. As a result, the DE librarian–whose part-time position did not include weekends–had to be vigilant about checking e-mail during weekends and absences nonetheless, particularly as students' deadlines approached, so not to leave the questions unanswered. While this arrangement was perhaps not ideal from a library staffing perspective, the individualized service provided to the students was in keeping with aforementioned ACRL recommendations. Because DE students were dealing with the same librarian for the duration of the course, a dialogue developed between the student and the librarian. Follow-up questions were common. A familiarity with the individual student's situation aided the librarian in answering subsequent questions. As a result, the DE librarian experienced the ironic phenomenon often noted by online teaching faculty, where distant communication becomes more personal than in-person communication. Berger (1999) writes:

> One of the most striking benefits of online education, from an instructor's point of view, is more personal dialogue with students. I have found the intimacy of dialogue to be much greater with the anonymity of Web-based instruction than in a typical classroom. Students reported that electronic communication freed them to be more revealing and to participate more than in the typical classroom setting. (p. 684)

Because the same librarian fielded most questions arising from the students in the course, she was readily able to identify common points of confusion that could then be addressed in the curriculum and in the *Guide*. Because the same librarian encountered similar questions from several different students, she was able to provide a level of consistency in responses, as well as provide reassuring feedback to often-isolated DE students that other students were having similar problems and questions.

INSTRUCTION

Library Use Instruction

Perhaps the greatest challenge for the library in moving the marketing course from an on-campus environment to distant synchronous format and finally to an online asynchronous environment was in the provision of library instruction. When the course was on campus librarians had the luxury of meeting with the group of students face-to-face to discuss the nature of the resources and demonstrate the databases. Similarly, when the course migrated to interactive television, librarians were still able to reach and teach the students in much the same way albeit via interactive television technology. When the course went online, however, librarians no longer had the same kind of opportunity.

In some cases, instruction was offered on an ad hoc basis as questions arose. Responses to questions often resembled mini-lectures. What could easily be demonstrated or explained in a face-to-face setting required more time, effort and wordsmithing to explain via phone or e-mail. While this personalized, point-of-need instruction may have been a boon to those students who recognized a need or faced a problem that compelled them to ask a question, it didn't replace traditional library instruction for all students.

How would students receive a comparable level of instruction and guidance in using library resources if they were never in the library and never at the same place at the same time? One solution was to take the existing *Marketing Information Guide,* embellish it and develop it into an online guide (http://www.uwec.edu/Admin/Library/Guides/sit_ana12. html) [Appendix A]. The online version of the *Guide* decreased the emphasis on print resources and added more online resources, including library databases and some freely accessible Internet sites. In addition to providing an annotated list of databases, the expanded *Guide* also attempted to explain how to use library resources and services, the information that had formerly been provided face-to-face in a classroom setting.

Another section, entitled Getting Started, was added to the online *Guide.* This section briefly discussed proprietary databases, free Internet sites and the proxy server. In addition, the Getting Started section provided information on getting books and articles from the library, and included links to tutorials on researching companies. The cursory treatment of these topics in the *Guide,* while disconcerting when compared to the onsite instruction, was somewhat intentional. As Nielsen (1997) reports, "People rarely read Web pages word by word; instead, they scan the page, picking out individual words and sentences." Among his suggestions for writing for the Web is to use half the word count, or less, than in conventional writing.

Another reason for keeping the *Guide's* text as brief as possible was in deference to research characteristics of MBA students observed on campus. In comparison to students in other disciplines, they tended to have less interest in learning the search process, preferring instead to have the desired information presented to them. This observation is supported by Cooper, Dempsey, Menon and Millson-Martula (1998, p. 59), who write, "People in the medical, legal, and corporate worlds are accustomed to having libraries perform more services for them." Too much textual information in the *Guide,* which wasn't presented as "required reading" per se, might discourage students from using it at all.

While feedback from students and research results reported by the instructor indicate that the *Guide* was valuable, it was not without shortcomings. Without the face-to-face component, it was difficult to direct the students' attention to certain salient points. Indeed, although information was provided in the *Guide,* it was not necessarily read, understood or absorbed. Several questions were received from the students that could have been answered by information in the *Guide,* indicating that the placement, presentation or wording of the information was not entirely effective.

In attempting to rectify this weakness for the subsequent marketing class, the instructor included additional library research information in his lecture, emphasizing and reiterating salient points from the *Guide,* such as the idea of using the proxy server and the value in using the subscription databases rather than relying solely on the free Internet. Information incorporated directly into the instructor's online lectures was more likely to be regarded as "essential" and therefore read. The *Guide* itself was revised to address questions that had arisen during the first run of the course. For example, the *Guide* was divided into sections corresponding to the sections of the Situation Analysis, with suggested databases listed under each section. While the *Guide* included a statement advising students that most of the databases would be fruitful for other sections of the Situation Analysis as well, questions that came to the DE librarian indicated that this point was usually overlooked. As a result, the information was bolded and moved to a more prominent place in the *Guide.*

The students were asked several questions about how to improve instruction in their post-course assessment of library support. The area that they indicated the most interest in using would be a tutorial in searching databases. Over two-thirds responded that they would be very likely to use this proposed feature. About half indicated that they would be very likely to use a tutorial on the online catalog, remote access to the library and an online lecture in researching. Only one-third indicated that they would be likely to use an online chat service with a librarian.

Course Instruction

Two questions were included in the post-course assessment that tied the value of this assignment back to the course. Students were asked if they felt if this was an appropriate assignment for this course. With the exception of one student, all indicated that they thought the project was appropriate.

The second question asked how likely (very, somewhat or not) they would be to utilize the research skills used in this course in future courses or work assignments. Two-thirds indicated they were very likely to use these skills. One-third indicated they were somewhat likely to use these skills and no one stated they were not likely to utilize these skills in the future.

RECOMMENDATIONS

Libraries continue to build their collection of online resources, which is a great boon to DE students. However, many essential print resources have no comparable online counterpart. Where a comparable online product exists, it is often beyond the means of the library–particularly small and medium-sized multidisciplinary libraries–to purchase it, especially if it is highly specialized and expensive, as are many online marketing databases and services. As universities grow their DE offerings they must be cognizant of the need for additional funding for library collections to support them. As the *ACRL Guidelines* state:

> Traditional on-campus library services themselves cannot be stretched to meet the library needs of distance learning students and faculty who face distinct and different challenges involving library access and information delivery. Special funding arrangements, proactive planning, and promotion are necessary to deliver equivalent library services and to maintain quality in distance learning programs. (ACRL, 1998)

Issues of availability are intrinsically linked to those of access. Simplify the process of connecting remotely to library resources when it's technically possible. Improve instruction and personal assistance when it is not.

Make sure the technology works early in the course, or even before the course begins if possible. Another online course at UW-Eau Claire requires that students complete a "technology pretest" as a prerequisite to taking the course. In addition to demonstrating that they can perform tasks such as sending and receiving e-mail, sending attachments, using a word processor, and using the appropriate courseware, students are required to connect to a library database via the proxy and find an article.

Access to reference service will be improved when it is readily available during times that DE students tend to need it, such as evening and weekend hours. For smaller and medium-sized libraries, such as McIntyre Library, expanding hours of reference service may not be feasible. However, flexibility in scheduling–such as staggering existing library staff work schedules to cover more evening and weekend hours, or supporting telecommuting to enable librarians to be "on call" from home–might be possible solutions. Cooperative real-time reference endeavors, such as the 24/7 Reference Project (http://www.247ref.org) offer the advantage of being always available, but the disadvantage of being less personal. Libraries at institutions engaged in multi-campus programs such as the UW System MBA program, may consider collaborating to offer cooperative library reference service on a smaller scale.

Document delivery service will be more useful to DE students–particularly to those in short-term courses–when electronic alternatives to mail-based document delivery service are provided. As McIntyre Library learned in the area of document delivery, urgent requests for services above and beyond those offered will be made, and it is important to retain enough flexibility in DE library services to be able to respond to such requests.

Improving library instruction for DE students poses perhaps the greatest challenge but also the greatest potential for innovation. Initial student response to developments and enhancements made to the *Guide* indicate that further development of the online *Guide* will be an effective means of providing point-of-need instruction for students. Likewise, positive results of integrating of library research issues into the curriculum offer promise that building upon this practice may be an effective method in providing library instruction. Based on student response to the questionnaire, campus librarians are exploring the possibility of developing short, concise online tutorials to address specific issues, such as discerning between free and proprietary databases, using basic database searching techniques, searching specific databases, and obtaining journal articles.

CONCLUSION

Overall, the initial offering of the course in the online environment was successful as is evidenced by the students' reactions and the instructor's assessment that the research projects submitted by DE students were of comparable quality to those submitted previously by on-campus students. The efforts in providing library service to the online Marketing course have served as a model for faculty in other disciplines as they put their courses online. The course offers evidence that even a research-intensive course can be supported at a distance by the library, but not without ample planning, faculty collaboration, flexibility and modification.

REFERENCES

Association of College and Research Libraries, Distance Learning Section. (1998). *Guidelines for Distance Learning Library Services*. Retrieved October 6, 2000, from the World Wide Web: <http://www.ala.org/acrl/guides/distlrng.html>.

Association of College and Research Libraries (2000). *Information Literacy Competency Standards for Higher Education*. [Brochure] Chicago, IL.

Berger, Natalie S. (1999) Pioneering experiences in distance learning: lessons learned, *Journal of Management Education*, 23 (6), 684-690.

Cooper, R., Dempsey, P.R., Menon, V., and Millson-Martula, C. (1998, Summer). Remote library users–needs and expectations. *Library Trends*. 147 (1), 42-64.

Dewald, N., Scholz-Crane, A., Booth, A., and Levine, C. (2000). Information literacy at a distance: instructional design issues, *The Journal of Academic Librarianship*, 26 (1), 33-44.

Mordan, B. A Pedagogical approach to designing a successful online learning experience. Retrieved October 17, 2000, from the World Wide Web: <http://acad.uwsuper.edu/morden/WebClass/LernStep/Lernstps.html>.

Nielsen, J. (1997, October). How users read on the Web, *Alertbox*. Retrieved October 17, 2000, from the World Wide Web: <http://www.useit.com/alertbox/9710a.html>.

APPENDIX A. Marketing Information Guide

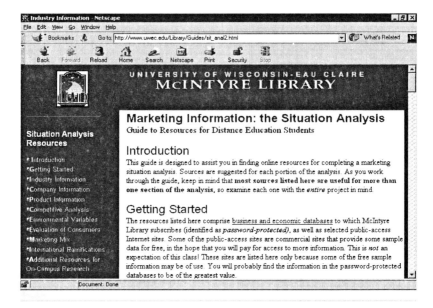

Copyright 2001, University of Wisconsin-Eau Claire. Used with permission.

"Plug and Play" in Context:
Reflections on a Distance Information Literacy Unit

Dana McFarland
Susan Chandler

SUMMARY. Royal Roads University Library has developed a Web-based information literacy unit for delivery to Masters of Business Administration students who are learning at a distance. For success the unit relies on the collaboration of librarians with business school and instructional design staff. The online approach contributes to an information literacy learning spiral that evolves throughout the degree programme. Other information literacy activities include face to face contact between learners and librarians during on site residencies together with online reference and research support. *[Article copies available for a fee from The Haworth Document Delivery Service: 1-800-HAWORTH. E-mail address: <getinfo@haworthpressinc.com> Website: <http://www.HaworthPress.com> © 2002 by The Haworth Press, Inc. All rights reserved.]*

KEYWORDS. Information literacy, distance learning, Masters Business Administration, Canada, research methods

Dana McFarland, MA, MLIS, is University Librarian, Royal Roads University, 2005 Sooke Road, Victoria, British Columbia, Canada, V9B 5Y2 (E-mail: dana.mcfarland@royalroads.ca).

Susan Chandler, MSc, is Coordinator of Distributed Learning and an Instructional Designer, Royal Roads University, 2005 Sooke Road, Victoria, British Columbia, Canada, V9B 5Y2 (E-mail: susan.chandler@royalroads.ca).

[Haworth co-indexing entry note]: " 'Plug and Play' in Context: Reflections on a Distance Information Literacy Unit." McFarland, Dana, and Susan Chandler. Co-published simultaneously in *Journal of Business & Finance Librarianship* (The Haworth Information Press, an imprint of The Haworth Press, Inc.) Vol. 7, No. 2/3, 2002, pp. 115-129; and: *Library Services for Business Students in Distance Education: Issues and Trends* (ed: Shari Buxbaum) The Haworth Information Press, an imprint of The Haworth Press, Inc., 2002, pp. 115-129. Single or multiple copies of this article are available for a fee from The Haworth Document Delivery Service [1-800-HAWORTH, 9:00 a.m. - 5:00 p.m. (EST). E-mail address: getinfo@haworthpressinc.com].

THE MANDATE AND MODEL
OF ROYAL ROADS UNIVERSITY

Royal Roads University (RRU) was founded in 1995 to deliver applied professional programs to mid-career learners. To meet the unique needs of this population the programs are outcomes based, applied, and delivered using a distributed model.

The distributed model is a combination of campus and distance learning, and requires students to complete short residencies (three to five weeks) on campus before they return to their communities to learn by distance. The advantage of this hybrid approach is that learners benefit from both the immediacy of face-to-face instruction and the flexibility and convenience of distance learning.

There are currently five graduate programs delivered using this distributed approach:

- Environment and Management
- Leadership and Training
- Distributed Learning
- Conflict Analysis and Management
- Business Administration

THE MBA PROGRAMME

The MBA is a two-year programme: in the first year learners are exposed to core business concepts in areas such as finance, marketing and accounting; in the second year learners, in addition to completing broad business courses, pursue their specialty area (Human Resources, Digital Technologies, or Public Relations).

The research course takes place during the fourth distance session, just prior to when the students complete their major project. The focus of the major project is on action research, and the expected workload around 360 hours. Students are required to identify a client who has a business problem. Learners work to analyze and research the problem, provide solutions, and possibly implement the recommendations. As the major projects involve real-life problems the types of research skills required can vary widely. For this reason, the research course is designed to expose students to a wide-range of research tools and approaches. Within this context, the information literacy unit becomes important as an applied lifelong business skill.

The unit on information literacy is delivered two weeks into the course, following a general introduction to the topic of research. The unit is positioned so that students acquire information research skills as part of a repertoire of business research tools.

HISTORY
OF THE "GENERIC" RESEARCH METHODS COURSE

Early in 1999, the Academic Management Committee of the University agreed to support the development of a graduate research methods course that could be delivered at a distance to learners across academic disciplines. One purpose was to use the course as a vehicle to advance the University's cross-institutional abilities. A second goal was to realize efficiencies in both initial course development and later revisions. In early discussions the library successfully advocated to include an information literacy unit as "a significant component in the new research methods course"[1] to be integrated with other units such as statistical analysis, research methodology, etc.

A content expert was engaged to work with an instructional designer to put the framework and much of the content in place, while the library was requested to develop the content and to propose assessment for the information literacy unit. The first target for delivery was to be a graduate class in Environment and Management in the late autumn of 1999. A librarian was released from other responsibilities to develop content for this project and the information literacy unit was researched and compiled over the course of about two weeks in September 1999.

PURPOSE AND DESIGN
OF THE INFORMATION LITERACY UNIT

In developing the information literacy unit, we had a number of key objectives.

* We were keen to learn from what had already been done in the area of online or distance development and delivery of such content.
* We wanted to be guided by sound principles with respect to adult learning preferences and learning in an online or distance setting.
* We needed to make the content relevant and engaging while keeping the unit generic enough to deliver across academic disciplines ranging from business to education to environmental science to policy studies.

- With our learners conducting most of their studies at a distance from the University, we needed to provide them with the skills to operate successfully in any academic library.
- We wanted to create the unit as part of a cohesive information literacy curriculum building on and adding depth to face-to-face instruction sessions in residency.

As a first step, the librarians worked to determine the learning outcomes for the unit, ultimately concluding that on completion of the unit learners should have:

- familiarity with typical services provided by a home library and by host libraries
- awareness of how academic libraries organize and provide access to print and electronic information
- understanding of the diverse nature and quality of Internet-based research resources
- ability to build, develop, and manage an effective information search
- strategies for evaluating the results of an information search.

These outcomes were compared to the standards, performance indicators, and outcomes described in the *Information Literacy Competency Standards for Higher Education* of the Association of College & Research Libraries (ACRL), at that time in draft.[2] In addition we matched our unit outcomes against the cross-institutional abilities of the University, specifically that each Royal Roads University graduate should achieve competency in areas that include communication, critical analysis, problem solving, human interaction, global awareness, and learning (setting goals, self-evaluation).[3]

With these outcomes in mind, we went on to investigate existing information literacy courses and modules with particular attention to what had been made for the online and distance environments. In summary we found:

- help guides specific to a database, interface, or discipline
- tutorials to acquaint users with a specific library's services and resources, including virtual orientations and "start here" guides
- instructional pieces with a conceptual approach, such as how to use boolean operators, introduction to the publication cycle, how to evaluate information found on the Internet.

Although we came across numerous very useful generic pieces, especially in the latter category, we found that there did not appear to be many modules or courses designed to give learners a cohesive introduction to information literacy skills, particularly within the conceptual framework that we proposed. For our purposes, the closest model at the time was the Electronic Information Literacy module developed by Ross Tyner at Okanagan University-College.[4] Although designed for an undergraduate audience, the approach to information literacy–presenting skills in a practical manner, yet as portable and transferable–was what we also had in mind.

Intensive writing of the unit content ensued, together with some consideration about the name of the unit. There was some feeling among our librarians that the term "information literacy" might bear a condescending ring to our mid-career, graduate learners. We decided to call the unit *Research in Information Sources: An Information Literacy Approach* in hopes of making the name friendly to learners, while keeping it identifiable to our professional peers. Content was organized to present several principal areas:

- What is the structure of published information?
- How to use academic library services including library organization principles and conventions.
- How to design and conduct an effective search strategy.
- How to search the Internet effectively.
- How to evaluate the results of an information search.
- What are the intellectual property issues involved graduate research?

Our object was not to replace the classroom and reference contact that librarians have with learners during each residency, which varies from one to three hours per learner per residency, depending on the programme. Rather, we saw this as an opportunity to present a conceptual framework and a detailed reference resource to enrich the brief and necessarily interrupted personal contact with librarians that occurs during residency intervals. Because the learners experience residencies interspersed with distance periods in the two-year duration of the degree, we hoped to build a 'learning spiral,' in which "learning is facilitated through an ongoing series of formal, continuous learning opportunities."[5] In the context of the Royal Roads University distributed learning model, we hoped to revisit information literacy issues from residency to residency, and in the information literacy unit at distance, with progressively greater sophistication.

For the first two deliveries, the information literacy unit was distributed only in print by mail along with the rest of the research methods course content. By April 2000, in time for a third delivery to a Conflict Analysis and Management class, the unit was also online and learners were able to access the content both in print and as a set of searchable Web pages.[6] In each instance different assessment strategies were employed to tailor what was otherwise a "plug and play" information literacy unit to the unique requirements of each discipline.

The first delivery to a Masters of Business Administration (MBA) class occurred in May and June 2000 with content provided both in print and online. There were two assessment pieces for this class which were developed by a librarian in consultation with the subject specialist instructor:

Individual Assignment 2A

Begin with the topic that you identified in Unit 1. Consider how specific or broad your topic is, and what subject areas it may relate to in the field of management. Define or redefine your topic so that it has moderate breadth that would likely relate well to the literature. If your topic is very specific or practical, you can use this assignment to find relevant background information. As you proceed in your information search, you may see that you have to refine your topic so that you find a reasonable amount of literature, but are not overwhelmed with references. For example, you may be interested in how a dominating management style sometimes is expressed in verbally aggressive behaviour in the workplace. If you begin by searching for several terms related to your topic you may get a limited return. On the other hand, if you simply search for conflict management style, you might be overwhelmed. But if you search for a strategic combination of terms such as personality and conflict management style, you may find a reasonable number of references.

Identify several key words and synonyms that describe your subject area. Be prepared to experiment with different combinations of terms. Using your key words, and consulting the unit content for strategies and tips, search:

- A library catalogue (you can search in a physical library or online, and you can choose either a public library or an academic library, depending on what is most appropriate for your topic),

- One or more of the online databases available via the Learning Resource Centre (http://library.royalroads.ca), and
- An Internet search engine.

Evaluate the strengths and weaknesses of each of the three types of information searches, with reference to specific criteria that you have decided to use to assess your search results. You do not need to write up your topic, nor do you need to list every source that you find. You may find it helpful to look at the sets of criteria referred to in this unit. Are you satisfied with the search outcome? What will you do the same or differently in your next research endeavour? Please submit a 900-word research report (300 words in each research area–library catalogue, online databases, and the Internet) to your Assignment drop-box by the due date listed in your online Schedules and Assignments page.

If you have questions or concerns as you conduct your information search, contact a librarian at <reflib@royalroads.ca>.

Team Assignment 2B

In your discussion group, identify and summarize guidelines (suggestions, recommendations, do's and don'ts) that would be useful for novice information searchers in conducting a search similar to the one you each have conducted in this unit.

FACILITATING THE INFORMATION LITERACY UNIT

The unit was initially designed with the expectation that the faculty member would be instructor for the research methods course: in other words, a faculty member in the discipline. Contact with a librarian would be through the library's existing reference service and the function of the librarian in that context would be as a guide, rather than as instructor.

This division of labour worked reasonably well in the first delivery to a Masters in Environment and Management class where the assessment was:

Learner Activities: Team Assignment

Discuss the following statement in light of the reading you have done on intellectual property.

The next phase of Canadian copyright law is expected to specifically address rights in the electronic environment. When you think about what is possible as opposed to what is presently legal, how do you think the law should attempt to establish a reasonable balance between the rights of creators and the rights of information users?

Post your individual team responses between December 1 and December 3. Then, select another team's response and critique it. Your critiques should be submitted via the drop-box between December 6 and December 9.

With this as the only assessment, we noted that learners tended not to retain much of the unit content, which was demonstrated in subsequent reference contacts. As a consequence, we began to develop other assessment strategies. These required librarian expertise for evaluation, and more time than our librarians were able to contribute. We began to look at other strategies to build in contact with a librarian as course-related resource.

The next time the course was delivered the assessment was made more detailed. The instructor (in this case a faculty member from the Conflict Analysis and Management Programme) identified that the content of the information literacy unit was too specialized for him to feel confident to evaluate the assignments. At this point a librarian was hired, on a contract basis, to develop evaluation criteria, grade the unit assignments, and provide written feedback to learners. Engaging a 'librarian as marker' was a step in the right direction, but the learners quickly identified this person as a resource and made requests that went beyond the contract deliverables. In response, the role of the instructor-librarian was expanded in subsequent deliveries of the course to include providing direction around the topic generally, facilitation of the online discussion groups, providing feedback to teamwork, and providing evaluation. In other words, the librarian assumed the role of the instructor for the information literacy unit.

Before delivering this model we wondered if it would be confusing for learners to have essentially two instructors. To minimize confusion the instructor-librarian introduced herself at the beginning of the course (by posting a photo and greeting) and indicated that she would be facilitating the unit on information literacy. By all accounts the learners had no difficulty working with two instructors, and saw the transition as being relatively seamless.

One challenge with this approach is that the librarian is required to have expertise in both online facilitation and information literacy. In this regard the challenge is no different for any other content area. Our approach has been to select for content area expertise first, a willingness to learn second, and technical proficiency third. To help instructors develop expertise in online facilitation and learner-centered instruction we have developed one and three-day workshops that can be delivered either face-to-face or online. The instructor-librarian was provided with support and short-term training in online facilitation both before and during delivery of thc unit.

ACHIEVING FACULTY BUY-IN

As one might expect, challenges arise in designing a research methods course for consumption by learners in disciplines that span both science and social science. Happily for us the most difficult of these issues have not been related to the information literacy unit, yet there have been some consequences for the unit.

As each programme reviewed the proposed generic research methods course, there were inevitably discipline-specific content changes that had to be made. In the case of one programme, the resulting course was so full that the course design team elected to append the information literacy unit as a recommended reading with no corresponding assessment. Accordingly the learners, who are busy people, typically did not give much attention to the unit and librarians saw the results in succeeding months. When this group of learners came to do their literature reviews, librarians were inundated with basic questions such as:

> I'm really struggling with how to do a search in order to read full-text online stuff.

> For the life of me I can't find the materials you distributed last summer and therefore I have been unable to get access to the LRC online resources.

> I have a list of magazine articles that I would like copies of, how do I do that?

> Can you tell me how I would determine if Royal Roads University has the following article? Is there a person/place I should be checking?

This unfortunate experience has been the exception, however. Other programmes, including the MBA, have integrated the unit fully into the research methods course and have attached some form of assessment to it. The Management school was the first to adopt a librarian fully as instructor for the unit and others have since followed that lead.

FEEDBACK: INSTRUCTORS

The three instructors we have worked with in different programs have all been receptive to working with the unit. There has been a growing comfort level, based on experience, with having a librarian as instructor to facilitate the unit. In fact, there was some discomfort among programme instructors when presented with the possibility of having to evaluate library-specific assessment. The librarian-instructor model grew out of this feedback and has been successfully implemented across three of our four programs. The fourth program has persisted in treating the unit as a recommended reading.

FEEDBACK: LIBRARIAN-INSTRUCTOR

The comments below from the librarian-instructor focus very much on technology and the challenges of facilitating in the distance mode. Like many instructors new to online teaching, she is completely at home with the content, but has worked to develop online teaching strategies.

> Overall, the online learning experience was a positive and enjoyable one, and generally things went well. It is great to work with students from such a wide range of backgrounds. A couple of disadvantages that I found . . .
>
> - it is difficult to judge the level of understanding of a group online, until the assignments arrive, by which time students have moved on to another unit. In a face-to-face environment, it is easier to check for blank looks, and quickly check to see that everyone is understanding what is going on.

The comment above reflects the need for additional training in online facilitation. In response, the librarian-instructor was sent resource material on how to "read" the virtual class. One example is the 'one-minute paper.'[7] Students are asked, at key points during the unit, to post important things they have learned and what questions remain uppermost in their minds.

- students were frequently stymied by changing or malfunctioning online tools. Often, group discussions were spent getting everyone up to speed technically, leaving little time to discuss issues. Students commented that it would be helpful to have uniform means of communication, such as always having a Q&A, or always communicating via the group e-mail.
- students come into the course with different comfort levels around technology. This can sometimes lead to great teamwork, as the more technically comfortable help the others along, but it can also lead to students missing out on important communication tools.

Royal Roads University does provide technical training and support for students prior to distance learning–nevertheless technical literacy remains one of our key challenges for delivering courses online, and cannot be taken for granted.

- It was hard for me to give up control with things like the Q&A discussions. How did I know if students were actually checking in? If I posted anything important to the Q&A, I'd generally send an e-mail advising that something important had been posted. Those who were checking regularly probably resisted the information overload, while those who weren't checking probably asked teammates what had been posted.[8]

This comment reflects the challenge for an online instructor of striking a balance between keeping everyone informed and connected while encouraging learners to be independent.

FEEDBACK: LIBRARIANS

Above we alluded to reference librarian feedback with respect to the efficacy of the information literacy unit. Librarians have noted a heavier load of reference questions while students are engaged in the course. Anecdotally, they report that if related assessment requires the learners to take a reflective, analytical approach to information searching, typically the reference questions and comments received following the course are sophisticated. For example:

Just to let you know–I have tried the online Science database. It is easy to use (in comparison to some of the others) and it has allowed me to get quick and easy access to science articles.

I am conducting preliminary research to come up with a MSc thesis project. Key words include: watershed restoration; habitat restoration; Pacific salmon; coho salmon; overwintering ponds; off-channel habitat development; Pacific Northwest region including B.C., Washington State; Oregon State.

I would like to check out the references given by [professor] for a case study. I can not seem to get them via the Canadian Business Index. Can you give me some advice about where to find old issues of Macleans magazine?

If there has been no assessment related to the information literacy unit librarians remark on high numbers of learners with basic questions even following the unit.

FEEDBACK: LEARNERS

In telephone and E-mail conversation with MBA learners about their experiences with the information literacy unit, we asked the following questions:

- Did you find the information literacy (library) unit of MB600 relevant to your work in the MBA programme?
- Did you feel that the content was at an appropriate intellectual level?
- Do you think that having completed the unit will help with your major project work?
- Do you think that the unit was as useful, more or less useful than your contact with librarians during residency?
- Did you find the assignment a useful learning opportunity?
- Are there suggestions that you would like to make regarding content, assignments or delivery?

Learner respondents felt that the unit was relevant, but that it might be more timely if it occurred earlier in the two-year degree programme. There was some sense that information literacy issues and skills should be presented in anticipation of any research needs–largely fuelled by a sense of unpreparedness for some early course work research requirements.

The intellectual level of the information literacy content was found to be acceptable, with recognition expressed that fellow students have varying levels of comfort and familiarity with libraries and library-related issues. One student remarked that "the level of language and intellect applied was both informative and helpful." On the conceptual level, another suggested that more might be done to draw out the differences between the structured information environment of libraries and databases as opposed to the Internet.

There have been mixed responses about the relevance of the information literacy unit to major project (thesis) work, and this seems to relate to the unique nature of the project. Some learners very much take an organizational consulting approach to what are essentially action research projects. It appears that in this context some feel that their associated research needs are minimal, less than in prior course work. In this the MBAs may be a unique group among the disciplines who take the course, although we would like to gather more information from other programmes on this point.

When considering the utility of the information literacy unit at a distance against contact with librarians during residency, students clearly identified what librarians also felt–that residency needs were different, more immediate and more practical, and that the personal contact with librarians was indispensable. At the same time there was a sense that distance delivery of the unit was appropriate, encouraging the knowledgeable exploration of local resources. One learner echoed our hope of creating a learning spiral, stating that he would like to see, even more than at present, the creation of a continuum of learning in this area, revisiting information literacy issues throughout the degree.

The MBA assessment pieces required both a team-based reflection on the research process as well as individual essays reflecting on a research process and the relative advantages and disadvantages of diverse types of information sources. Learner respondents found in favour of these exercises as useful learning opportunities. A number of learners remarked that they had expected to put less time into information searching in support of the exercises than turned out to be the reality. One student commented that although the essay requirement was very practical, the process of searching for and evaluating information led him to consider the future of information and how it is structured and disseminated. There was a suggestion that assessments and activities might be made more interactive, perhaps taking the form of an online scavenger hunt that could engage teams and build on group synergy.

Additional comments related to University Library matters such as hours, staffing, contact and service issues related to distance, and collection development. Although we were not necessarily expecting these sorts of comments to emerge through this process, we were pleased that learners took the opportunity to communicate about these matters. We were also able to infer from learner comments something about patterns in using other libraries while at distance. It was reinforced for us that local library access is viewed as a priority in addition to the support that we provide from on site, and that both public and academic libraries are visited. A number of learners also made reference to the value, learned through experience and through the unit, of seeking the assistance of a local or a Royal Roads librarian early in the research process.

REFLECTIONS, DIRECTIONS AND CHALLENGES

An early challenge that dogged the first two deliveries was the development of the two-instructor model for the research course to allow a librarian to take the lead for the information literacy unit. With this in place subsequent deliveries have gone much more smoothly, and the person in this position has been able to fulfill a useful liaison role with the library, passing on resource and service-related feedback that might otherwise never have surfaced. However, on the path to developing the present arrangement we learned that when engaging a librarian-instructor to facilitate this unit it is important to clarify the expectations, in terms of contact hours. Unless the librarian has experience teaching online, he or she may be overwhelmed, like any instructor new to the online environment, by the degree of facilitation required and the intensity of attention that online learners require.

Technical development of the unit may take a new direction in the future. To date the content has been delivered in print, as html pages, and in Adobe Acrobat format for download via course Web site. Although emphasizing development using nonproprietary software tools until recently, the University has lately begun to experiment with some course delivery using WebCT. We may consider moving the unit to this platform to allow for the development of more interactivity as well as online assessment tools.

Through repeated deliveries across diverse programmes we have asked ourselves if the information literacy unit has to be part of the research methods course. The course was a convenient place to lodge it when the opportunity arose, but it may not be the only possible situation or even the most desirable one, depending on the programme. Perhaps, as one MBA student suggested, the unit should be "up front and centre" before they undertake any distance study and the associated challenges of information seeking in that environment. An important factor is that the unit becomes relevant through a connection with some programme imperative, ideally with an assessment tool so that the content is synthesized and applied. As University programmes and course offerings evolve, librarians and instructional designers will work to integrate information literacy content, and the unit specifically, so that it is made as meaningful as possible in time and context.

Making the unit meaningful also means paying ongoing attention to its place in the continuum of graduate information literacy instruction throughout the course of a two-year degree programme. We must be committed to maintaining communication among librarians, instructional designers and programme faculty and coordinators so that information literacy distance learning, addressing learner information needs 'in the field,' builds on learning about University-specific resources that occur in residency, and so that instruction at each point on the learning spiral is customized and occurs in close proximity to the information need. In this way the information literacy unit becomes one in an array of integrated strategies to promote the effective, knowledgeable, and lifelong use of information by distance learners.

NOTES

1. Royal Roads University, Academic Management Committee, Minutes, 7 April 1999.

2. Association of College & Research Libraries, *Information Literacy Competency Standards for Higher Education*, 8 August 2000, <http://www.ala.org/acrl/ilcomstan. html> (15 November 2000).

3. Royal Roads University, *Cross-Institutional Abilities Draft Standards*, 18 March 1999. Presently under review.

4. Ross Tyner, *Electronic Information Literacy*, 25 August 2000, <http://www. ouc.bc.ca/libr/eil/research/intro.html#contents> (15 November 2000). This module has been updated and redeveloped since our work began.

5. Paul J. Mack, *A Spiral Plan for Delivery and Evaluation of Continuous Professional Development*, 1998, ERIC ED 426981.

6. Royal Roads University, Library, *Research in Information Sources: An Information Literacy Approach*, 17 August 2000, <http://www.royalroads.ca/lrdl/infolit/ default.htm> (15 November 2000).

7. K.P. Cross and T.A. Angelo, *Classroom Assessment Techniques: A Handbook for Faculty* (San Francisco: Jossey-Bass, 1993).

8. Beth Davies, "thoughts on online learning," 14 October 2000, personal E-mail.

Creating a Distance Education Tool-Set for Course Based Business Information Instruction

Amanda Wakaruk

SUMMARY. Shaped by new technologies, demand, and a growing base within higher education, distance education programs have expanded and evolved over the past decade. Professors have incorporated distance education tools into their instructional skill-sets and librarians must do the same in order to remain relevant and practicable to the growing numbers of distance learning students. Over the past year, I have created and maintained a system of tools focused on instructing distance education students enrolled in the College of Business and Public Administration at Old Dominion University in Norfolk, Virginia. These tools include a Web based research tutorial, Web based course guides, and classroom instruction in videoconference format. This paper will provide practical strategies for creating and maintaining a complementary distance education tool-set with a focus on course based business information instruction. *[Article copies available for a fee from The Haworth Document Delivery Service: 1-800-HAWORTH. E-mail address: <getinfo@haworthpressinc.com> Website: <http://www.HaworthPress.com> © 2002 by The Haworth Press, Inc. All rights reserved.]*

KEYWORDS. Distance education, bibliographic instruction

Amanda Wakaruk, BComm, MLIS, is Business Reference Librarian, Perry Library, Old Dominion University, VA (E-mail: awakaruk@odu.edu). She has experience working in a reference and instructional capacity in public, special, and academic libraries.

[Haworth co-indexing entry note]: "Creating a Distance Education Tool-Set for Course Based Business Information Instruction." Wakaruk, Amanda. Co-published simultaneously in *Journal of Business & Finance Librarianship* (The Haworth Information Press, an imprint of The Haworth Press, Inc.) Vol. 7, No. 2/3, 2002, pp. 131-140; and: *Library Services for Business Students in Distance Education: Issues and Trends* (ed: Shari Buxbaum) The Haworth Information Press, an imprint of The Haworth Press, Inc., 2002, pp. 131-140. Single or multiple copies of this article are available for a fee from The Haworth Document Delivery Service [1-800-HAWORTH, 9:00 a.m. - 5:00 p.m. (EST). E-mail address: getinfo@haworthpressinc.com].

INTRODUCTION

My first experience with distance learning was as an undergraduate student; I attended an organizational behavior course that was broadcast using two way audio and video between campuses 300 miles apart. At the time, this was cutting edge technology offered by an educational leader in the arena of distance education. What I remember most from that first videoconference class was not a sense of wonderment with the new medium or frustration with the instructor's steep technological learning curve, but the freedom offered by this new option in education. As a student, distance courses allowed me to balance my time between employment and classroom commitments with relative ease and without sacrificing the courses I felt I needed to include in my education. Today, using video to deliver courses is common; over half of all U.S. postsecondary institutions that offer courses through distance education utilize this delivery format.[1] Furthermore, the number of higher education institutions offering distance education courses (through a variety of media) increased from 33 percent to 44 percent between the fall of 1995 and the 1997-1998 academic year, with another 20 percent of polled institutions planning to start offering distance education courses within the next three years.[2] As the technology has evolved and expanded, so has the freedom and flexibility enjoyed by distance education students. As with all advances in academic instruction, librarians are responsible for integrating relevant techniques into the provision of library services.

Although relatively new to academic librarianship (having joined the profession in early 2000), I have had the opportunity to work at flattening my own technological learning curve in the area of distance education. Within the scope of business information instruction, I have created and implemented a variety of Web based resources for both undergraduate and graduate students in addition to teaching undergraduate students in the videoconference classroom. This paper will provide you with some of the strategies I have learned and created in order to develop and maintain a suite of distance learning tools for business students. For ease of reference, I have organized this paper by instruction tool, starting with the video classroom and ending with Web based research tutorials. This structure moves from the general academic to a business centered focus.

CLASSROOM INSTRUCTION: VIDEOCONFERENCING

Videoconferencing is the transmission of video, audio, and/or data from a broadcaster to a receiver. Types of transmission media include satellite, television cable, Internet, and microwave. Flow can be either one directional (instructor to off-site students) or interactive (instructor and students interact in a synchronous environment). My own experience teaching with videoconference technology includes the use of two way audio, one way video. In this scenario, the instruction session is broadcast from the primary classroom via satellite to students in off-site classrooms (downlink locations) and via the Internet to students receiving the broadcast at home or work using personal computers (often referred to as Web based streaming). In addition, the primary classroom or studio is set up as a traditional classroom and students are able to attend the session in person. Note that this scenario is only one possible configuration that can be created with video based instruction.

Students receiving the broadcast from satellite classrooms can interact with the instructor and the rest of the class via audio transmission (satellite classrooms are equipped with microphones for this purpose). While students receive incoming video of the session, they do not broadcast video. Furthermore, the primary classroom requires a dedicated workstation in order to interact with the group of students receiving the transmission over the Internet. This group of students uses Internet Relay Chat (better known as IRC) software to communicate with the rest of the class. The chat session is monitored by an in-class teaching assistant or student who alerts the instructor to incoming messages from the Internet students. The instructor then repeats the question for the benefit of the class as a whole. Finally, in-class students communicate with off-campus students by using microphones and video cameras. In this scenario, the instructor is giving the same lecture to three distinct student groups. The main challenge of working in this environment is to consciously include every group in the discussion: those in the class, those in satellite classrooms, and those at home or work.

Like transmission configuration, instructional aids used in the video classroom vary by institution. Examples of instructional aids include white boards, writing tablets, and workstations. White boards (roughly $6' \times 4'$ in size) are used in the same fashion as the traditional chalkboard, with the video camera zooming in to capture the instructor's written work. Writing tablets work the same way, with the exception of size and location; they are usually $8 \ 1/2'' \times 11''$ and located on the instructor's desk. The desk itself usually includes at least one workstation (used for PowerPoint presentations or Internet access).

Preparing for a Video Classroom

The best way to prepare to use video tools is to familiarize yourself with the limitations and capabilities of the system used at your institution. Prior to conducting any videoconference courses, I completed an in-house training series aptly titled "Teaching on Television." This series of eleven workshops not only introduced me to the technology available to instructors at Old Dominion University, but also to the people behind the scenes.

Course based library instruction is ideally a collaborative effort between librarian and professor. In the video classroom at least one other person is added to the mix–the broadcast technician. This person acts on the instructor's behalf (and at their behest) to manipulate and configure the actual broadcast. To clarify–if the instructor wants to switch the on-screen image from their PowerPoint presentation to the white board to the writing tablets to their body/facial image and back again, all they have to do is voice these desires and the technician completes the actual change in broadcast configuration. While this may seem simple, an open dialogue with your technician is critical for a successful instruction session. For example, during my first video instruction session the technician came into the studio (primary classroom), introduced himself, and ensured that I was comfortable with the technology. One section of the session included a live database demonstration, which I soon determined was difficult for satellite students to see on their monitors. To remedy this problem, the technician showed me how to zoom in on the screen image to improve clarity (*instructors* normally control *workstation based* configurations as opposed to *transmission based* configurations). My next video class required the same type of demonstration. Confident with my ability to use the technology, I neglected to seek out and meet the broadcast technician. When the time came to conduct the live demonstration, I realized the equipment in that particular studio was slightly different than the equipment had been in the previous studio. This resulted in more than a few wasted minutes trying to find someone to talk me through the procedure for zooming that I had used in my first class. To make matters worse, the screen captures I had saved for just this type of situation were not large enough to be legible to either satellite or Internet students. This type of frustration can be avoided by discussing your class plan and technical needs to the broadcast technician prior to the session. Much like working with faculty members to provide traditional classroom instruction, success in this area depends on your capacity to network and form positive cross-departmental working relationships.

Developing an acute awareness of presentation legibility and student participation can also help make the video instruction session successful. Presentation legibility, a factor taken for granted or often easily improved in a traditional classroom, requires greater attention when conducting a video instruction session. Students receiving the transmission over satellite and Internet media are unable to view material with the same degree of clarity as their in-class counterparts. The solution is relatively simple for white boards and writing tablets–use a larger handwritten script! Unfortunately, legibility problems with PowerPoint presentations are not as easy to fix during the session. The Center for Learning Technologies at Old Dominion University has created the following guidelines for PowerPoint presentations that are being broadcast to off-campus students:

- use a light, solid background color (e.g., white, ivory or cream)
- create a 20% border around all text
- ensure that wording is concise
- use a heavy sans serif font, minimum 36 point type size (e.g., Arial, Helvitica, Tahoma)
- use title, sentence, or lower case text; do not use uppercase text
- do not use animated transitions (e.g., audio or visual) between slides
- avoid/limit the use of images.

Web pages and related image files can also be difficult to view. One technique that can be used to enlarge the text on Web pages is the menu driven View–Text Size–Increase (Explorer) or View–Increase Font (Netscape–short cut command "Ctrl +]"). Unfortunately, this technique does not work with all Web based tools (e.g., Dow Jones Interactive). Another option for improving Web page legibility is to use screen captures. After capturing the screen as an image file, use an appropriate application (e.g., PaintShop Pro) to enlarge the image. A good rule of thumb is to enlarge the image to the extent required for the text size to be viewed as if it were 36 points. In addition, screen captured images of all Web based resources should be kept on a floppy disk as an alternative to real time access in the event of Internet, network or Web server problems. Finally, be sure to tell students what Web pages you are visiting and spell out the URL. In this way, the audio transmission can provide information lost in the video transmission.

Steps should also be taken to prevent the distortion of your own image. It is important not to wear excessively shiny jewelry or clothing that is black, white, or has a tight geometric or "busy" pattern, as the former can create glare and the latter can be difficult to view. Solid, subdued colors are recommended. In addition, quick movements are both difficult for the technician to follow and more likely to result in a choppy and/or disjointed transmission. To remedy this, instructors are encouraged to remain seated for the duration of the session. Unfortunately, this solution not only makes using the white board difficult, it can also feel restrictive for those of us who are accustomed to using body movement to engage the class (e.g., hand gestures, walking, etc.). Extensive planning and preparation are required to produce an instruction session that is both engaging and sedentary.

Visual contact and body language are not always available as cues, which makes the communication process feel more labor intensive. Student-instructor interaction should be planned into your session. Try to think of the camera lens as another in-class student and be sure to direct general comments and questions towards this piece of equipment. You may also find that open-ended questions are not always enough to initiate and maintain student interaction. Furthermore, the time delay can make the "ten second rule" feel like sixty seconds. If possible, try to get a student class list prior to your instruction session. Calling on people by name and location early in the session may improve student attention and participation. Another technique is to ask students to write down at least one question about each segment of your instruction session. In-class assignments can also be useful, but be sure to confirm ahead of time that all students have access to the same type of equipment and information tools at their downlink sites.

Setting clear goals and keeping to your timeline is as important in the video classroom as it is in the traditional classroom. Begin each session by indicating your objectives and finish each session by summarizing what was accomplished. Try to keep the segments of your session shorter than twenty minutes and vary activities (e.g., ten minutes of navigating the library Web site followed by a brainstorming session for a search strategy). Finally, I have found that using other distance learning tools in conjunction with video based classroom instruction is extremely beneficial. For example, I usually spend some of the session exploring relevant Web based research tutorials or introducing students to course based research guides. Because distance education students are relatively independent learners, I try to think of the video session as both an instructional and referral tool (i.e., if they do not fully understand the material covered in the instruction session, they should at least know where they can find the tools to teach themselves the same material at a later date).

COURSE BASED RESEARCH GUIDES

I began creating course based research guides in HTML format to eliminate paper handouts and improve accessibility for students that could not attend classroom sessions. These guides have become important reference tools for my distance education students. Not only do they replace the traditional handout, they also include hotlinks to Web based resources and research related tools (e.g., business and general research tutorials). Content covered within the guide itself can include everything from a step by step procedure for searching Investext by SIC code to a list of industry specific trade publications.

While the main component of the research guide will vary by class and professor requirements, the majority of the HTML coding can be stored on a template, as many features are reproduced in each guide. For example, contact information (including e-mail addresses) for both the professor and myself are always included, as is a standard institutional copyright statement and the following line of advise to my students: "Do not waste time struggling with your research! Contact me if you are having trouble finding what you need." Many students that are reluctant to ask questions in front of their class will feel comfortable using e-mail as a mechanism to get the assistance they require. Using a standard page layout and an HTML template makes it relatively simple to create new research guides as required.

In addition to discussing these guides in classroom instruction sessions, I also send the professor the URL and include a link to the guide on our library's "Research Assistance" Web page. Of all the distance learning tools I have used with distance education students, I have had the most positive feedback from the course based research guides. They are simple to create and provide students with the specificity and practicality they need to complete their research assignments.

WEB BASED RESEARCH TUTORIALS

Another tool that I often refer to in instruction sessions and link to from course research guides is the research tutorial. This is a multi-module Web based tutorial that takes the student through successively advanced stages of library research procedures. I am fortunate to work with reference librarians that have produced numerous library research tutorials over the past two years. One of these tutorials, created by our Instruction Services Librarian, Cynthia Wright Swaine, was designed to assist the library neophyte with basic research procedures (all other tutorials created by the staff at Old Dominion University Libraries are subject or course specific in nature). Having the ability to use this type of tutorial as a referral for first year students has allowed me to focus my efforts on creating a research tutorial specifically designed for upper level business students.

Like the course research guides, I started the *Industry and Company Research Tutorial* as a supplement to on-campus instruction at the Perry Library. With a few minor alterations, I was able to make this tool relevant for distance education and on-campus students alike. The first step of tutorial creation was an assessment of faculty and student needs. The procedure I used was informal, but provided me with the information I required to create a relevant instructional tool.

First, I observed the behavior of business students in traditional classroom instruction sessions, at the reference desk, and using PCs in both computer lab and reference room settings. Next, I surveyed the business faculty, via e-mail, about desired tutorial components. I found surveying to be only slightly useful, as my response rate was low. However, the results did help me confirm that a multi-module "Industry Research, Company Research" format would be of the most benefit to the majority of departments within the college (i.e., accounting, marketing, finance, and management). Finally, I spoke with professors informally and following library instruction sessions.

The information I gathered, coupled with my own experience using online tutorials, led me to create a tutorial that includes print and electronic research tools, provides students with practical examples using our database subscriptions, and is flexible enough to be relevant for students from multiple departments of the business college. It is important to note that all of our electronic subscriptions are available to distance learning students through the use of a proxy server. In addition, students have access to WorldCat, which helps locate print resources referred to in the tutorial (print resources are referred to as alternative sources and not used in any specific examples within the tutorial).

The four modules of the tutorial are organized as follows:

- Getting Started: an introductory section that refers true library neophytes to other, more generic library tutorials;

- Industry Information: based on completing an industry profile template, students are taught to use a variety of tools, including SIC/NAICS codes, Investext, Dow Jones Interactive, and Associations Unlimited;
- Company Information: based on finding corporate information, students are introduced to SEC documents and given tips for using ABI/Inform;
- Test Yourself: this final section allows students to test their comprehension of earlier modules by filling out and submitting a ten question online quiz, which provides students with immediate feedback on the accuracy of their answers.

In addition to the above modules, I also created supporting pages including a resource list and a glossary. The resource list provides information about all the research tools covered in the tutorial and relevant search tips for all available business database subscriptions (i.e., supported Boolean operators, truncation, and proximity commands). This resource list is linked from almost all course based research guides and I usually refer to it at some point during classroom sessions.

While the tutorial was time consuming and certainly expanded my HTML knowledge, the final product provides distance education students with research assistance independent of library building hours or location.

CONCLUSION

The library instruction program for distance education students in the area of business at Old Dominion University remains in its infancy. When possible and appropriate, I adapt and change components as necessary. For the sake of convenience and practicality, I have created linkages between the distance education tools outlined in this paper. Instruction sessions include references to Web based tutorials and course research guides, course research guides include links to Web based tutorials, and asynchronous communication is encouraged through the use of e-mail to some extent in all of the above. These linkages also serve as a natural bridge between the business course and the library instruction program.

NOTES

1. National Center for Education Statistics. *Distance Education at Postsecondary Education Institutions: 1997-1998* [online]. Washington, DC: Office of Educational Research and Improvement, U.S. Department of Education, December 1999 [cited 11 September 2000]. Available from World Wide Web: (http://nces.ed.gov/pubsearch/pubsinfo.asp?pubid=2000013).

2. Ibid.

RESOURCES

American Center for the Study of Distance Education
http://www.ed.psu.edu/ACSDE/

Distance Education Clearinghouse
http://www.uwex.edu/disted/home.html

Distance Learning Resource Network–DLRN's Technology Resource Guide
http://www.dlrn.org/library/dl/guide.html

ELITE Project
http://www.le.ac.uk/li/distance/eliteproject/elib/videoconf.html

Industry and Company Research Tutorial
http://www.lib.odu.edu/research/tutorials/amanda/bus/index.htm

Old Dominion University Libraries–Research Assistance
http://www.lib.odu.edu/research/

Resources for Distance Learning Library Services
http://www.lib.odu.edu/services/disted/dersrcs.html

A Teacher's Guide to Distance Learning
http://fcit.coedu.usf.edu/distance/

Videoconferencing for Learning
http://www.distance-educator.com/portals/instructors/article7.html

Library Services for Distance Learners at Drexel University's LeBow College of Business

Ken Johnson

SUMMARY. Provides an example of experiences at the W. W. Hagerty Library in extending services to the distance learning programs at Drexel University's LeBow College of Business. Addresses the goal of offering equivalent services to all distance learning programs through the library Web site and extension of traditional services. Discusses library services provided, the awareness and instruction initiative of the Business Librarian, off-campus access to research databases via the proxy address, and service challenges experienced. Relates how Hagerty Library incorporates services to all distance learning programs into its strategic plan. Also discusses issues of funding, time commitment and measures of use in serving distance learning programs. *[Article copies available for a fee from The Haworth Document Delivery Service: 1-800-HAWORTH. E-mail address: <getinfo@haworthpressinc.com> Website: <http://www.HaworthPress.com> © 2002 by The Haworth Press, Inc. All rights reserved.]*

KEYWORDS. Distance learning, business schools, reference services, remote campuses, business reference, Drexel, ACRL, guidelines, proxy

Ken Johnson is Information Services Librarian, W. W. Hagerty Library, Drexel University. He serves as liaison to the LeBow College of Business and the Hospitality Management program.

[Haworth co-indexing entry note]: "Library Services for Distance Learners at Drexel University's LeBow College of Business." Johnson, Ken. Co-published simultaneously in *Journal of Business & Finance Librarianship* (The Haworth Information Press, an imprint of The Haworth Press, Inc.) Vol. 7, No. 2/3, 2002, pp. 141-154; and: *Library Services for Business Students in Distance Education: Issues and Trends* (ed: Shari Buxbaum) The Haworth Information Press, an imprint of The Haworth Press, Inc., 2002, pp. 141-154. Single or multiple copies of this article are available for a fee from The Haworth Document Delivery Service [1-800-HAWORTH, 9:00 a.m. - 5:00 p.m. (EST). E-mail address: getinfo@haworthpressinc.com].

INTRODUCTION

Academic library services to distance learning programs of all types face one major challenge–distance. Libraries that support the distance learning programs of business schools must overcome this challenge in order to provide services equivalent to those provided on campus. To state the obvious, libraries that neglect to extend services to distance learning programs disenfranchise what has become a thriving component of many business schools. This case study will explain how, at Drexel University, the Business Librarian extends services to the LeBow College of Business distance learning MBA program and how the W. W. Hagerty Library (http://www.library.drexel.edu) incorporates services to all distance learning programs into the distance learning policy and overall strategic plan. This case study also will address related issues like funding for distance learning support, measures of use, time commitments, and service challenges.

BACKGROUND

The Bennett S. LeBow College of Business offers an MBA degree in both a remote campus and an online environment. For winter term 2001, LeBow has an enrollment of 381 graduate MBA students in two remote campus programs and an online MBA program. The remote campus programs have an enrollment of 146 students and the online MBA program has an additional 235 students. The ability of the LeBow College of Business to provide distance learning MBA programs has become a strong selling point for the college in the highly competitive Philadelphia education market. In the Philadelphia metropolitan area, prospective students have fourteen MBA programs from which to choose (Philadelphia, 2000).

The W. W. Hagerty Library appoints one Business Librarian to act as the liaison for the LeBow College of Business. Part of his responsibility is to provide support and services to the LeBow remote campus and online MBA programs.

Drexel University is an urban campus located in the University City section of Philadelphia and has an enrollment of 13,128 undergraduate and graduate students for the fall quarter 2000. In addition to the LeBow College of Business program, the University offers distance learning opportunities in the College of Engineering and the College of Information Science and Technology.

LIBRARY SERVICES PROVIDED

Hagerty Library provides off-campus access to all traditional services through the library Web site, with the goal to provide the distance learning community with library services equivalent to those services provided on-campus (Hagerty, 1999). To support the LeBow distance learning community, the Business Librarian has embraced an awareness and assistance initiative as a part of his liaison and reference duties. This section also will address service challenges experienced by the Business Librarian.

Awareness and Assistance

Regarding the awareness and assistance initiative the Business Librarian annually conducts a library introduction workshop at the two remote campus MBA programs and at the annual online MBA orientation weekend. During an hour-long workshop, he explains the scope of the library services available to the students and expounds upon the Library's goal to provide services equivalent to those available on campus. Students receive a folder emblazoned with the Library's logo, the business card of the Business Librarian, and multiple handouts tailored to their business research needs. The workshop then proceeds to cover such items as the Research Assistance Web pages (http://www.library. drexel.edu/research/business.htm). These pages act as a portal to the Business Librarian and business information resources available through the library Web site.

Following the basic introduction to library services and the Research Assistance portal, the students spend the remaining time covering the major business databases available for research. Most importantly, they learn that all of these databases are available from their home computer using a proxy address and a unique library identification number. The off-campus access procedures will be explained in the next section.

The goal of the workshop is for the students and faculty members to understand that the Library's Web site functions as a service, providing access to business research databases, financial information, and books, as well as a quick link to the Business Librarian's reference service via e-mail or telephone.

Off-Campus Access

For distance learners, access to the print and electronic book collection, the journals (print and electronic), electronic reserves, and the research databases all begins at the Hagerty Library Web site (http://www.library.

drexel.edu). Linden's article title best sums up this concept, "The library's Web site *is* the library" (Linden, 2000).

In an effort to meet the goal of equivalent service, the Library employs a book and journal delivery service to all distance learners at Drexel. The Interlibrary Loan (ILL) department acts as the delivery agent by mailing library books to students free of charge. The regular checkout period of twenty-eight days with one renewal applies. Students request books by using the Web-based ILL form (http://innopac. library.drexel.edu/screens/ill.html). The only charge to the student is the return shipping cost. ILL also delivers copies of print journal articles that are not available electronically. Of course, students are not required to return copies of journal articles.

Electronic reserves is another example of how Hagerty Library provides equivalent service to distance learners. The electronic reserves system allows professors to place course reading materials and other study materials on the library Web site for easy access by distance learners. The Reserve department staff scans reading materials specified by professors and loads the files onto the Reserve module of the library catalog. Electronic reserves can save a professor and distance learning students much time by placing required reading materials in one location. A distance learning student simply searches the electronic reserves sections for the desired materials, and downloads or prints the files as necessary.

Most distance learning students also need to use the wide array of subscription-based electronic resources available through the Hagerty Library Web site. The procedure to gain access to these services warrants some explanation.

Off-campus access to library resources, especially the subscription-based databases, depends on an authentication system whereby each patron has a unique library identification number, more commonly referred to as the "barcode" number. For on-campus students, this barcode number is attached to the student's photo identification card when issued. The on-campus student must visit the Library's Access Services department to have his or her account activated. An active account allows students to make use of all library services either on-campus or off-campus.

By definition, distance learning students rarely step foot on campus. For this reason, all distance learning students, including those from LeBow, must have their barcode issued at an orientation class or delivered through e-mail. Each term, the Library requires that the professor or an academic department representative furnish a list of all newly-enrolled students to the Access Services department head. The department head then verifies each student as currently enrolled and issues an activated library barcode number. The professor or academic department representative then distributes the barcodes to the students either at the remote campus class or by e-mail.

Once a student holds an activated barcode number, the Hagerty Library considers the student a fully functioning library patron. The student may request books, use the Interlibrary Loan service and, most importantly, make the necessary proxy setting change in their Web browser that allows access to the subscription-based electronic resources.

While making a proxy setting change may seem a complicated process, the setting change only has to be made one time. The proxy setting change allows the Hagerty Library to permit off-campus access to all of its subscription-based databases. Licensing agreements for these databases require that access be limited only to current Drexel students, faculty and staff. By requiring all off-campus users to complete a proxy setting change, Hagerty Library can provide off-campus access and stay within the rules of the licensing agreements. Hagerty Library uses an automatic proxy configuration that works within a Web browser to reroute requests to the restricted databases through the Library's computer system. Students find instructions on how to set up the automatic proxy configuration on the same Web page that provides links to the databases (http://www.library.drexel.edu/er/er.html). By rerouting the requests through the Library's system, a student, faculty or staff member can be validated and allowed into the desired database. The last step is for the person to enter his of her library barcode number. Once entered, the Library's computer system grants access to the database.

Service Challenges

In his experience with the LeBow distance learning MBA programs, the Business Librarian has discovered certain challenges that have affected service quality. These challenges shall be broken down into the categories of access and techno-challenges.

Access Challenges

As discussed earlier in this article, the Hagerty Library requires a unique library barcode number for each student. As described in the previous section, an academic department representative must deliver a list of new students to Library's Access Services department head in order for the students to receive the library barcode number. This effort requires much organization on the part of the LeBow department representative and the Library. The LeBow representatives have proven to be quite organized, but problems often arise. For example, during a recent term, two students who registered for remote MBA courses were included on a class list, but their tuition bills had not been processed. When the Access Services department head checked the enrollment status of these students, they could not be found in the system and a library barcode number could not be issued. Only days later, when the students were officially enrolled, could the Access Services department issue the library barcode number. Solving these sorts of bureaucratic snafus requires much patience and persistence on the part of all parties involved.

Another access challenge, relating to the student's access from home, arose when the Business Librarian addressed one of the remote campus distance learning classes. Some students explained that their employer had furnished them a home computer with Internet access, but that even at home, they found themselves behind the corporation's computer system firewall. Such computer security prevents any computer behind the firewall from making a proxy setting change. Hagerty Library normally addresses the workplace firewall issue by informing the students to change the setting at home because the workplace system is beyond the Library's control. However, these particular students could not escape the corporate firewall because their employer supplies both the computer and Internet access. After much brainstorming by the class, the Business Librarian and the students determined that the best solution was for these students to establish an Internet account with another Internet service provider or test the free Internet service providers to see if one would accept a proxy setting change. Of course, the Business Librarian also distributed the contact number for the Library Systems department.

Techno-Challenges

Anyone who has given a presentation will sympathize with the challenge of presenting in an unfamiliar setting. When traveling to a new location, one must quickly become familiar with the technical capabilities of each room. Issues such as slow Internet access speed, substandard projection capabilities, and inadequate workstation software could all pose threats to a "live" Web presentation.

To eliminate any surprises, the Business Librarian arrived approximately 45 minutes before class time in order to assess the capabilities of each classroom. As a backup, he brought along a laptop, a projector, and fifty feet of Internet cable. One of the rooms had a fairly new personal computer with adequate Internet speed and screen projection capabilities, but the computer did not have Adobe Acrobat Reader software loaded. In addition, this classroom was located on a corporate campus that was protected by a system firewall. Moreover, the Business Librarian found himself unable to change the proxy setting to demonstrate the databases. Fortunately, he brought along a canned PowerPoint presentation for backup with screen captures of the databases.

The second classroom had only a projection screen and a network jack. The Business Librarian needed both his laptop computer and projector to begin the presentation. In this case, the network had no firewall protection so he could make the necessary proxy change to demonstrate the Web site and business databases.

Certain techno-challenges, like classroom and equipment capabilities, can be handled with proper planning (i.e., get there early). Other issues, such as firewall protection on free corporate computers, only serve to keep librarians humble.

DISTANCE LEARNING
AS PART OF THE OVERALL STRATEGIC PLAN

The commitment to serve the entire distance learning community at Drexel University falls under the goals of Hagerty Library's overall strategic plan (http://www.library.drexel.edu/facts/middlestates/pdf/strategic7_pln.pdf). The administration and staff of Hagerty Library developed and began to implement the strategic plan in 1998 and 1999, and the Library Advisory Committee adopted the current strategic plan in April 2000. The strategic plan sets forth support for distance learning programs as one of the Library's major service goals. Objectives towards meeting this goal include developing a distance learning policy and appointing a liaison to the distance learning programs. The Business Librarian works within these established goals and objectives to serve the LeBow distance learning MBA programs.

Distance Learning Policy

To prepare a comprehensive distance learning policy, the library administration reviewed the needs of the Drexel distance learning community and consulted the Association of College and Research Libraries (ACRL) guidelines for distance learning library services (Association, 2000). In accordance with the needs of the distance learning community and the ACRL guidelines, Hagerty Library established the aforementioned goal to provide services to distance learners equivalent to those services provided on-campus. The resulting distance learning policy and procedures (http://www.library.drexel.edu/services/distancelearning. html), adopted by the Hagerty Library in October 1999, explain the equivalent service goal and list the services offered and requirements necessary for the distance learning community to gain off-campus access to library resources. The procedure for gaining off-campus access to the Library's services and resources has been explained earlier in this paper.

Chief among the needs of the distance learning community is twenty-four hour access to the library catalog, journals and research databases. The Library meets this need through the Hagerty Library Web site. By making the required proxy setting change in their Web browser, distance learners have access to all library resources whenever needed. The policy also explains procedures for students to have books and copies of journal articles delivered to their homes.

Liaison Duties

In addition to creating a distance learning policy, the Hagerty Library strategic plan established another objective of appointing a Librarian liaison for off-campus programs. The library administration originally assigned this task to the Business Librarian. Within three months the Business Librarian discovered that the job of serving all distance learning programs at Drexel was too wide-ranging and varied for one person. Consequently, the objective was changed so that each subject librarian now serves the distance learning programs of his or her assigned college. Hagerty Library has six librarians that represent Drexel's six colleges and schools. Currently, only three of the colleges, the College of Engineering, the Bennett S. LeBow College of Business, and the College of Information Science and Technology, have distance education programs. This new arrangement allows the subject librarians to extend their established working relationship with faculty members who now find themselves teaching distance learning courses. Hagerty Library finds this arrangement appropriate for Drexel University.

RELATED ISSUES

Other issues, like funding for library services, time commitments, and measures of use, all have an impact on service to the distance learning programs at Drexel, including the LeBow College of Business. Each issue warrants discussion.

Funding for Library Services

Financial commitments, to support Drexel's distance learning programs, also fall under the administrative goals of the Hagerty Library strategic plan (http://www.library.drexel.edu/facts/middlestates/pdf/strategic7_pln.pdf). In January 1998, Library Dean, Carol Montgomery, received a substantial increase in funding for library services and infrastructure from the Provost. The Provost increased funding to revitalize a library that the University had neglected for years, and to prepare for the upcoming accreditation review by the Middle States Association of Colleges and Schools in 2001. Montgomery applied much of this funding increase towards Web-based access to traditional library research databases, electronic journal collections, and electronic books. Regarding business resources, the library added or improved Web-based access to ABI/Inform, Lexis/Nexis, Business&Industry, General Businessfile, the CCH Tax Research Network, and Standard & Poor's NetAdvantage. For electronic journals, the Library acquired the Elsevier journals through Science Direct, MCB University Press titles, and selected electronic journals from Wiley Interscience, to name just a few. All of these databases and electronic journal collections serve the research needs of the LeBow College of Business distance learning programs.

In addition, Montgomery moved aggressively towards establishing an electronic journals only environment. During 1998, Montgomery gained support for this effort from the faculty members on the Library Advisory Committee. At the same time, she reinstated the faculty copy service that had been discontinued a few years earlier. This service delivers journal articles to faculty members via regular mail, e-mail, or fax. In the opinion of this author, the reinstitution of the faculty copy service helped ease potential fears that the faculty was losing access to their beloved print journals.

To implement this electronic journals plan, all of the Librarians have participated in an intense evaluation process of print journal holdings to decide if an equivalent electronic version of a traditional print resource exists. The Librarians have operated under the guideline that if an electronic equivalent of the print exists and can be acquired, then the print will be cancelled. In turn, the Library has applied money saved from the cancellation of print titles towards increased access to electronic titles.

Between 1998 and 2000, the Library reduced its print subscriptions from about 1,500 titles down to approximately 800. The Library replaced many of the print titles with the electronic counterpart and cancelled some titles for lack of use. In 2001, the Library expects to subscribe to only about 300 print tiles. Over the same time period, the Library built its electronic offerings to over 6,000 unique electronic titles and intends to add more (Montgomery, 2000). One may learn more about Hagerty Library's efforts to create an electronic only journal collection by reading Montgomery's article in the October 2000 issue of *D-Lib Magazine* (http://www.dlib.org/dlib/october00/montgomery/10montgomery.html).

Feedback from the Drexel community regarding the Library's allocation of funds towards electronic resources, especially electronic journals, has been mostly positive. In-house users of the Hagerty Library have learned quickly that they can access journals from anywhere on- or off-campus. From the Business Librarian's conversations with business faculty and students, including a few distance learners, the LeBow College of Business has been pleased with the move to electronic journals. In addition, the College of Engineering, College of Information Science and Technology, and the Sciences programs have been pleased with the increased offerings of electronic journals. Other programs, such as the Design Arts and Humanities programs, have concerns that electronic equivalents do not exist for some of their journals, and that these print journals will be cancelled without their input. Montgomery has made concessions to these programs, but remains steadfast in her conviction to convert to electronic journals as quickly as possible and to allocate more funds towards electronic resources for all Drexel programs.

Time Commitment

The Hagerty Library staff shares the responsibility of supporting the remote access needs of the Drexel community. The time commitment necessary to manage the electronic resources requires a full time position. In 1998, a new position, Electronic Resources Manager (ERM), was created for managing all technical and access issues relating to electronic resources. The person in this position handles all licensing agreements with the database vendors and makes certain our contracts allow for off-campus access that is essential for distance learners. The ERM also contacts the vendors directly when problems arise and communicates to the Information Services (IS) librarians any database problems or improvements. In turn, the IS librarians field most reference calls and e-mails regarding the use of these electronic resources. Minor troubleshooting problems, such as setting up the proxy address, are handled by the IS staff.

The Library Systems department, including the Webmaster, supports the Electronic Resources Manager and Information Services librarians by resolving network problems, technical access questions from students, and Web site design issues. Each of these individuals and departments works as a team to support remote access to the library and by default the distance learning community. The Hagerty Library's dedication to support remote access through the behind the scenes efforts of the Electronic Resources manager and the Library Systems department increases the quality of resources and service provided to the entire distance learning community, including the LeBow distance learning MBA programs.

For the Business Librarian, the time commitment necessary to serve the distance learning MBA programs requires a flexible work schedule. All remote campus MBA classes convene in the evening, and the online MBA orientation meets over a weekend. The Business Librarian believes attending these classes and the orientation weekend an essential job duty, and based on the positive feedback he receives from students and faculty, the effort has paid dividends in increased awareness of electronic resources for business research.

Due to the increased awareness of the electronic resources, the Business Librarian receives about three e-mail or telephone questions each month from distance learning students. He answers these questions within the normal workday. On weekends, he checks his work e-mail account at least once, and responds to questions when possible. Even with traveling to the distance learning sites and responding to e-mail queries over the weekend, the Business Librarian believes the time committed to LeBow distance learning MBA programs falls within a normal work week.

Measures of Use

Librarians may expect that service to distance learners would produce a quantifiable increase in library use statistics. At Hagerty Library, the increase has proven either very small with regards to book requests and reference questions or not quantifiable when measuring the use of electronic resources.

The Business Librarian, as stated earlier, receives about three reference queries each month from LeBow distance learners. The Information Services department, which handles all reference queries, does not keep separate statistics on questions from distance learners, so it is possible that other librarians at the Reference desk handle a few more queries each month. Still, questions from distance learners do not create a noticeable burden on either the Business Librarian or the Information Services department.

The Interlibrary Loan (ILL) department handles requests for books and journal articles from distance learners. ILL has received only one book request and zero journal requests from Drexel's distance learning students since the implementation of the distance learning policy in 1999. This one book request did not come from a business student. To explain why the use of physical print materials has been so low, this author reviewed the available course syllabi for the LeBow distance learning courses, and discovered that course readings are normally provided to the students by the professor. Also, the remote campus MBA programs are all located within one hour of the Drexel campus. Students in these programs may choose to travel to the Hagerty Library and use the library in the traditional manner. However, the Library staff may wish to review the distance learning policy to remove any possible barriers to the students' use of print materials.

Hagerty Library expects that most distance learners use the electronic resources more than any other library service. The Business Librarian believes this to be especially true for business research. Unfortunately, neither the database vendors nor the library's automated system provides quantifiable figures. The vendor's usage reports do show a high volume of use that validates the Library's expectations, especially for the business services like ABI/Inform and the *Wall Street Journal*. Yet, these reports do not provide the detail necessary to assess the volume of use by distance learners. Most often, the reports tally the number of logins, search requests, or individual titles accessed. These figures do not detail the location where students log in.

The Library's automated system (Millennium from Innovative Interfaces) also fails to provide a count of distance learner access. The Millennium system employs the same student categories as assigned by Drexel's student records system called Bannerweb. Bannerweb categorizes students as being either undergraduates or graduates. It does not distinguish distance learners within these student groups. Hence, when a student logs on to a library database from home, the student enters his or her unique library barcode number into the Millennium verification system to gain access. Millennium proceeds to tally the student as an undergraduate or graduate, but not as a distance learner. Unless Drexel University creates a separate category for distance learners, the Library may never be able to quantify use of its electronic resources by distance learners.

In summary, Hagerty Library cannot accurately assess the amount of use by the LeBow distance learning programs or by any distance learning group at Drexel. For the future, it may be necessary for the Business Librarian to discuss with faculty the kind of business research and resources required for the distance education courses. With this method, the Business Librarian would at least be able to gain empirical evidence of use.

CONCLUSION

Certain aspects of the experience at Drexel may be typical for academic libraries that support business schools offering distance learning programs. Other aspects may be unique. Hopefully, this case study provides a relevant example of a library that provides specialized outreach and instruction to its business distance learning program, and integrates support for all distance learning programs into its overall strategic plan.

To serve the future needs of the LeBow programs, the Business Librarian must continue outreach and instruction efforts to the faculty and students. Working under the assumption that the LeBow distance learning programs will expand, outreach and awareness efforts by the Business Librarian will be crucial to integrate library services into the distance education experience. In addition, the Business Librarian must stay abreast of new electronic resources that improve the business research capabilities of distance learning students as well as all of Drexel's business students.

It cannot be overstressed that libraries which support the distance learning programs of business schools must provide services equivalent to those provided on campus. Without such a commitment, the library may find itself neglecting a significant portion of its population.

REFERENCES

Association of College and Research Libraries. 2000. "Guidelines for Distance Learning Library Services" [Online]. Available at URL: <http://www.ala.org/acrl/guides/distlrng.html> [January 23, 2001–access date].

Linden, Julie. 2000. "The library's Web site *is* the library: designing for distance learners." *College & Research Libraries News* 61, no. 2: 91, 101.

Montgomery, Carol. 2000. "Measuring the Impact of an Electronic Journal Collection on Library Costs." *D-Lib Magazine* 6, no. 10. Available at URL: <http://www.dlib.org/dlib/october00/montgomery/10montgomery.html> [February 15, 2001–access date].

Philadelphia Business Journal. 2000. "MBA Programs," in the *2000 Book of Business Lists* (Philadelphia: Philadelphia Business Journal): 122.

W.W. Hagerty Library. 1999. *Distance Learning Policy and Procedures* [Online]. Philadelphia: Drexel University, W.W. Hagerty Library. <http://www.library.drexel.edu/services/distancelearning.html> [February 6, 2001 access date].

W.W. Hagerty Library. 2000. *Hagerty Library Strategic Plan: Draft 4/13/00* [Online]. Philadelphia: Drexel University, W.W. Hagerty Library, 2000. Available at URL: <http://www.library.drexel.edu/facts/middlestates/pdf/strategic7_pln.pdf> [February 6, 2001–access date].

Guidelines and Standards
Applicable for Library Services
to Distance Education Business Programs

Barton Lessin
Rhonda McGinnis
Rick Bean

SUMMARY. There are four recent, readily available publications that serve as guidelines or standards for distance library services. Two statements published by the AACSB, The International Association for Management Education, address many aspects of business education and represent a much broader view than solely the role of libraries in support

Barton Lessin is Assistant Dean, Wayne State University Library System, Detroit, MI. He serves as chair of the Association of College and Research Libraries Standards and Accreditation Committee and its Information Literacy Competency Standards for Higher Education Task Force. He was a founding member of ACRL's Distance Learning Section and is the creator of the Off-campus Library Services Conference.

Rhonda McGinnis is Business Librarian, Wayne State University, Detroit, MI. She is a member of the Business and Finance Division and College and University Libraries Roundtable of the Special Libraries Association and the Business Reference and Services Section of the American Libraries Association.

Rick Bean is Director, Library and Research Services, Keller Graduate School of Management, Oakbrook Terrace, IL. Previously, he was Coordinator of Library Services, O'Hare and South Campuses, DePaul University, Chicago, IL and a reference librarian at two Chicago-area public libraries. He is a member of the Association for College and Research Libraries' Distance Learning Section.

[Haworth co-indexing entry note]: "Guidelines and Standards Applicable for Library Services to Distance Education Business Programs." Lessin, Barton, Rhonda McGinnis, and Rick Bean. Co-published simultaneously in *Journal of Business & Finance Librarianship* (The Haworth Information Press, an imprint of The Haworth Press, Inc.) Vol. 7, No. 2/3, 2002, pp. 155-205; and: *Library Services for Business Students in Distance Education: Issues and Trends* (ed: Shari Buxbaum) The Haworth Information Press, an imprint of The Haworth Press, Inc., 2002, pp. 155-205. Single or multiple copies of this article are available for a fee from The Haworth Document Delivery Service [1-800-HAWORTH, 9:00 a.m. - 5:00 p.m. (EST). E-mail address: getinfo@haworthpressinc.com].

155

of distance business programs. The Association of College and Research Libraries "Guidelines for Distance Library Services" speaks directly to the matter of distance library service. Although not oriented specifically to business programs, this statement can be very useful for librarians who serve distance education business programs. Most recent of these four statements are the Information Literacy Competency Standards For Higher Education. This article considers each of these statements and examines their usefulness to librarians who are planning, developing, implementing or enhancing services in support of distance education business programs. *[Article copies available for a fee from The Haworth Document Delivery Service: 1-800-HAWORTH. E-mail address: <getinfo@haworthpressinc.com> Website: <http://www.HaworthPress.com> © 2002 by The Haworth Press, Inc. All rights reserved.]*

KEYWORDS. Library service, distance education, business students, guidelines, standards

INTRODUCTION

The use of standards in higher education is frequently and correctly associated with the pursuit of the status that accompanies accreditation. Standards are prepared by the accrediting association, either a regional or discipline-based group, and used by members of an institution to describe how that institution has met or exceeded the educational and organizational expectations reflected in the standards document. The accreditation process is voluntary and provides the institution with an opportunity for the self-study and review of all aspects of its operations or that of a specific department or program. The standards serve as the catalyst for the self-study by stating what are, in the opinion of the reviewing association, the norms by which the institution should conduct itself. These standards also provide the institution with a framework for comparison with its peer institutions within higher education. This process has proven its worth over the last 115 years, dating from the establishment of the regional accrediting associations and then later the creation of discipline-specific associations.[1] Within this latter group, the AACSB–The International Association for Management Education–was an early participant. Among several standards and guidelines considered in this article are two statements from the AACSB that are basic to the evaluation of academic business programs and, in particular, to academic business programs offered to students engaged in learning at a distance from the traditional home campus of the institution that presents them. The first of these is a standard that is a part of the accreditation process; the other is a set of guidelines recently published by the AACSB as an aid to institutions of higher education that have already or are planning to extend their business program to distance education students.

Standards within higher education are also used beyond the accreditation process in the context of "an acknowledged measure of comparison for quantitative or qualitative value; criterion; norm."[2] The quickly developing arena of distance education for business students combined with the competitive environment to attract and retain qualified students calls for librarians associated with new programs as well as more mature programs to compare their services and resources to one another and with national norms. This comparison can help to assure solid informational access and support appropriate to business education programs. Comparison of this type is also used to demonstrate a qualitative advantage over one's programmatic rival in an effort to successfully market a distance education business program to perspective student enrollees.

There are two additional statements that can be used by librarians who are charged to support academic business programs at a distance. An Association of College and Research Libraries guideline has had the distance learner in mind since its original publication in 1982. Although the text of this statement has changed over the intervening eighteen years, it has also remained very consistent in its support of equitable services and resources, the responsibility of the parent organization, the need for appropriate levels of personnel, financial and other resources in support of the distance learner and the academic program of which he is a part. A newer standard that addresses information literacy is an important contribution to the mix of resources available to the librarian with responsibility to distance learners. The Information Literacy Competency Standards for Higher Education is one of the most recent and among the more significant outcomes that have resulted in response to the 1989 American Library Association's Presidential Committee Report on Information Literacy.[3] Even at the date of its publication more than eleven years ago, that committee's report included brief explanations as to why information literacy is important to the business community and therefore business education. The information literacy standards are a reflection of an international interest in information literacy and how its skills set can benefit students and prepare them to be better life-long learners.

This article explores each of these four guidelines/standards to determine if and how library services are addressed and whether librarians can use these statements to the benefit of the distance education students served by their institutions.

AACSB ACCREDITATION STANDARDS AND THE ASSOCIATION'S QUALITY ISSUES IN DISTANCE LEARNING "GUIDELINES"

AACSB–The International Association for Management Education–is perhaps the best known and most widely used association for accreditation of academic business programs. This not-for-profit corporation has a history extending back to 1916 when it was founded by seventeen of the most prestigious and well-known schools of business in the U.S. The AACSB Web site indicates that as of April 2000, this association had accredited 390 business programs of which 380 are located in North America.[4] AACSB evaluates and accredits programs at the undergraduate, masters and doctoral level as well as undertaking other association based initiatives. Of primary importance to this article is the fact that the some 85% of the U.S. institutions offering business and management degrees are accredited by the AACSB. Given the impact of the AACSB on the accreditation of business and management programs, it is not surprising that this organization's standards are seen as very important for the review of academic programs and the library programs that support them both in the traditional setting and the distance learning environment.

The AACSB accreditation standards are included in the 1999 publication "Achieving Quality and Continuous Improvement through Self-Evaluation and Peer Review."[5] Nowhere in this statement is there any direct mention of libraries or library support. Although most if not all business education programs rely heavily on information resources, these standards address this matter only indirectly.

Section IN.1 of the Standards apply to library support regardless of the location of the academic program. It reads "The school should provide and manage resources to meet the instructional responsibilities created by the programs offered."[6] While section IN.1 does not provide direction as to how an institution can successfully accomplish this, neither does it limit the manner by which a self-study might be prepared.

The institution is free to craft that document in a way that is appropriate to the institution, its goals and objectives, and the degrees it offers.

Any librarian involved with an academic business program offered at a distance would benefit by combining these Standards with a newer document from AACSB titled "Quality Issues In Distance Learning."[7] This latter document provides a set of guidelines for the consideration of academic business programs offered at a distance from an institution's traditional campus. These guidelines are timely and include useful statements that speak to both information literacy and distance library services. AACSB clearly notes that the guidelines do not "create new accreditation standards for distance learning" and are meant only to complement other documents from that association.[8]

It is important that the task force that authored the AACSB guidelines included early within its introductory paragraphs an acknowledgement of the merging of distance learning with campus-based learning. Here the task force specifically noted services and resources traditionally associated with the library. "Remote access to learning materials, databases and libraries, electronic communication, . . . and other features of distance learning increasingly are used in campus-based instruction" (p. 7). This acknowledgement is consistent with AACSB's position that these guidelines do not create new standards, but rather assist in the evaluation of distance programs. This is again reiterated in the Mission section of the AACSB guidelines where it is stated that "The school must ensure the outcomes of the distance learning programs are of comparable quality with on-campus programs" (p. 11). Further, the task force clearly states that the AACSB guidelines are not prescriptive, having rather the intention of providing a "source of ideas to ensure that the necessary quality is inherent in the program" (p. 8). While perhaps not stated in the same language, this position is very similar to that found in the Association of College and Research Libraries "Guidelines for Distance Library Services."

Five recommendations in the AACSB guidelines are particularly notable for their potential impact on the library and its services. Recommendation 3 suggests that the academic program gather information "from all stakeholder constituencies" (p. 4). Given the role of the library in support of business education, it is realistic that the library should be considered a constituent party and approached for comment. This recommendation, if followed, would provide library staff with an opportunity to participate in the discussions concerning the organizational support of business programs at a distance. Recommendation 8 speaks to evaluation of the faculty. Here we find language that is similar to that found with information literacy. Evaluation and feedback are integral parts of information literacy that permit the faculty person to recognize whether the students are learning as expected. Recommendation 13 suggests that resource assessment be a "regular part of an annual distance learning program review" (p. 6). The library and its services should be considered as resources to be assessed in this context. Recommendation 14 speaks to the development of "explicit intellectual property rights policies for materials used in distance learning programs" (p. 6). This recommendation could be directed to the use of faculty materials in a distance learning environment and appropriate steps by the institution to assure copyright and royalty payments for the use of those materials in keeping with the law. It could also refer to the appropriate use of copyrighted materials by students involved in distance business programs. This latter issue is also addressed in Standard 5 of the "Information Literacy Competency Standards for Higher Education" discussed later. Recommendation 16 does not mention the library but encourages the development of "support services before initiating distance learning programs" (p. 6). In some instances, the library may be overlooked in the planning and development of distance education programs and later expected to play catch-up with a program that has already been initiated. This recommendation suggests that a more inclusive, thoughtful, and proactive approach to new programs be undertaken with regard to libraries. This same recommendation speaks to working with non-campus partners and the need to survey students to determine support needs.

The "Instructional Resources" section of the AACSB guidelines address library services directly and indirectly. It refers to a need for emphasis on "access to and utilization of, learning resources" (p. 24). Bullet point two in this section of the guidelines directly speaks to the need for library support stating "Students should have access to, and be required to make use of, library and computing facilities, including electronic access . . ." (p. 24). It suggests that students be given training and assistance to assure their technological competence as a part of their academic program. This is consistent with the underpinnings of information literacy as noted later in this article. The AACSB guidelines also state in clear language that those institutions offering graduate programs or scholarship should support the library and other services at a level appropriate to those missions.

These guidelines make a point that has been heard for years within the community of librarians that support distance academic programs. This has to do with the realization that the resources for distance academic programs need to be equitable with those on-campus but need not replicate them in all aspects (p. 25). While it may be unreasonable to build a library facility to support a geographically distributed educational program, it is eminently reasonable to assure that students have the ability to access needed information through other means. This may include electronic resources, Interlibrary Loan, contracts or agreements with information providers or facilities in close proximity to the distance education faculty and students, or a combination of services that compare favorably with the access that is enjoyed on a traditional academic campus. Indeed equitable service could well imply that those teaching and learning at a distance are sometimes offered more or better service by the library than their on-campus counterparts. This stems from the challenges that can arise as a result of the geographic separation that is inherent in distance programs. For example, a library on campus is likely to provide a fee-based service permitting students to obtain copies of needed periodical articles. The same institution may provide a predetermined number of free article copies per week to students learning at a distance because they are unable to easily visit the library and make the needed copies for themselves. The emphasis in both the AACSB position and in the Association of College and Research Libraries "Guidelines for Distance Library Services" is based on comparability and the needs of those being served by the academic program.

It is somewhat surprising given other attention to libraries that the AACSB guidelines fail to include the library and its services within the category titled "Consumer Information for Students" (p. 15). It seems reasonable to expect that an institution would want to share information about its library services to distance students and to perhaps use this facet of its operation to distinguish its program from others. This presumes, of course, that the institution offers library services of merit. This one oversight aside, the AACSB "Quality Issues in Distance Education" guidelines offer a useful, non-prescriptive statement that is sensitive to the need for library service. It offers a substantive guide for librarians as well as others to evaluate library services; this is an important tool that can be used effectively by librarians to address issues of merit concerning library support to distance business programs.

ASSOCIATION OF COLLEGE AND RESEARCH LIBRARIES GUIDELINES FOR DISTANCE LIBRARY SERVICES

Long before computers were as widely used within higher education as they are today, in advance of the explosion of the Internet and World Wide Web, and prior to the recent development of distance education, the Association of College and Research Libraries had guidelines for services in support of students taking classes distant from an institution's main campus. The guidelines extend back to 1982 and are a good example of how forward-thinking the leaders of the Association of College and Research Libraries have been in this area of librarianship.[9] It is likely that the explosion of off-campus academic programs in the 1970s, marked by institutions that included Northern Colorado, Maryland, and many others, had an influence on the development of this statement. These guidelines were revised in 1990[10] and 1998[11] and are once again in the process of revision.[12] (See Appendix A for the 1990 edition.) When approved and distributed the new version will offer possible outcomes of distance library services that can be used by institutions to help further assess their distance support efforts.

The committees that fashioned these statements shared several common interests. There was in each case a clear effort to use language that was not readily characterized as belonging to one or another discipline. It seems apparent that the intention was to prepare guidelines that could be used in providing library services to distance education students regardless of the subject matter of the curriculum involved. There is, for example, nothing in the "Guidelines for Distance Library Services" that would preclude their use in support of business curricula. Another shared interest seemed to be an equitable treatment of the off-campus learner. While the authors seem to recognize the differences inherent in the on-campus and off-campus learning environments in regard to the kind of library support appropriate and reasonable, there is an effort to assure that the off-campus learner is treated equitably. This becomes most apparent beginning with the 1989 Guidelines and continues into the latest versions.[13] Writing about the 1997 draft statement that eventually became the 1998 Guidelines, Duggan states "The Association of College and Research Libraries has provided guidelines for library services to off-site students for years. The guidelines are to the point: 'The home library is the primary source of materials; the off-campus librarian is the primary means of access and delivery . . . .'"[14] A third common thread that runs through these statements is the avoidance of language that might be construed as prescriptive. From their beginning in 1982 and continuing to the present and on to the forthcoming version of the "Guidelines for Distance Library Services" one reads the word "should" rather than "must" as the word that defines how libraries are expected to apply the contents of this statement. A great deal of interpretive flexibility is directed to the institution. This statement is clearly intended to provide guidance and assistance rather than requiring institutions and members to comply with a set of rules. Kirk and Bartelstein stated that "The guidelines follow national accreditation standards and offer strong language on the necessity of resources and services equal to those that support on-campus programs. At the same time they encourage innovative and novel approaches from librarians."[15]

These Guidelines under one name or another have included a number of component parts. Many of these have been consistently a part of this statement. Following the introductory paragraphs, one finds a list of defined terms and assumptions that were applied to the Guidelines and their revision. There is also a listing (1998) of fourteen actions that the "librarian-administrator" of the distance library services should minimally do. Recommendations concerning finances, personnel, and facilities/equipment are also included. The current document additionally speaks to the need to secure access to both print and electronic resources. Here, as elsewhere throughout the Guidelines, attention is focused squarely on the institution offering the distance education program as well as the individuals responsible for managing the library services. The Guidelines similarly provide an "essential" group of activities in support of "informational, bibliographic, and user needs." The Guidelines speak to the need of the institution to provide "records" that can be used to demonstrate how to achieve the intent of the statement. There are seventeen examples of the kinds of information that can help to meet this goal. The document closes with an explanation of the process that was used in the creation of the Guidelines; this is fully consistent with the process described below. There is a strong emphasis on the contributions of librarians from around the world that offered comments on the draft and assisted in the work of the authoring committee. The substantial list of "experts" in their chosen field of library services is a good indication of the opportunity that librarians can have in influencing the revision of these as well as other ACRL standards and guidelines that might be used in support of distance library services for business students.

The review process that the Association of College and Research Libraries applies to all of its guidelines and standards helps to assure that each is reasonably current. Procedures call for the review of a statement of this type on a five-year cycle.[16] While it is true that the review timing does not always match the intent of the Association's Board of Directors, the responsible section or committee is advised as to its obligation and there is another committee that has oversight responsibility (Standards and Accreditation Committee) for assisting in this review. The actual process does not require change. However, in order to comply with the established procedure, the committee charged with the review process must determine whether or not change is needed. If no change is required, the committee is expected to explain how it came to this determination as well as its choice to maintain the then current language. Part of this may involve seeking the advice and comment of library leaders known to have an interest in the topic of the particular standard or guideline under consideration. Use of listserv lists and Web sites also helps in the solicitation of comments that assist the review committee in making its decision as to the need for language changes. If a reconsideration of the text or a determination of the value of the document itself is required, a revision or even a rescission of the document may be recommended. Language changes result in the committee preparing a draft statement that is shared with the membership of the Association as a whole. The draft is published in *C&RL News* and posted on the Association's Web site. An open hearing is held by the authoring committee (this may be a sub-committee of the review committee) providing the membership with an opportunity to discuss the draft and to voice thoughts about the draft guideline or standard and its appropriateness to the services or type of library it addresses. This process helps to keep guidelines and standards current and reflect the best thinking of the Association membership. As of the preparation of this article, none of the other statements considered here carried with it a review process with as much opportunity for on-going change and assurance for currency as this. Despite this excellent process, it is clear that not every academic business librarian is in a position to comment on the Guidelines for Distance Library Services. Many of these librarians are members of other professional associations, notably the Special Libraries Association, and would neither routinely attend the annual or midwinter American Library Association conference nor comment on suggested changes to a draft document through the use of the Web.

The authors of this article were interested in determining whether or not the "Guidelines for Distance Library Services" is actually being used in support of academic business programs at a distance. To achieve this end, a survey was prepared and distributed to a number of listserv lists that focus on issues pertinent to librarians serving business and distance learning. (See Appendix B.) A special effort was made to encourage only academic librarians to reply. Corporate librarians whose perspectives may be very different than the focus of this article frequent these same lists. Although the total number of responses was not large, the outcome of this data gathering resulted in some insight to the familiarity of librarians with these particular Guidelines, where they learned about them, and whether they are using the Guidelines in support of the students and faculty they serve.

The survey was distributed to three listserv lists in June 2000. These included <offcamp@lists.wayne.edu>, <buslib-l@listserv.boisestate.edu/>, and <slabf@lists.psu.edu>. Forty-five librarians from the U.S. and one librarian from Canada responded. Of this number, two (2) (4.35%) responses were from community college librarians, four (4) (8.7%) from college librarians, one (1) (2.17%) from an institute, one (1) from a school, and the remaining 38 (82.61%) responses were from university librarians. Nine (9) (19.57%) said that their employer offered business classes while thirty-seven (37) or 80.43% said that their institution offered a business degree program.

Forty-one (41) (89.13%) of the respondents answered that they were familiar with the "Guidelines for Distance Library Services." This high number is somewhat surprising in that it is likely that not all business librarians regularly read *C&RL News* or access the Association of College and Research Libraries Web site. At the same time, this may be an excellent reflection of the impact of distance education on the lives of business librarians. Only five (5) responded by indicating that they were unfamiliar with this statement. Librarians answering the survey were given five options indicating where they recall learning about this statement. Those answering in the affirmative could select one or multiple responses. Of these forty-one respondents who indicated a prior knowledge of the Guidelines, thirty-seven responded by identifying one of more sources of that knowledge.

- 25 (67.57%) of the respondents explained that they recalled reading about these Guidelines on the Association of College and Research Libraries Web site.
- 23 (62.16%) learned about the Guidelines from another librarian.
- 22 (59.46%) remembered hearing about the Guidelines at a meeting or conference.
- 22 (59.46%) read about the Guidelines in one or more issues of *C&RL News*.
- 7 (18.92%) indicated something other than the options presented including "involved in the development of the Guidelines," "the Off-Camp listserv," and "member of the Distance Learning Section."
- 6 (16.22%) recalled learning about the Guidelines as a result of one of the association's opening hearings on this statement.

Thirty-eight (38) respondents indicated that they had (22, 57.89%) or had not (16, 42.11%) used the Guidelines in the course of their work in support of distance education services for business students. Those responding positively to this question were provided with four options.

- 17 (77.27% of those responding to this question) used the Guidelines to guide the development new or enhanced distance library services for business students.
- 12 (54.55%) indicated that the Guidelines were used to compare a library services program with a national standard.
- 12 (54.55%) used the Guidelines to solicit funding support for the distance library services at their institution.
- 9 (40.91%) indicated that the Guidelines were employed to demonstrate compliance with a national standard.
- 4 (18.18%) indicated other responses including: "to develop job descriptions for distance librarian positions and . . . mission/goals for distance library services," "for an accreditation visit," "have shared the guidelines with administrators (. . .) and indicated that this library supports and follows them," and "referred to Guidelines as guiding principles for our services in narrative for self-study for regional accreditation."

Finally, those indicating that they had used the Guidelines were asked if they found them helpful. Of the twenty-two responses in this category, twenty-one (21, 95.45%) responded in the affirmative and one (1, 4.55%) in the negative. These individuals were further asked to comment on the reasons that they found the Guidelines useful.

- 19 (90.48% of respondents to this question) indicated that the Guidelines provided help for thinking inclusively about distance services.
- 14 (66.67%) said that the Guidelines were useful as a clearly articulated statement about distance services.
- 13 (61.90%) suggested that the Guidelines pointed them to obvious weaknesses in an existing support program.
- 5 (23.81%) said that they used the Guidelines as a reflection of the status of the Association of College and Research Libraries.

It seems reasonable to assume if the results of this survey are indicative of the larger population of business librarians that many librarians who support business students at a distance know about the ACRL

"Guidelines for Distance Library Services." Many of these librarians have used this statement in the work of supporting these students and academic business curricula and find it a useful statement for these endeavors.

INFORMATION LITERACY COMPETENCY STANDARDS FOR HIGHER EDUCATION

There is one additional standard that is appropriate to any discussion involving academic libraries and the provision of support services to business students at a distance. (See Appendix C.) A task force of academics representing higher education associations created the "Information Literacy Competency Standards for Higher Education."[17] The Association of College and Research Libraries, the American Association for Higher Education (AAHE), Association of Library and Information Science Educators (ALISE), and the Middle States Commission on Higher Education were represented. This task force worked quickly, relying heavily on conference telephone calls to complete its charge to write the Standards in about one year's time. Great care was used to solicit comment on the draft of these Standards during an open meeting at the annual American Library Association (ALA) meeting in 1999 and during a presentation at the spring 1999 AHEE Assessment Forum. Feedback from these two sessions, in addition to that captured from the posting of the draft on the ACRL Web site, helped to form and amend the draft. Nana Lowell, from the University of California-Berkeley, served the task force as its assessment consultant and further evaluated the draft. The formal presentation of the Standards occurred during the ALA Midwinter meeting in January 2000; the ACRL Board approved the Standards as prepared at that time. Subsequently, this important document has been endorsed by the AAHE, and the ACRL continued the work of the originating task force with the intent of creating an action plan for the further endorsement of the Standards by other higher education associations. The Information Literacy Competency Standards for Higher Education are in no small part the result of leadership taken by Maureen Sullivan, then ACRL President, to create the authoring task force and Patti Iannuzzi, Associate University Librarian and Director of the Doe-Moffitt Libraries at the University of California-Berkeley, to ably lead the task force to its stated goal.

There are five standards, each of which is accompanied by specific performance indicators and outcomes. The Standards provide benchmarks that allow learners to integrate a set of information skills valuable for the college/university experience as well as the real-world environment. The goal of information literacy is to help individuals become competent in the use and management of information for their entire lives, not just their time within higher education. An individual is defined as information literate when she has achieved a level of mastery in each of the areas represented by the five standards. The Standards state that an information literate individual is able to understand the nature and extent of an information need (Standard 1), access needed information effectively and efficiently (Standard 2), evaluate information and incorporate the new information into her knowledge base or value system (Standard 3), use information effectively to accomplish a purpose (Standard 4), and understand many of the economic, legal, and social issues about the use of information and to use information ethically and legally (Standard 5). The performance indicators and outcomes are provided in an effort to facilitate assessment. The language chosen for the Standards, indicators, and outcomes is generic and the Standards were crafted to avoid any preference for one discipline or set of disciplines rather than others. A recent faculty meeting at Marygrove College in Michigan on the subject of information literacy reinforced the success of the Standards in this particular arena.[18] When asked if changes were needed in the language to reflect the needs of specific disciplines, no member of the faculty, including those from the business program, offered any change to the existing language or suggested language problems that minimized the value of these Standards for the discipline that he or she represented. This took place after the standards had been seen and discussed well in advance of the meeting.

The Association of College and Research Libraries has taken a leadership role in the distribution of the Standards. It has also used its influence to encourage other higher education associations to endorse the Standards and to integrate them with their work. Thus far, the Association of College and Research Libraries has approached some eleven other associations and each of the six regional accrediting associations about the Standards. The Association of College and Research Libraries has also provided on-going Web access to the Standards. Members of the authoring task force as well as other members of the association have given conference presentations across the globe in order to have others become more familiar with the Standards and how they can be used. The Standards have been translated in Japanese and Spanish and Chinese, Korean, and Finnish translations are pending. They are being used in universities and colleges in Spain, Japan, and Mexico with a local variant of the Standards in use in Australia. All this points to a global initiative that will benefit students and individuals worldwide.

The survey referred to earlier in this article was also employed to collect data concerning the possible use of the Information Literacy Competency Standards for Higher Education. The findings differed somewhat from those for the Guidelines for Distance Library Services.

There were forty-six (46) total responses to the question that asked whether or not the individual responding was familiar with the Information Literacy Competency Standards for Higher Education. Of the total, 29 (63.04%) responses indicated that the librarians answering the survey were familiar with these Standards while 17 (36.94%) were not. One negative response included a demonstrative note that reads "No, but I will certainly intend to head for the ACRL (Web) site as soon as I finish filling out this form!" About 25% fewer librarians serving business students were familiar with the Standards than with the "Guidelines for Distance Library Services."

Those responding that they were familiar with these Standards were asked where they recall learning about them. The greatest number of those answering indicated that they found the Standards in *C&RL News* (16, 55.17% of those responding). The other choices were:

- The ACRL Web site (15, 51.72% of respondents)
- Other librarians (13, 44.83%)
- Direct correspondence from ACRL President Larry Hardesty (11, 37.93%)
- Presentation or poster session at a conference (6, 20.69%)
- ACRL open hearing on the Standards (0, 0%)
- Under the "Other" category, one individual indicated that the Standards were located on the Bi-L listserv.

These numbers differ significantly from the responses to the equivalent question about the "Guidelines for Distance Library Services." In each of the comparable categories, the responses were higher for the Guidelines than the Standards. Twelve percent fewer respondents recalled reading the Standards on the Web vs. reading the Guidelines on the Web. About 14% fewer recalled hearing about the Standards from a colleague than the percentage reporting about the Guidelines. Almost 36% fewer indicated that they had heard about the Standards as a part of a meeting or conference presentation than the same introduction for the Guidelines. Much of this can be explained by the relative newness of the Standards. The Guidelines are only a little older than the Standards;

however, familiarity with the former among librarians who serve business students at a distance is perhaps greater owing to earlier versions as well as the current one. It is likely that the percentage of those familiar with each of these statements will grow less disparate as more and more librarians know the Standards better and appreciate their value to the education of business students learning at a distance.

Responding to a question meant to determine the use of the Standards, twenty (20, 71.43% of those responding to this question) indicated that they had or planned to use the Standards, while eight (8, 28.57%) said that they had not and did not plan to do so. This positive response compares very favorably to the same question relating to the Guidelines with a larger percentage (71.43% vs. 57.89%) indicating that they planned to use the Standards rather than the Guidelines in support of business students at a distance. One might hypothesize that this is again a reflection of the relative newness of the Standards. In this case, information literacy may represent an area where a lack of familiarity exists and where librarians are looking for guidance in bringing this skills set to students. The Standards are a valuable tool to aid librarian and faculty member alike, and therefore a higher percentage of respondents may have indicated their willingness to apply the Standards in their work with distance students.

The twenty librarians who responded positively to this question were further asked to indicate the one or several reasons that they planned to use the Standards.

- All 20 (100%) planned to use the Standards to guide the development of new or enhanced services.
- 13 (65%) will use the Standards to compare services with a national benchmark.
- 8 (40%) suggested that they would use the Standards to demonstrate compliance with the national standard.
- 5 (25%) completed the survey indicating that they planned to use the Standards to solicit funding in support of distance students.
- One respondent added that she planned "to make students aware that finding information is only one step in the research process." Sixteen of the twenty positive responses (80%) indicated that they viewed the Standards as helpful.

The number of responses concerning information literacy was limited. Nonetheless, these responses provide useful insight as to how some librarians view the new Standards. It is encouraging that a reasonably high percentage of respondents know about the Standards and plan to use them in their work.

It is important to ask if there are any indications that information literacy is needed for business students. On what basis should the new Standards be included among those considered here as appropriate for the business and distance education environments? First and foremost it is crucial that the goal of information literacy be emphasized. It is to create information literate individuals who can be more successful in the understanding and use of information while attending school and college or university as they gain the skills that will assure their ability to effectively use information throughout their careers and lifetimes. This in mind, it seems only reasonable that this set of skills would be fully appropriate to the business student while engaged in an academic program as well as on the job.

A short story may help to more clearly illustrate the importance of information literacy to the student of business. Ray Benton, Jr. (Loyola University Chicago) included a research component in several of his marketing courses. During those classes, he invited a librarian to teach the information competency segment. Some time ago Dr. Benton heard from one of his students who had graduated and begun work in the marketing industry. She told him that she had observed her employers paying large amounts of money to consultants to do research. The student went to her employer and explained that she had learned these skills at Loyola and that she could do the work herself thus saving company resources. She was given the opportunity to apply the skills that she had earlier learned in the marketing class, did well, and received a large bonus while saving the company thousands of dollars in consulting fees.[19] Not only was the individual made more knowledgeable through the acquisition of information literacy skills, her employer benefited from that skills set as well.

Beyond this anecdote, it is perhaps best to look toward the work of the National Forum on Information Literacy (NFIL), "a coalition of over 75 education, business, and governmental organizations working to promote awareness of the need for information literacy and encouraging activities leading to its acquisition."[20] The NFIL Web site offers a number of useful reports that bear on the focus of this article. Diane Frankel's testimony to NFIL is a good example. Frankel stated that "what individuals, businesses, and families need is the skill to put this information to work to help make good decisions."[21] She also refers to a document "A Progress Report on Information Literacy: An Update on the American Library Association Presidential Committee on Information Literacy: Final Report, March 1998." She states "The report notes that information-literate citizens know how to use information to their best advantage at work and in everyday life."[22] Then she lists examples such as the head of a non-profit organization using the local library to find information on potential fundraising sources and a patron who wants to set up a business and get information on applying for a small business loan.

Ronald Hall, from the Michigan Small Business Development Center, led a discussion during the May 12, 2000 NFIL meeting on the relationship between information literacy and economic development focusing on small business.[23] Among the information needs of business that he cited are:

- Information on medical insurance for employees
- Technology
- Changes in global marketplace
- E-commerce models and transactions
- Management and operations (e.g., strategic planning)
- Information about employees.

He also mentioned that most small business have no librarians/information specialists or "networks" of expertise and that they lack knowledge of potential customers and workforce needs of potential employees.

Patricia Katopol of the Aspen Institute addressed the NFIL meeting May 21, 1999 and reported on an earlier (April 1999) discussion within FOCAS (Forum on Communications and Society).[24] FOCAS is a CEO level body that is convened annually to address subjects relating to the societal impact of the communications and information sectors. The initiatives generated at the FOCAS conference were:

- Promote greater awareness of IL
- Assess and hold educators and political leaders at all levels accountable for students' IL proficiency
- Give teachers the preparation and support they need
- Involve parents
- Develop a technology-based educational alternative
- Increase funding for information literacy.

With often overwhelming amounts of information to consider, opportunities for enhanced teaching and learning, and global implications for success in information knowledge and use, it seems that information literacy has a place in the consideration of service to distance education business students. It is likely to have an ever-growing impact as we continue through the current decade and beyond.

It would be misleading to suggest that all one needed to do is somehow magically integrate information literacy into the teaching/learning environment to have students benefit from this set of skills. There are certainly some challenges to achieving this kind of integration. Four issues are of particular importance in this context. One of these is the relationship of information literacy to technology. With so much information available on the Web and via technological devices of various sorts, it seems reasonable to look upon technological competence as a kind of information literacy infrastructure issue. It would be difficult if not impossible for an individual to become information literate lacking technological competence at a level that would permit easy and successful access to some of the vast resources of information available in electronic format. Institutions and organizations need to take appropriate steps that will assure that each individual is technologically competent and therefore prepared for the information literacy skills set. A second issue has to do with faculty development. It seems clear that professional development can and should play an important role in helping business faculty to understand information literacy and how it can be applied to their benefit and that of their students. As most curricula are packed with concepts that must be successfully conveyed and learned during a specific quarter or semester, faculty may react to information literacy by suggesting that there simply is not the time available to include this set of skills. The goal must be integration with the curriculum in a way that enhances learning and facilitates the assessment of that learning. This can and is being accomplished through collaborative work between faculty and librarians often without reducing the time needed for other purposes. Assessment is a third challenge and one where information literacy can prove most helpful in determining the level of comprehension of teaching by individuals and groups. How to assess is a highly significant issue. Finally, there is the matter of integration with institutional goals and objectives. Information literacy works best when it is combined in a meaningful way within the goals and objectives of the institution rather than external to them much as some "deus ex machina" in an ancient play.

CONCLUSION

Librarians who serve business students and faculty at a distance have at their disposal three useful guidelines/standards for planning, implementing and enhancing the services that they proffer. Not only are these statements comprehensive in their treatment of distance library support services, but they are each recently revised with the oldest, dating to less than three years ago. This timeliness is exceedingly significant given the changes in technology that are impacting all areas of the academic process.

The AACSB "Quality Issues In Distance Learning" represents a significant departure from the AACSB Standards "Achieving Quality and Continuous Improvement Through Self-Evaluation and Peer Review," in that the former speaks specifically and frequently about libraries, library services, and information resources. This document is a particularly significant tool for librarians and it can be used effectively for substantive discussions with academic administrators responsible for distance education programs. The recommendations as well as other parts of this document are clearly supportive of library services and view them as integral to the overall distance academic program for business students. These guidelines were not prepared with prescriptive language. This allows a librarian to interpret the guidelines in a manner consistent with the mission, goals, and objectives of her institution. As the AACSB accredits an overwhelming majority of the business degree programs in the United States, these guidelines must be seen as a key measure of the suitability of business programs generally as well as the libraries that support them. It should not go unnoticed that this set of guidelines differs somewhat from the "Guidelines for Distance Library Services" and the "Information Literacy Competency Standards for Higher Education" in focus and intent. This is understandable since the AACSB "Issues" covers the entire business academic program and has not been limited to either the library or information literacy concerns.

The Association of College and Research Libraries "Guidelines for Distance Library Services" is an excellent statement that continues to be refined and improved. It is perhaps the best known and most widely used set of guidelines for distance library services regardless of discipline. The survey undertaken for this article suggests that a preponderance of librarians who serve business students at a distance are familiar with these guidelines. Equally important, a majority of those responding indicated that they have or intend to use these Guidelines in support of the library services program of which they are a part. If the percentages indicated by the survey are a reasonable reflection of the greater population of academic business librarians, this set of Guidelines is viewed as an important and well-known tool in support of distance business students. That this is a generic rather than discipline-specific set of guidelines does not seem to interfere with the level of interest in this document or its perception as a useful instrument for librarians supporting academic business at a distance.

The "Information Literacy Competency Standards for Higher Education" are somewhat less well known among librarians who support academic business programs at a distance than the other statements mentioned in this article. This is likely a reflection of the relatively recent publication of this document. Of those responding to the survey, a high percentage indicated that they have used or plan to use these Standards in supporting business students at a distance. Fully 100% of those responding and planning to use these Standards in their work anticipated that the Standards would help to guide the development of their institution's distance library services for business students. One of the most important potential uses of the Information Literacy Standards is that of collaboration between librarians and teaching faculty who convey the distance business curriculum. These standards represent an on-going national and international effort to integrate information literacy into academic curricula with the expected outcome of helping students to be successful life-long learners and information literate members of society. The "Information Literacy Competency Standards for Higher Education" is a blueprint for enhanced student learning. These Standards can facilitate librarian/faculty discourse and collaboration that can result in better prepared students, enhanced academic outcomes, and students who are ready to deal with the challenges of information in their work and personal lives.

The fourth statement discussed in this article, albeit brief, the AACSB "Achieving Quality and Continuous Improvement Through Self-Evaluation and Peer Review," is less valuable for librarians as a standard given its broad brush approach to the issue of instructional resources. This is in no way to minimize the importance of this latter document to the overall accreditation process.

The combination of these four guidelines/standards provides interested librarians with a strong portfolio of tools that can be used in support of accreditation self-study for business education at a distance. These statements can also be used independent of accreditation studies to open dialogues with academic administrators as to the kind and level of library support appropriate to distance business. Each of the statements discussed in this article can be employed to encourage innovative responses to the challenges of access arising from the inherent difficulties with geographic separation of the business program's participants from the institution's main campus and its library.

ACKNOWLEDGEMENTS

The authors wish to extend their thanks to the following people for their assistance in the preparation of this article: Karen Martinez, AACSB; Milton R. Blood, AACSB; Colleen Vanderlinden, Wayne State University Science and Engineering Library; Barbara Price, Wayne State University School of Business Administration; Hugh Thompson, Association of College and Research Libraries; Margot Sutton, Association of College and Research Libraries; Craig Gibson, George Mason University; Linnea Dudley, Marygrove College; Lenora Berendt, Loyola University; and Lori Goetsch, University of Maryland.

NOTES

1. *Encyclopedia of Education*, 1971, v.1, p. 50, s.v. "Accreditation."

2. *The American Heritage Dictionary of the English Language*, 1980, p. 1256, s.v. "standard."

3. American Library Association President's Committee Report on Information Literacy. Available: <http://www.ala.org/acrl/nili/ilit1st.html>.

4. AACSB the International Association of Management Education. "AACSB–About Us." Available: <http://www.aacsb.edu/aboutus.html>.

5. AACSB–the International Association of Management Education. "Achieving Quality and Continuous Improvement Through Self-Evaluation and Peer Review." Available: <http://www.acsb.edu/baccrd1.html>.

6. AACSB–the International Association of Management Education. "Instructional Resources and Responsibilities." Available: <http://www.aacsb.edu/stand6.html>.

7. AACSB–the International Association of Management Education. *Quality Issues in Distance Education*. (St. Louis, Mo.: AACSB–the International Association of Management Education, 1999).

8. *Ibid*, p. 2 and Blood, Milton R. Telephone conversation with author, August 15, 2000.

9. Association for College and Research Libraries. "Guidelines for Extended Campus Library Services." *College & Research Libraries News* 43, no. 3 (March 1982): 86-88.

10. Association for College and Research Libraries. "ACRL Guidelines for Extended Campus Library Services." *College & Research Libraries News* 51, no. 4 (April 1990): 353-55.

11. Association for College and Research Libraries. "Guidelines for Distance Learning Library Services: the Final Version, Approved July 1998." *College & Research Libraries News* 59, no. 9 (October 1998): 689-94. Also Available: <http://www.ala.org/acrl/guides/distlrng.html>.

12. The 2000 version of the Association of College and Research Libraries Guidelines for Distance Library Services was reviewed by the Standards and Accreditation Committee and sent forward to the Association of College and Research Libraries Board with a recommendation for approval and distribution to the membership on July 8, 2000.

13. The Philosophy section of the 1989 Guidelines states clearly that the parent institution offering off-campus courses or programs "should provide library service to the extended campus community equitable with that provided to the on-campus community. " This section also states that "effective and appropriate services for extended campus communities may differ from those services offered on campus." (Association for College and Research Libraries. "Guidelines for Extended Campus Library Services." *College & Research Libraries News* 51, no. 4 (April 1990): 354).

14. Dugan, Robert E. (1997) "Distance Education: Provider and Victim Libraries." *Journal of Academic Librarianship* 23 (4), 315-318.

15. Kirk, Elizabeth E. and Andrea M. Bartelstein. (1999) "Libraries Close in on Distance Education." *Library Journal*, 124 (6), 40-42.

16. Association of College and Research Libraries. Standards and Accreditation Committee. (2000) *Policies and Procedures Manual*, Section 8.2.

17. Association for College and Research Libraries. "Information Literacy Competency Standards for Higher Education: the Final Version, Approved January 2000." *College & Research Libraries News* 61, no. 3 (March 2000): 207-15. Also Available: <http://www.ala.org/acrl/ilcomstan.html>.

18. Faculty meeting, Marygrove College, Detroit, Michigan on August 23, 2000.

19. Berendt, Lenora and Raymond Benton, Jr. (1999) "Taking Care of Business: Collaborating with Faculty to Create an Information Literacy Course." An unpublished discussion presented at the Association of College and Research Libraries National Conference in Detroit, MI, April 9.

20. National Forum on Information Literacy. "National Forum on Information Literacy [Homepage]." Available: <http://www.iinfolit.org>.

21. Diane Frankel speaking on the Institute of Museum and Library Services' Office of Library Services FY 2000 Budget Request to the House Appropriations Subcommittee on Labor, Health and Human Services, Education, and Related Agencies. 18 March 1999. Available: <http://www.imls.gov/whatsnew/leg/archive/031899.htm>.

22. American Library Association Presidential Committee on Information Literacy. "A Progress Report on Information Literacy: An Update on the American Library Association Presidential Committee on Information Literacy: Final Report, March 1998" quoted in Diane Frankel speaking on the Institute of Museum and Library Services' Office of Library Services FY 2000 Budget Request to the House Appropriations Subcommittee on Labor, Health and Human Services, Education, and Related Agencies. 18 March 1999. Available: <http://www.ala.org/acrl/nili/nili.html>.

23. Ronald Hall. "Information Literacy and Economic Development" (presented at a meeting of the National Forum on Information Literacy, Washington, DC, 12 May 2000). Available: <http://www.infolit.org/meetings/nfil_summary_May2000.html>.

24. Patricia Katopol. "Information Policies Discussion: Update on Forum on Communications and Society, Aspen Institute" (presented at a meeting of the National Forum on Information Literacy, Washington, DC, 21 May 1999). Available: <http://www.infolit.org/meetings/052199a.htm>.

APPENDIX A

Association of College and Research Libraries
Guidelines for Distance Learning Library Services*

These Guidelines were approved by the ACRL Board of Directors at the 1998 Midwinter Meeting and by the ALA Standards Committee at the 1998 Annual Conference.

Library resources and services in institutions of higher education must meet the needs of all their faculty, students, and academic support staff, wherever these individuals are located, whether on a main campus, off campus, in distance education or extended campus programs, or in the absence of a campus at all; in courses taken for credit or non-credit; in continuing education programs; in courses attended in person or by means of electronic transmission; or any other means of distance education. The "Guidelines" delineate the elements necessary to achieving these ends. The "Guidelines" are intended to serve as a gateway to adherence to the ACRL Standards in the appropriate areas.

The audience for the "Guidelines" includes administrators at all levels of post-secondary education, librarians planning for and managing distance learning library services, other librarians and staff working with distance learning program staff, faculty, and sponsors of academic programs, as well as accrediting and licensure agencies.

The decision to revise the 1990 "Guidelines" was made initially by the DLS Guidelines Committee, then the official mandate came from the DLS Executive Board at its final 1996 Midwinter meeting. The 1990 "Guidelines" resulted from the first revision of the original 1981 "Guidelines." As in that initial revision, the current decision to revise was based on the following identical, though increasingly critical, factors: non-traditional study becoming a more commonplace element in higher education; an increase in diversity of educational opportunities; an increase in the number of unique environments where educational opportunities are offered; an increased recognition of the

---

*Available: http://www.ala.org/acrl/guides/distlrng.html>.

need for library resources and services at locations other than main campuses; an increased concern and demand for equitable services for all students in higher education, no matter where the "classroom" may be; a greater demand for library resources and services by faculty and staff at distance learning sites; and an increase in technological innovations in the transmittal of information and the delivery of courses. To these may be added the decrease in central campus enrollments, the search for more cost-effective sources for post-secondary education, and the appearance and rapid development of the virtual or all-electronic university, having no physical campus of its own.

Definitions

Distance learning library services refers to those library services in support of college, university, or other post-secondary courses and programs offered away from a main campus, or in the absence of a traditional campus, and regardless of where credit is given. These courses may be taught in traditional or non-traditional formats or media, may or may not require physical facilities, and may or may not involve live interaction of teachers and students. The phrase is inclusive of courses in all post-secondary programs designated as: extension, extended, off-campus, extended campus, distance, distributed, open, flexible, franchising, virtual, synchronous, or asynchronous.

Distance learning community covers all those individuals and agencies, or institutions, directly involved with academic programs or extension services offered away from a traditional academic campus, or in the absence of a traditional academic campus, including students, faculty, researchers, administrators, sponsors, and staff, or any of these whose academic work otherwise takes them away from on-campus library services.

Originating institution refers to the entity, singular or collective, its/their chief administrative officers and governance organizations responsible for the offering or marketing and supporting of distance learning courses and programs: the credit-granting body. Each institution in a multi-institutional cluster is responsible for meeting the library needs of its own students, faculty, and staff at the collective site.

Library denotes the library operation directly associated with the originating institution.

Librarian-administrator designates a librarian, holding a master's degree from an ALA-accredited library school, who specializes in distance learning library services, and who is directly responsible for the administration and supervision of those services.

Philosophy
The "Guidelines" assume the following precepts:

- Access to adequate library services and resources is essential for the attainment of superior academic skills in post-secondary education, regardless of where students, faculty, and programs are located. Members of the distance learning community are entitled to library services and resources equivalent to those provided for students and faculty in traditional campus settings.
- The instilling of lifelong learning skills through information literacy instruction in academic libraries is a primary outcome of higher education. Such preparation is of equal necessity for the distance learning community as it is for those on the traditional campus.
- Traditional on-campus library services themselves cannot be stretched to meet the library needs of distance learning students and faculty who face distinct and different challenges involving library access and information delivery. Special funding arrangements, proactive planning, and promotion are necessary to deliver equivalent library services and to maintain quality in distance learning programs. Because students and faculty in distance learning programs frequently do not have direct access to a full range of library services and materials, equitable distance learning library services are more personalized than might be expected on campus.
- The originating institution is responsible, through its chief administrative officers and governance organizations, for funding and appropriately meeting the information needs of its distance learning programs in support of their teaching, learning, and research. This support should provide ready and equivalent library service and learning resources to all its students, regardless of location. This support should be funded separately rather than drawn from the regular funding of the library. In growing and developing institutions, funding should expand as programs and enrollments grow.
- The originating institution recognizes the need for service, management, and technical linkages between the library and other complementary resource bases such as computing facilities, instructional media, and telecommunication centers. The originating institution is responsible for

assuring that its distance learning library programs meet or exceed national and regional accreditation standards and professional association standards and guidelines.

- The originating institution is responsible for involving the library administration and other personnel in the detailed analysis of planning, developing, and adding or changing of the distance learning program from the earliest stages onward.
- The library has primary responsibility for identifying, developing, coordinating, and providing resources and services, which meet both the standard and the unique information needs of the distance learning community. The librarian-administrator, either centrally located or at an appropriate site, should be responsible for ensuring that all requirements are met.
- Effective and appropriate services for distance learning communities may differ from, but must be equivalent to, those services offered on a traditional campus. The requirements of academic programs should guide the library's responses to defined needs. Innovative approaches to the design of special procedures or systems to meet these needs is encouraged.
- When resources and services of unaffiliated local libraries are to be used to support information needs of the distance learning community, the originating institution is responsible, through the library, for the development and periodic review of formal, documented, written agreements with those local libraries. Such resources and services are not to be used simply as substitutes for supplying adequate materials and services by the originating institution.
- The distance learning library program shall have goals and objectives that support the provision of resources and services consistent with the broader institutional mission.

Management

The chief administrative officers and governance organizations of the originating institution bear the fiscal and administrative responsibilities, through the active leadership of the library administration, to fund, staff, and supervise library services and resources in support of distance learning programs. As the principal and direct agent of implementation, the librarian-administrator should, minimally:

1. assess and articulate, on an ongoing basis, both the electronic and traditional library resource needs of the distance learning community, the services provided them, including instruction, and the facilities utilized;
2. prepare a written profile of the distance learning community's information needs;
3. develop a written statement of immediate and long-range goals and objectives for distance learning, which addresses the needs and outlines the methods by which progress can be measured;
4. promote the incorporation of the distance learning goals and objectives into those of the library and of the originating institution as a whole;
5. involve distance learning community representatives, including administrators, faculty, and students, in the formation of the objectives and the regular evaluation of their achievement;
6. assess, using the written profile of needs, the existing library support for distance learning, its availability, and appropriateness;
7. prepare and/or revise collection development and acquisitions policies to reflect the profile of needs;
8. participate with administrators, library subject specialists, and teaching faculty in the curriculum development process and in course planning for distance learning to ensure that appropriate library resources and services are available;
9. promote library support services to the distance learning community;
10. survey regularly distance learning library users to monitor and assess both the appropriateness of their use of services and resources and the degree to which needs are being met;
11. initiate dialog leading to cooperative agreements and possible resource sharing and/or compensation for unaffiliated libraries;
12. develop methodologies for the provision of library materials and services from the library and/or from branch campus libraries or learning centers to the distance learning community;
13. develop partnerships with computing services departments to provide the necessary automation support for the distance learning community; and
14. pursue, implement, and maintain all the preceding in the provision of a facilitating environment in support of teaching and learning.

Additional areas of management responsibility are covered in sections on finances, personnel, facilities, resources, and services.

Finances

The originating institution should provide continuing, optimum financial support for addressing the library needs of the distance learning community sufficient to meet the specifications given in other sections of these "Guidelines," and in accordance with the appropriate ACRL Standards and with available professional, state, or regional accrediting agency specifications. This financing should be:

1. related to the formally defined needs and demands of the distance learning program;
2. allocated on a schedule matching the originating institution's budgeting cycle;
3. designated and specifically identified within the originating institution's budget and expenditure reporting statements;
4. accommodated to arrangements involving external agencies, including both unaffiliated and affiliated, but independently supported, libraries;
5. sufficient to cover the type and number of services provided the distance learning community; and
6. sufficient to support innovative approaches to meeting needs.

Personnel

Personnel involved in the management and coordination of distance learning library services include the chief administrators and governance organizations of the originating institution and the library administration and other personnel as appropriate, the librarian-coordinator managing the services, the library subject specialists, additional professional staff in the institution, support staff from a variety of departments, and the administrator(s), librarian(s), and staff from the distance learning site(s).

The originating institution should provide, either through the library or directly to separately administered units, professional and support personnel with clearly defined responsibilities at the appropriate location(s) and in the number and quality necessary to attain the goals and objectives for library services to the distance learning program including:

1. a librarian-administrator to plan, implement, coordinate, and evaluate library resources and services addressing the information needs of the distance learning community;

2. additional professional and/or support personnel on site with the capacity and skills to identify informational needs of distance learning library users and respond to them directly;
3. classification, status, and salary scales for distance learning library personnel that are equivalent to those provided for other comparable library employees while reflecting the compensation levels and cost of living for those residing at distance learning sites; and
4. opportunities for continuing growth and development for distance learning library personnel, including continuing education, professional education, and participation in professional and staff organizations.

Facilities

The originating institution should provide facilities, equipment, and communication links sufficient in size, number, scope, accessibility, and timeliness to reach all students and to attain the objectives of the distance learning programs. Arrangements may vary and should be appropriate to programs offered. Examples of suitable arrangements include but are not limited to:

1. access to facilities through agreements with a non-affiliated library;
2. designated space for consultations, ready reference collections, reserve collections, electronic transmission of information, computerized data base searching and interlibrary loan services, and offices for the library distance learning personnel;
3. a branch or satellite library; and
4. virtual services, such as Web pages, Internet searching, using technology for electronic connectivity.

Resources

The originating institution is responsible for providing or securing convenient, direct physical and electronic access to library materials for distance learning programs equivalent to those provided in traditional settings and in sufficient quality, depth, number, scope, currentness, and formats to:

1. meet the students' needs in fulfilling course assignments (e.g., required and supplemental readings and research papers) and enrich the academic programs;
2. meet teaching and research needs; and

3. accommodate other informational needs of the distance learning community as appropriate.

When more than one institution is involved in the provision of a distance learning program, each is responsible for the provision of library materials to students in its own courses, unless an equitable agreement for otherwise providing these materials has been made. Costs, services, and methods for the provision of materials for all courses in the program should be uniform.

Programs granting associate degrees should provide access to collections which meet the "Association of College and Research Libraries (ACRL) Guidelines for Two-Year College Learning Resources Programs" and the "Statement on Quantitative Standards." Programs granting baccalaureate or master's degrees should provide access to collections that meet the standards defined by the "ACRL Standards for College Libraries." Programs offering doctorate degrees should provide access to collections that meet the standards defined by the "ACRL Standards for University Libraries."

Services

The library services offered to the distance learning community should be designed to meet effectively a wide range of informational, bibliographic, and user needs. The exact combination of central and site staffing for distance learning library services will differ from institution to institution. The following, though not necessarily exhaustive, are essential:

1. reference assistance;
2. computer-based bibliographic and informational services;
3. reliable, rapid, secure access to institutional and other networks including the Internet;
4. consultation services;
5. a program of library user instruction designed to instill independent and effective information literacy skills while specifically meeting the learner-support needs of the distance learning community;
6. assistance with nonprint media and equipment;
7. reciprocal or contractual borrowing, or interlibrary loan services using broadest application of fair use of copyrighted materials;
8. prompt document delivery such as a courier system and/or electronic transmission;
9. access to reserve materials in accordance with copyright fair use policies;

10. adequate service hours for optimum access by users; and
11. promotion of library services to the distance learning community, including documented and updated policies, regulations and procedures for systematic development, and management of information resources.

Documentation

To provide records indicating the degree to which the originating institution is meeting these "Guidelines" in providing library services to its distance learning programs, the library, and when appropriate, the distance learning library units, should have available current copies of at least the following:

1. printed user guides;
2. statements of mission and purpose, policies, regulations, and procedures;
3. statistics on library use;
4. statistics on collections;
5. facilities assessment measures;
6. collections assessment measures;
7. data on staff and work assignments;
8. institutional and internal organization charts;
9. comprehensive budget(s);
10. professional personnel vitae;
11. position descriptions for all personnel;
12. formal, written agreements;
13. automation statistics;
14. guides to computing services;
15. library evaluation studies or documents;
16. library and other instructional materials and schedules; and
17. evidence of involvement in curriculum development and planning.

Library Education

To enable the initiation of an academic professional specialization in distance learning library services, schools of library and information science should include in their curriculum courses and course units this growing area of specialization within librarianship.

Revising the "Guidelines"

This revision of the 1990 ACRL "Guidelines" for Extended Campus Library Services was prepared by Harvey Gover, chair of the Guidelines Committee of the ACRL Distance Learning Section (DLS), formerly the Extended Campus Library Services Section. The revision is based upon input from members of the Guidelines Committee, members of the DLS Executive Board, the general membership of DLS, and other librarians and administrators involved in post-secondary distance learning programs from across the nation and around the world.

Major portions of the input for revision came from two open hearings: the first held on February 17, 1997, at the Midwinter Conference of the ALA in Washington, D.C. and the second on June 28, 1997, at the ALA Annual Conference in San Francisco, California.

In response to requests for revision suggestions–which appeared in widely read national academic and library publications, distance education listservs, through the DLS Web site, and print publications–numerous other individuals, consortia, and representatives of professional and accrediting associations provided information on their own efforts to ensure excellence of library services for post-secondary distance learning programs.

Among the groups responding were: the Canadian Association of College and University Libraries of the Canadian Library Association; College Librarians and Media Specialists (CLAMS); the Commission on Colleges of the Northwest Association of Schools and Colleges (NASC); The Consortium for Educational Technology for University Systems (CETUS); the Interinstitutional Library Council (ILC) of the Oregon State System of Higher Education (OSSHE); Libraries and the Western Governors University Conference; the Southern Association of Colleges and Schools (SACS); and the Western Cooperative for Educational Telecommunications of the Western Interstate Commission for Higher Education (WICHE).

Guidelines Committee Members

Members of the Guidelines Committee who initiated or contributed to the revision process include: Stella Bentley, University of California at Santa Barbara; Jean Caspers, Oregon State University; Jacqueline A. Henning, Embry-Riddle Aeronautical University; Sharon Hybki-Kerr, University of Arkansas, Little Rock; Gordon Lynn Hufford, Indiana University East; Ruth M. Jackson, West Virginia University; Chui-Chun Lee, SUNY-New Paltz; G. Tom Mendina, University of Memphis; Virginia S. O'Herron, Old Dominion University; Mae

O'Neal, Western Michigan University; Bill Parton, Arkansas Tech University; Mercedes L. Rowe, Mercy College; Dorothy Tolliver, Maui Community College Library; and Steven D. Zink, University of Nevada, Reno.

Others outside the Committee who contributed significantly to the cycle of revision include: Thomas Abbott, University of Maine at Augusta; Janice Bain-Kerr, Troy State University; Nancy Burich, University of Kansas, Regents Center Library; Anne Marie Casey, Central Michigan University; Tony Cavanaugh, Deakin University, Victoria, Australia; Monica Hines Craig, Central Michigan University; Mary Ellen Davis, ACRL; Tom DeLoughry, Chronicle of Higher Education; Jill Fatzer, University of New Orleans, ACRL Board, Task Force on Outcomes; Jack Fritts, Southeastern Wisconsin Information Technology Exchange Consortium (SWITCH); Barbara Gelman-Danley of SUNY Monroe Community College, Educational Technology, and the Consortium for Educational Technology for University Systems; Kay Harvey, Penn State, McKeesport; Maryhelen Jones, Central Michigan University; Marie Kascus, Central Connecticut State University; Barbara Krauth, Student Services Project Coordinator for the Western Cooperative for Educational Telecommunication of the Western Interstate Commission for Higher Education (WICHE); Eleanor Kulleseid, Mercy College; Rob Morrison, Utah State University; Kathleen O'Connor, Gonzaga University; Alexander (Sandy) Slade, University of Victoria, British Columbia, Canada; Mem Catania Stahley, University of Central Florida, Brevard Campus; Peg Walther, City University, Renton, Washington; Virginia Witucke, Central Michigan University; Jennifer Wu, North Seattle Community College and College Librarians and Media Specialists (CLAMS).

Special recognition is due Virginia S. (Ginny) O'Herron who served throughout this cycle of revision as both a member of the Guidelines Committee and as Chair of the ACRL Standards and Accreditation Committee (SAC). In this dual role O'Herron was instrumental in securing the placement of the Guidelines draft on the agendas not only of SAC, but also of the ACRL Board and the ALA Committee on Standards. In addition to her considerable contribution to the revision process as a member of the Guidelines Committee, O'Herron was then the primary facilitator of the final approval process.

–Harvey Gover

APPENDIX B

Survey: Library Services to Distance Education Business Students

The results of this survey will be used in conjunction with an article now in preparation for The Haworth Press, Inc. on library services to distance education business students. Librarians from academic libraries that serve students engaged in distance education business classes or degree programs are encouraged to complete this survey. Time required for completion of the survey ranges from thirty seconds to ten minutes depending on the length of answers. This survey may be completed by more than one librarian at the same institution. Privacy will be protected and neither the name of individual institutions nor librarians will appear as a part of the publication.

Please return the completed survey as an e-mail attachment to aa3327@wayne. edu. Thank you in advance for your assistance.

1. Please indicate the name of the institution where you are employed:

2. Does the library where you are employed support distance (check only one):
   _____ Business or business-related classes
   _____ Business or business-related degree program

3. Are you familiar with the ACRL *Guidelines for Distance Library Services?*

   _____ Yes
   _____ No

If the answer to #3 was No, proceed to question 9.

4. Where have you read or heard about the *Guidelines for Distance Library Services?* (Check all that apply.)
   _____ ACRL hearing
   _____ Conference or seminar presentation
   _____ *C&RL* News article
   _____ ACRL Web site
   _____ Other librarians
   _____ Other. Please describe briefly.

5. Have you ever employed the ACRL *Guidelines for Distance Library Services* in support of library services to distance education business students?

_____ Yes

_____ No

If the answer to this question was No, proceed to question 9.

6. How did you use the guidelines? (Check as many as apply.)

_____ To help compare services with the national benchmark

_____ To solicit funding in support of distance students

_____ To demonstrate compliance with a national standard

_____ To guide the development of new or enhanced services

_____ Other. Please use as many lines as needed to explain.

7. Do you believe that the *Guidelines* were helpful in the use(s) indicated?

_____ Yes

_____ No

8. If the answer to #7 was Yes, please indicate the reason(s) for this. Check as many answers as apply.

_____ Clearly articulated statement

_____ Status of ACRL

_____ Pointed to obvious weaknesses in an existing support program

_____ Provided help for thinking inclusively about distance services

_____ Other. Please use as much space as needed.

9. Are you familiar with *the Information Literacy Competency Standards for Higher Education?*

_____ Yes

_____ No

If the answer to #9 was No, proceed to question 14.

10. Where have you read or heard about the *Information Literacy Competency Standards for Higher Education?* (Check all that apply.)

_____ Direct mailing from ACRL President Hardesty

_____ ACRL hearing

_____ Conference or seminar presentation

_____ *C&RL* News article

_____ ACRL Web site

_____ Other librarians

_____ Other. Please describe briefly.

11. Have you ever employed or do you have plans to employ the *Information Literacy Competency Standards for Higher Education* in support of library services to distance education business students?

    _____ Yes

    _____ No

If the answer to this question was No, proceed to question 14.

12. If the answer to #8 was Yes, how did you use these standards? (Check as many as apply.)

    _____ To help compare services with the national benchmark

    _____ To solicit funding in support of distance students

    _____ To demonstrate compliance with a national standard

    _____ To guide the development of new or enhanced services

    _____ Other. Please use as many lines as needed to explain.

13. If the answer to #8 was Yes, do you believe that the *Information Literacy Competency Standards for Higher Education* were helpful in the use(s) indicated?

    _____ Yes

    _____ No

14. Please indicate by checking below if you would like to receive a copy of the data generated by this survey.

    _____ Send a copy of the data to (your e-mail address):

APPENDIX C

Information Literacy Competency Standards for Higher Education*

Information Literacy Defined

Information literacy is a set of abilities requiring individuals to "recognize when information is needed and have the ability to locate, evaluate, and use effectively the needed information."[1] Information literacy also is increasingly important in the contemporary environment of rapid technological change and proliferating information resources. Because of the escalating complexity of this environment, individuals are faced with diverse, abundant information choices–in their academic studies, in the workplace, and in their personal lives. Information is available through libraries, community resources, special interest organizations, media, and the Internet–and increasingly, information comes to individuals in unfiltered formats, raising questions about its authenticity, validity, and reliability. In addition, information is available through multiple media, including graphical, aural, and textual, and these pose new challenges for individuals in evaluating and understanding it. The uncertain quality and expanding quantity of information pose large challenges for society. The sheer abundance of information will not in itself create a more informed citizenry without a complementary cluster of abilities necessary to use information effectively.

Information literacy forms the basis for lifelong learning. It is common to all disciplines, to all learning environments, and to all levels of education. It enables learners to master content and extend their investigations, become more self-directed, and assume greater control over their own learning. An information literate individual is able to:

- Determine the extent of information needed
- Access the needed information effectively and efficiently
- Evaluate information and its sources critically

---

*Provided courtesy of the Association of College and Research Libraries. Available: <http://www.ala.org/acrl/ilcomstan.html>.

- Incorporate selected information into one's knowledge base
- Use information effectively to accomplish a specific purpose
- Understand the economic, legal, and social issues surrounding the use of information, and access and use information ethically and legally

Information Literacy and Information Technology

Information literacy is related to information technology skills, but has broader implications for the individual, the educational system, and for society. Information technology skills enable an individual to use computers, software applications, databases, and other technologies to achieve a wide variety of academic, work-related, and personal goals. Information literate individuals necessarily develop some technology skills.

Information literacy, while showing significant overlap with information technology skills, is a distinct and broader area of competence. Increasingly, information technology skills are interwoven with, and support, information literacy. A 1999 report from the National Research Council promotes the concept of "fluency" with information technology and delineates several distinctions useful in understanding relationships among information literacy, computer literacy, and broader technological competence. The report notes that "computer literacy" is concerned with rote learning of specific hardware and software applications, while "fluency with technology" focuses on understanding the underlying concepts of technology and applying problem-solving and critical thinking to using technology. The report also discusses differences between information technology fluency and information literacy as it is understood in K-12 and higher education. Among these are information literacy's focus on content, communication, analysis, information searching, and evaluation; whereas information technology "fluency" focuses on a deep understanding of technology and graduated, increasingly skilled use of it.[2]

"Fluency" with information technology may require more intellectual abilities than the rote learning of software and hardware associated with "computer literacy," but the focus is still on the technology itself. Information literacy, on the other hand, is an intellectual framework for understanding, finding, evaluating, and using information–activities which may be accomplished in part by fluency with information technology, in part by sound investigative methods, but most important, through critical discernment and reasoning. Information literacy initiates, sustains, and extends lifelong learning through abilities which may use technologies but are ultimately independent of them.

Information Literacy and Higher Education

Developing lifelong learners is central to the mission of higher education institutions. By ensuring that individuals have the intellectual abilities of reasoning and critical thinking, and by helping them construct a framework for learning how to learn, colleges and universities provide the foundation for continued growth throughout their careers, as well as in their roles as informed citizens and members of communities. Information literacy is a key component of, and contributor to, lifelong learning. Information literacy competency extends learning beyond formal classroom settings and provides practice with self-directed investigations as individuals move into internships, first professional positions, and increasing responsibilities in all arenas of life. Because information literacy augments students' competency with evaluating, managing, and using information, it is now considered by several regional and discipline-based accreditation associations as a key outcome for college students.[3]

For students not on traditional campuses, information resources are often available through networks and other channels, and distributed learning technologies permit teaching and learning to occur when the teacher and the student are not in the same place at the same time. The challenge for those promoting information literacy in distance education courses is to develop a comparable range of experiences in learning about information resources as are offered on traditional campuses. Information literacy competencies for distance learning students should be comparable to those for "on campus" students.

Incorporating information literacy across curricula, in all programs and services, and throughout the administrative life of the university, requires the collaborative efforts of faculty, librarians, and administrators. Through lectures and by leading discussions, faculty establish the context for learning. Faculty also inspire students to explore the unknown, offer guidance on how best to fulfill information needs, and monitor students' progress. Academic librarians coordinate the evaluation and selection of intellectual resources for programs and services; organize, and maintain collections and many points of access to information; and provide instruction to students and faculty who seek information. Administrators create opportunities for collaboration and staff development among faculty, librarians, and other professionals who initiate information literacy programs, lead in planning and budgeting for those programs, and provide ongoing resources to sustain them.

Information Literacy and Pedagogy

The Boyer Commission Report, Reinventing Undergraduate Education, recommends strategies that require the student to engage actively in "framing of a significant question or set of questions, the research or creative exploration to find answers, and the communications skills to convey the results . . . "[4] Courses structured in such a way create student-centered learning environments where inquiry is the norm, problem solving becomes the focus, and thinking critically is part of the process. Such learning environments require information literacy competencies.

Gaining skills in information literacy multiplies the opportunities for students' self-directed learning, as they become engaged in using a wide variety of information sources to expand their knowledge, ask informed questions, and sharpen their critical thinking for still further self-directed learning. Achieving competency in information literacy requires an understanding that this cluster of abilities is not extraneous to the curriculum but is woven into the curriculum's content, structure, and sequence. This curricular integration also affords many possibilities for furthering the influence and impact of such student-centered teaching methods as problem-based learning, evidence-based learning, and inquiry learning. Guided by faculty and others in problem-based approaches, students reason about course content at a deeper level than is possible through the exclusive use of lectures and textbooks. To take fullest advantage of problem-based learning, students must often use thinking skills requiring them to become skilled users of information sources in many locations and formats, thereby increasing their responsibility for their own learning.

To obtain the information they seek for their investigations, individuals have many options. One is to utilize an information retrieval system, such as may be found in a library or in databases accessible by computer from any location. Another option is to select an appropriate investigative method for observing phenomena directly. For example, physicians, archaeologists, and astronomers frequently depend upon physical examination to detect the presence of particular phenomena. In addition, mathematicians, chemists, and physicists often utilize technologies such as statistical software or simulators to create artificial conditions in which to observe and analyze the interaction of phenomena. As students progress through their undergraduate years and graduate programs, they need to have repeated opportunities for seeking, evaluating, and managing information gathered from multiple sources and discipline-specific research methods.

Use of the Standards

Information Literacy Competency Standards for Higher Education provides a framework for assessing the information literate individual. It also extends the work of the American Association of School Librarians Task Force on Information Literacy Standards, thereby providing higher education an opportunity to articulate its information literacy competencies with those of K-12 so that a continuum of expectations develops for students at all levels. The competencies presented here outline the process by which faculty, librarians and others pinpoint specific indicators that identify a student as information literate.

Students also will find the competencies useful, because they provide students with a framework for gaining control over how they interact with information in their environment. It will help to sensitize them to the need to develop a metacognitive approach to learning, making them conscious of the explicit actions required for gathering, analyzing, and using information. All students are expected to demonstrate all of the competencies described in this document, but not everyone will demonstrate them to the same level of proficiency or at the same speed.

Furthermore, some disciplines may place greater emphasis on the mastery of competencies at certain points in the process, and therefore certain competencies would receive greater weight than others in any rubric for measurement. Many of the competencies are likely to be performed recursively, in that the reflective and evaluative aspects included within each standard will require the student to return to an earlier point in the process, revise the information-seeking approach, and repeat the same steps.

To implement the standards fully, an institution should first review its mission and educational goals to determine how information literacy would improve learning and enhance the institution's effectiveness. To facilitate acceptance of the concept, faculty and staff development is also crucial.

Information Literacy and Assessment

In the following competencies, there are five standards and twenty-two performance indicators. The standards focus upon the needs of students in higher education at all levels. The standards also list a range of outcomes for assessing student progress toward information literacy. These outcomes serve as guidelines for faculty, librarians, and others in developing local methods for measuring student learning in the context of an institution's unique mission. In addition to assessing all students' basic information literacy skills, faculty and librarians should also work together to develop assessment instruments and strategies in the context of particular disciplines, as information literacy manifests itself in the specific understanding of the knowledge creation, scholarly activity, and publication processes found in those disciplines.

In implementing these standards, institutions need to recognize that different levels of thinking skills are associated with various learning outcomes–and therefore different instruments or methods are essential to assess those outcomes. For example, both "higher order" and "lower order" thinking skills, based on Bloom's Taxonomy of Educational Objectives, are evident throughout the outcomes detailed in this document. It is strongly suggested that assessment methods appropriate to the thinking skills associated with each outcome be identified as an integral part of the institution's implementation plan.

For example, the following outcomes illustrate "higher order" and "lower order" thinking skills:

"Lower Order" thinking skill: Outcome 2.2.2. Identifies keywords, synonyms, and related terms for the information needed.

"Higher Order" thinking skill: Outcome 3.3.2. Extends initial synthesis, when possible, to a higher level of abstraction to construct new hypotheses that may require additional information.

Faculty, librarians, and others will find that discussing assessment methods collaboratively is a very productive exercise in planning a systematic, comprehensive information literacy program. This assessment program should reach all students, pinpoint areas for further program development, and consolidate learning goals already achieved. It also should make explicit to the institution's constituencies how information literacy contributes to producing educated students and citizens.

Notes

1. American Library Association. Presidential Committee on Information Literacy. Final Report. (Chicago: American Library Association, 1989.) http://www.ala.org/acrl/nili/ilit1st.html
2. National Research Council. Commission on Physical Sciences, Mathematics, and Applications. Committee on Information Technology Literacy, Computer Science and Telecommunications Board. Being Fluent with Information Technology. Publication. (Washington, D.C.: National Academy Press, 1999) http://www.nap.edu/reading room/books/BeFIT/
3. Several key accrediting agencies concerned with information literacy are: The Middle States Commission on Higher Education (MSCHE), the Western Association of Schools and College (WASC), and the Southern Association of Colleges and Schools (SACS).
4. Boyer Commission on Educating Undergraduates in the Research University. Reinventing Undergraduate Education: A Blueprint for America's Research Universities. http://notes.cc.sunysb.edu/Pres/boyer.nsf/

Standards, Performance Indicators, and Outcomes

Standard One. The information literate student determines the nature and extent of the information needed.

Performance Indicators:
1. The information literate student defines and articulates the need for information.

Outcomes Include:
1. Confers with instructors and participates in class discussions, peer workgroups, and electronic discussions to identify a research topic, or other information need
2. Develops a thesis statement and formulates questions based on the information need
3. Explores general information sources to increase familiarity with the topic
4. Defines or modifies the information need to achieve a manageable focus
5. Identifies key concepts and terms that describe the information need
6. Recognizes that existing information can be combined with original thought, experimentation, and/or analysis to produce new information

2. The information literate student identifies a variety of types and formats of potential sources for information.

Outcomes Include:
1. Knows how information is formally and informally produced, organized, and disseminated
2. Recognizes that knowledge can be organized into disciplines that influence the way information is accessed
3. Identifies the value and differences of potential resources in a variety of formats (e.g., multimedia, database, website, data set, audio/visual, book)
4. Identifies the purpose and audience of potential resources (e.g., popular vs. scholarly, current vs. historical)
5. Differentiates between primary and secondary sources, recognizing how their use and importance vary with each discipline
6. Realizes that information may need to be constructed with raw data from primary sources

3. The information literate student considers the costs and benefits of acquiring the needed information.

Outcomes Include:
1. Determines the availability of needed information and makes decisions on broadening the information seeking process beyond local resources (e.g., interlibrary loan; using resources at other locations; obtaining images, videos, text, or sound)
2. Considers the feasibility of acquiring a new language or skill (e.g., foreign or discipline-based) in order to gather needed information and to understand its context
3. Defines a realistic overall plan and timeline to acquire the needed information

4. The information literate student reevaluates the nature and extent of the information need

Outcomes Include:
1. Reviews the initial information need to clarify, revise, or refine the question
2. Describes criteria used to make information decisions and choices

Standard Two. The information literate student accesses needed information effectively and efficiently.

Performance Indicators:
1. The information literate student selects the most appropriate investigative methods or information retrieval systems for accessing the needed information.

Outcomes Include:
1. Identifies appropriate investigative methods (e.g., laboratory experiment, simulation, fieldwork)
2. Investigates benefits and applicability of various investigative methods
3. Investigates the scope, content, and organization of information retrieval systems
4. Selects efficient and effective approaches for accessing the information needed from the investigative method or information retrieval system.

2. The information literate student constructs and implements effectively-designed search strategies.

Outcomes Include:

1. Develops a research plan appropriate to the investigative method
2. Identifies keywords, synonyms and related terms for the information needed
3. Selects controlled vocabulary specific to the discipline or information retrieval source
4. Constructs a search strategy using appropriate commands for the information retrieval system selected (e.g., Boolean operators, truncation, and proximity for search engines; internal organizers such as indexes for books)
5. Implements the search strategy in various information retrieval systems using different user interfaces and search engines, with different command languages, protocols, and search parameters
6. Implements the search using investigative protocols appropriate to the discipline

3. The information literate student retrieves information online or in person using a variety of methods.

Outcomes Include:

1. Uses various search systems to retrieve information in a variety of formats
2. Uses various classification schemes and other systems (e.g., call number systems or indexes) to locate information resources within the library or to identify specific sites for physical exploration
3. Uses specialized online or in person services available at the institution to retrieve information needed (e.g., interlibrary loan/document delivery, professional associations, institutional research offices, community resources, experts and practitioners)
4. Uses surveys, letters, interviews, and other forms of inquiry to retrieve primary information

4. The information literate student refines the search strategy if necessary.

Outcomes Include:

1. Assesses the quantity, quality, and relevance of the search results to determine whether alternative information retrieval systems or investigative methods should be utilized
2. Identifies gaps in the information retrieved and determines if the search strategy should be revised
3. Repeats the search using the revised strategy as necessary

5. The information literate student extracts, records, and manages the information and its sources.

Outcomes Include:
1. Selects among various technologies the most appropriate one for the task of extracting the needed information (e.g., copy/paste software functions, photocopier, scanner, audio/visual equipment, or exploratory instruments)
2. Creates a system for organizing the information
3. Differentiates between the types of sources cited and understands the elements and correct syntax of a citation for a wide range of resources
4. Records all pertinent citation information for future reference
5. Uses various technologies to manage the information selected and organized

Standard Three. The information literate student evaluates information and its sources critically and incorporates selected information into his or her knowledge base and value system.

Performance Indicators:
1. The information literate student summarizes the main ideas to be extracted from the information gathered.

Outcomes Include:
1. Reads the text and selects main ideas
2. Restates textual concepts in his/her own words and selects data accurately
3. Identifies verbatim material that can be then appropriately quoted

2. The information literate student articulates and applies initial criteria for evaluating both the information and its sources.

Outcomes Include:
1. Examines and compares information from various sources in order to evaluate reliability, validity, accuracy, authority, timeliness, and point of view or bias
2. Analyzes the structure and logic of supporting arguments or methods
3. Recognizes prejudice, deception, or manipulation
4. Recognizes the cultural, physical, or other context within which the information was created and understands the impact of context on interpreting the information

3. The information literate student synthesizes main ideas to construct new concepts.

Outcomes Include:
1. Recognizes interrelationships among concepts and combines them into potentially useful primary statements with supporting evidence
2. Extends initial synthesis, when possible, at a higher level of abstraction to construct new hypotheses that may require additional information
3. Utilizes computer and other technologies (e.g., spreadsheets, databases, multimedia, and audio or visual equipment) for studying the interaction of ideas and other phenomena

4. The information literate student compares new knowledge with prior knowledge to determine the value added, contradictions, or other unique characteristics of the information.

Outcomes Include:
1. Determines whether information satisfies the research or other information need
2. Uses consciously selected criteria to determine whether the information contradicts or verifies information used from other sources
3. Draws conclusions based upon information gathered
4. Tests theories with discipline-appropriate techniques (e.g., simulators, experiments)
5. Determines probable accuracy by questioning the source of the data, the limitations of the information gathering tools or strategies, and the reasonableness of the conclusions
6. Integrates new information with previous information or knowledge
7. Selects information that provides evidence for the topic

5. The information literate student determines whether the new knowledge has an impact on the individual's value system and takes steps to reconcile differences.

Outcomes Include:
1. Investigates differing viewpoints encountered in the literature
2. Determines whether to incorporate or reject viewpoints encountered

6. The information literate student validates understanding and interpretation of the information through discourse with other individuals, subject-area experts, and/or practitioners.

Outcomes Include:
1. Participates in classroom and other discussions

2. Participates in class-sponsored electronic communication forums designed to encourage discourse on the topic (e.g., email, bulletin boards, chat rooms)
3. Seeks expert opinion through a variety of mechanisms (e.g., interviews, email, listservs)

7. The information literate student determines whether the initial query should be revised.

Outcomes Include:
1. Determines if original information need has been satisfied or if additional information is needed
2. Reviews search strategy and incorporates additional concepts as necessary
3. Reviews information retrieval sources used and expands to include others as needed

Standard Four. The information literate student, individually or as a member of a group, uses information effectively to accomplish a specific purpose.

Performance Indicators:
1. The information literate student applies new and prior information to the planning and creation of a particular product or performance.

Outcomes Include:
1. Organizes the content in a manner that supports the purposes and format of the product or performance (e.g., outlines, drafts, storyboards)
2. Articulates knowledge and skills transferred from prior experiences to planning and creating the product or performance
3. Integrates the new and prior information, including quotations and paraphrasings, in a manner that supports the purposes of the product or performance
4. Manipulates digital text, images, and data, as needed, transferring them from their original locations and formats to a new context

2. The information literate student revises the development process for the product or performance.

Outcomes Include:
1. Maintains a journal or log of activities related to the information seeking, evaluating, and communicating process
2. Reflects on past successes, failures, and alternative strategies

3. The information literate student communicates the product or performance effectively to others.

Outcomes Include:
1. Chooses a communication medium and format that best supports the purposes of the product or performance and the intended audience
2. Uses a range of information technology applications in creating the product or performance
3. Incorporates principles of design and communication
4. Communicates clearly and with a style that supports the purposes of the intended audience

Standard Five. The information literate student understands many of the economic, legal, and social issues surrounding the use of information and accesses and uses information ethically and legally.

Performance Indicators:
1. The information literate student understands many of the ethical, legal and socio-economic issues surrounding information and information technology.

Outcomes Include:
1. Identifies and discusses issues related to privacy and security in both the print and electronic environments
2. Identifies and discusses issues related to free vs. fee-based access to information
3. Identifies and discusses issues related to censorship and freedom of speech
4. Demonstrates an understanding of intellectual property, copyright, and fair use of copyrighted material

2. The information literate student follows laws, regulations, institutional policies, and etiquette related to the access and use of information resources.

Outcomes Include:
1. Participates in electronic discussions following accepted practices (e.g., "Netiquette")
2. Uses approved passwords and other forms of ID for access to information resources
3. Complies with institutional policies on access to information resources
4. Preserves the integrity of information resources, equipment, systems and facilities
5. Legally obtains, stores, and disseminates text, data, images, or sounds
6. Demonstrates an understanding of what constitutes plagiarism and does not represent work attributable to others as his/her own

7. Demonstrates an understanding of institutional policies related to human subjects research

3. The information literate student acknowledges the use of information sources in communicating the product or performance.

Outcomes Include:
1. Selects an appropriate documentation style and uses it consistently to cite sources
2. Posts permission granted notices, as needed, for copyrighted material

Approved by: ACRL Board, January 18, 2000.

Using Computer-Based and Electronic Library Materials in the Classroom: It's Not the Technology, It's the System!

Michael Moch

SUMMARY. From the perspective of a professor who wants to take full advantage of the new technology in the classroom, the frustrations of integrating disparate components are exacerbated because of the lack of coordination among those responsible for the various elements of the technology. *[Article copies available for a fee from The Haworth Document Delivery Service: 1-800-HAWORTH. E-mail address: <getinfo@haworthpressinc.com> Website: <http://www.HaworthPress.com> © 2002 by The Haworth Press, Inc. All rights reserved.]*

KEYWORDS. Technology, classroom, electronic, library, system

INTRODUCTION

I have been teaching business courses at the undergraduate and graduate level for over 27 years. My subject matter requires a close linking

Michael Moch is Professor of Management at Michigan State University and former chair of the department. Professor Moch has taught Organizational Theory, Organizational Behavior, Management of Technology, and Strategic Management. He has widely participated in presentations at professional meetings, and published numerous articles and a book.

[Haworth co-indexing entry note]: "Using Computer-Based and Electronic Library Materials in the Classroom: It's Not the Technology, It's the System!" Moch, Michael. Co-published simultaneously in *Journal of Business & Finance Librarianship* (The Haworth Information Press, an imprint of The Haworth Press, Inc.) Vol. 7, No. 2/3, 2002, pp. 207-214; and: *Library Services for Business Students in Distance Education: Issues and Trends* (ed: Shari Buxbaum) The Haworth Information Press, an imprint of The Haworth Press, Inc., 2002, pp. 207-214. Single or multiple copies of this article are available for a fee from The Haworth Document Delivery Service [1-800-HAWORTH, 9:00 a.m. - 5:00 p.m. (EST). E-mail address: getinfo@haworthpressinc.com].

between theory and practice and between theory and current events. During my teaching career, many suggestions for improving both the applicability and the timeliness of my material have been made and implemented. Casebooks help applicability but frequently lack timeliness. Requiring daily reading of selected daily publications facilitates timeliness, but these readings have problematic applicability to concepts presented in class. The advent of online electronic resources presents the instructor with the best way to date to reconcile these two desirable attributes. It is now possible to identify articles in daily periodicals and classify them into virtual cases in real time. Class preparations and testing can be altered and administered in real time. Applications and timeliness therefore can both be maximized.

In the last few years I have initiated efforts to realize the potential of online electronic information resources. I have implemented (1) automated graphics in PowerPoint for class and out-of-class use, (2) an online collection of pre-selected newspaper articles categorized by class topic for case use, (3) an online quizzing system, (4) automated online grade reporting, and (5) student peer evaluations for case presentations. There have been software problems, network problems, hardware problems, design problems, and student receptivity problems. These problems can appear to be insurmountable. However, they can be overcome so long as the user follows two simple maxims: (a) do it yourself, and (b) never give up. The only problem that I could not overcome involved the integration of all the necessary components. The instructor working alone even with reasonable consultation cannot accomplish this integration. The components can be made to work. But can they be made to work *together*???

PowerPoint and Automated Graphics. I now have all my coursework encapsulated in a series of PowerPoint slide presentations. These not only reduce subsequent preparation time, they also allow for updating as events or my own learning require. The upfront investment is more than worth the effort. On the other hand, it is easy to get seduced into being "too fancy" for the medium. Animation has provided marginal returns. Students complain when they cannot print out the animated slides, and updating is a problem when you have to alter an animation that has been hidden under other animations. Students, I have found, prefer simple slides. They can be printed out. Even relatively simple animations can obfuscate more than clarify.

Of course support for computer presentations is essential. In reality, at this university, the Web people operate under a different administrative system than the network people. Moreover, the Business College network people are independent of the University network people. The University maintains the console in the classroom; the College people, therefore, can (and sometimes do) refuse to assist with console hardware problems, even though they are right down the hall.

To get support from the University network support staff, one has to call from a phone in the classroom. The phone frequently is removed (either stolen or removed by physical plant people who fear it will be stolen). When it is present, there is a number posted on it to call in case of emergencies. Since the physical plant people put the phone there, the number is the number for physical plant emergencies, not for computer support emergencies. There is no number for computer support emergencies. When a problem arises with the computer console, therefore, I can easily contact someone who can send a maintenance person over to replace a broken light, but I cannot contact someone who can fix the console. If the problem is with the computer projector, the computer support staff cannot help. I must contact media services. They, however, are terribly understaffed and cannot handle emergency services.

If all works well, and I try to use the University console, it takes 5 minutes to boot up from campus, because of all the security, checking, erasing, and reloading required for machines that can be (and are) used by many different users. I have a class off-campus. The console at the off-campus site takes 25 minutes to boot up, due to bandwidth issues. Even if I get to class 30 minutes early, one problem booting up means you don't get access to the network until as much as 30 minutes into the class. If there are two problems booting up, an hour can elapse before the system is ready to use. The system, therefore, has a built-in disincentive to use it. The alternative is to bring my own laptop, but this defeats one of the reasons why consoles were installed in the classrooms.

I tend not to use the Web in class, because I cannot access the Web server from the console without considerable time-consuming local reconfiguring for every boot-up. This is because the standard configuration has been applied University-wide and the Business College does not want everyone in the University to have access to its server. Needless to say, The Business College Webmaster is administratively independent of the Office of University Computing (and the Business College's own network people). The Webmaster, for example, cannot give me access to the College network server. The alternative is to use my own laptop for class or to capture Web pages before class and store them on a zip disk for subsequent access using the console. In short, I do as much as possible myself. I cannot depend on external support.

In the past, projector breakdowns have been incessant. Now, they are infrequent but can be disastrous when they occur. Projectors are maintained by an office of University Media Services that is independent of both Business College Web and network people and independent of University computer people. Getting assistance with projector problems therefore requires the instructor to be familiar with an entirely different bureaucratic structure. To address this problem, our department purchased a projector for use when the classroom projector breaks. So long as two projectors do not break simultaneously, this generally solves the problem. Of course, it substantially increases departmental expenses while it takes pressure off University Media Services.

The College Webmaster designed and implemented a system for posting class materials for students. This has worked well for faculty who are not concerned about security. Password protection on the system, to the extent it works at all, is an all-or-nothing option. Some faculty want their class materials protected; others do not. When the network people implemented password protection, they discovered problems with authentication they could not adequately resolve. They therefore took all security features from the site. This means, according to the University legal people, that I cannot post material on my course site if it has a copyright, even though I may have secured copyright permission for my students. I had to mount these materials on another server, and arrange for my own authentication. Students seeking access to this resource must now enter two IDs and two passwords: one to access the University from outside and one to access materials from my server. I succeeded, but I had to do it myself.

The Online Library. I try to make contemporary articles from the business press available to my students in a way that allows them to see how the articles relate to specific topics in my class. I used to publish compendiums of articles for each class. With the advent of online electronic libraries, we now have the option of giving students access without out the tedious cut-and-paste process required for hardcopy publication. The potential is enormous. In practice, however, there are significant problems.

Fair use practices for hardcopy are fairly well established. Simply put a hardcopy on reserve and each student can make one copy. Publishing compendiums of articles represented more of a problem, but copyright permission procedures were also well established. The University established an office to facilitate copyright acquisition for such products.

Electronic resources are another matter. Upon consultation with the University, I was told that publishers have not agreed to transpose fair use precedents from hardcopy to an electronic medium. Even if I were to compile a collection using my own subscription to an online service (e.g., the electronic version of the *Wall Street Journal*), password protect it and locate it on a Business College or Department server, I would still have to pay the publisher a license fee and a fee for each access of each article. One publisher quoted $500 for a license for a class and $0.50 for each article. Since I post many articles (hundreds) from which students can choose, the cost to the university for this service is enormous. They understandably decline to pay it.

The alternative was to tell students to access articles from the electronic resources available online through the University library (e.g., Dow Jones Interactive, Lexis-Nexis). Every student then has to enter the article title and search for him/herself. Article titles in some publications (notably the *Wall Street Journal* Online edition) can vary from vendor to vendor. Titles from *Wall Street Journal* Online do not always match with titles for the same article available through Dow Jones Interactive. If I download a title from the online edition, students may not find it in the electronic database available through the University. More importantly, access to the electronic resource on campus has been limited to several simultaneous users. Only so many can access it at one time. Given the number of student complaints about (1) not finding an article because of title variants and (2) being unable to access the electronic resource because of a limited number of site licenses, I determined I would build my own system. I was able to get copyright permission from the publisher's marketing office that was unavailable at an acceptable price from their copyright permission people. The process, however, was tedious. I also had to edit each article using the editing features in my browser and promise to password protect my collection. This exposed me to the authentication problems mentioned earlier.

UMI produced a product (Sitebuilder) that allows faculty to build an online library of article titles, organized any way the faculty member wants. Simply search for and secure the article, click on the save feature to identify a URL at UMI, and insert the URL as a hyperlink for the title listed in a syllabus or an online list of titles. I developed a wonderful online library resource using this system, including full text articles from the Wall Street Journal. The problem developed when Sitebuilder software was upgraded. The Library subscription to Proquest (UMI) did not include the *Wall Street Journal*. I had been able to create the links due to a glitch in the system. All links to the articles that I had made were lost in the upgrade. I no longer had access to a key resource via Proquest.

Had the University subscribed to my information resource through Proquest, I would have been able to access and post *Wall Street Journal* articles using Sitebuilder. Now, I am back to doing everything myself (and never giving up).

While I was building my system using Sitebuilder, Proquest lost its access to *Harvard Business Review*. It is now (March 2001) found in Lexis/Nexis in addition to EBSCO, to which the MSU Libraries do not subscribe. In order to make these articles available to my students, I would have had to download them from Lexis/Nexis into my own passworded Web site.

This situation puts faculty like myself into the position of either violating copyright law or depriving students of easy access to crucial course material. Students can click to the Lexis/Nexis site and retrieve the assigned readings on their own. This, however, erects a significant barrier between the student and the materials they need. Students must search using words in the title, and this retrieves many more articles than the one assigned. For non-*HBR* articles (e.g., the *Wall Street Journal*) some titles in Lexis/Nexis may be different from the one available in hardcopy and listed in the syllabus (editors sometimes change titles). Thus, students may not retrieve the article assigned. In addition, my class is the first one taken by new students on campus. The students do not yet know how to access L/N, nor do I have class time to devote to this. Yet faculty who try to resolve this problem by assembling all reading material electronically at one site risk exposure to copyright violation. The safest and easiest alternative, therefore, is to avoid the electronic medium altogether, hardly a desirable outcome.

An Online Quizzing System. I wanted to be able to quiz students in the classroom to identify areas needing greater emphasis. I was assigned a classroom in which students could plug in their laptops, and I worked with a University level office responsible for developing the software. The University had decided to develop its own software for online testing rather than purchase it from an outside vendor. It is very costly to use one's classroom as a testing site for new software. Bugs abound, and student frustration with the developing system can undermine your own status and legitimacy. The potential, however, is substantial. Never give up!

I soon determined that online quizzing should not be done in class. The time needed by all is the time needed by the slowest student. In addition, once the students have booted up, they stay online. I have found them e-mailing, downloading unrelated material, and even playing games during remaining class time. Without a master-slave system of computers in the room, this is impossible to control or even monitor. In addition, some ports in the room were broken or vandalized. Additional time outside of class was required to include these students in the quizzing process. I moved the quizzing outside of class. Students would submit their quiz answers just before class; I would then compile the results and start the class by reviewing the quiz results and by focusing on material the students did not understand. This worked well.

Automated Online Grade Reporting. Grade reporting has become a serious problem at the University. For privacy reasons, we are not allowed to post grades in public places, even by student ID number. Yet students want (and deserve?) feedback before final grades are distributed. Handing results back in class is time-consuming, cumbersome, and prone to error. Moreover, since there are no classes after final exams a colleague developed a grade reporting system online. Students access the system through the Web, insert their student ID number and select a class in which they are enrolled and the feedback item (e.g., grade, paper, etc.) on which they want their grade. The system then e-mails them their grade, along with supportive information (e.g., component grades, weights, etc.). The system works wonderfully for on-campus students. Off-campus students had to configure their computers to access the University's proxy server. Some off-campus students who tried to access the system from their workplace ran into problems attributable to their company's firewall. This problem could not be resolved.

Student Peer Evaluations. Group work presents unique assessment problems. I found that some students were inclined to "free-ride" on their more ambitious or hard-working colleagues. Accordingly, a colleague developed a student peer evaluation system. Students access the system, enter their student ID number and the class requiring peer assessment. They then click to rate each of their team members on a series of dimensions. The system then generates a report, including descriptive statistics, which allows the instructor to identify students who are rated particularly poorly or particularly highly by their fellow team members. This system has worked very well. Without this system, it simply would take too much time to consider peer evaluations. Problems with the system are problems I would experience with any peer-evaluation system (e.g., the phenomenon of increasing within-team rancor as the semester progresses).

Summary. The applications that have worked best are applications generated by myself or by colleagues. Applications have been problematic to the extent they require coordination with other College or University offices/resources. The greatest difficulties have come when resources from multiple outside offices need to be coordinated. I have found that they cannot effectively be coordinated from the bottom up (i.e., by me). Outside resources take their orders and priorities from above, and these differ across offices. Hence, the problem is not the technology per se. The problem is the administrative system.

Were the University foolish enough to ask me for my advice, I would recommend that funds that would otherwise be spent creating a series of support services be allocated to individuals within academic departments to develop, purchase and apply instruments for using electronic resources in the classroom. I would then advertise and diffuse those that work and accept failure with grace. This approach, however, would have only limited utility. Some resources simply must be administered centrally. The University, for example, could not locate subscription purchases of significant online resources to individuals within departments. To some extent, we must continue to muddle our way through the myriad possibilities until we find solutions that realize the potential we all know is there.

The mission of the University Libraries appears to be to provide faculty and student access to information resources. The library people do this very well, given the limited resources with which they have to work. Electronic information resources offer potential for a significant improvement in access. We now have more resources more easily available than ever before and this is wonderful. However, integrating these resources and delivery tools to provide coherent and organized information resources for specific classes has become a major impediment to realizing the full potential of the new technology. At Michigan State University we are using the new technology to do things the old way. Since everyone is responsible for only a small piece of the electronic information resource picture, integration is left to the faculty members. They generally are not up to the task. They do not have sufficient time or expertise to address the myriad administrative and technical issues. They have enough trouble simply staying abreast of their own fields. Nevertheless, they are the only ones in a position to accomplish the task. If progress is to be made, therefore, we must follow the two maxims: Do as much as possible yourself and never give up.

Index

Page numbers followed by f indicate figures; those followed by t indicate tables.